REPORT

ON THE

EXPLORATION OF THE YELLOWSTONE RIVER,

BY

BVT. BRIG. GEN. W. F. RAYNOLDS.

COMMUNICATED BY

THE SECRETARY OF WAR,

IN COMPLIANCE WITH

A RESOLUTION OF SENATE, FEBRUARY 13, 1866.

WASHINGTON:
GOVERNMENT PRINTING OFFICE.
1868.

40TH CONGRESS, 1st Session. | SENATE. | Ex Doc. No. 77.

REPORT

OF

THE SECRETARY OF WAR,

COMMUNICATING,

In compliance with a resolution of the Senate of February 13, 1866, *the report of Brevet Brigadier General W. F. Raynolds, on the exploration of the Yellowstone and the country drained by that river.*

JULY 19, 1867.—Read; ordered to lie on the table. Motion to print referred to the Committee on Printing.

JULY 17, 1868.—*Resolved,* That the report proper of General Raynolds, upon his exploration in the valley of the Yellowstone river, be printed, with the maps, but without the illustrations; and that three thousand extra copies be printed and bound for the use of the Senate; and that the Secretary of the Senate be directed to return the appendices to General Raynolds's report to the Chief Engineer of the army of the United States.

WAR DEPARTMENT,
Washington City, July 19, 1867.

SIR: In compliance with the Senate's resolution of February 13, 1866, calling for the report of Major Raynolds, United States engineers, of his exploration of the Yellowstone, and the country drained by that river, I have the honor to transmit herewith a communication of the Chief of Engineers, of July 18, with the report desired, just now completed.

Your obedient servant,

EDWIN M. STANTON,
Secretary of War.

Hon. B. F. WADE,
President of the Senate.

ENGINEER DEPARTMENT,
Washington, July 18, 1867.

SIR: Referring to letters of this department of the 14th February, 1866, and 7th May, 1867, and in compliance with Senate resolution of the 13th February, 1866, I have the honor to transmit herewith the report of Brevet Brigadier General William F. Raynolds, major of engineers, upon his exploration of the Yellowstone and Missouri rivers, just completed, and comprised in the following papers, viz:

1. Captain Raynolds' report and journal.
2. Lieutenant Maynadier's report.
3. Reports of detached parties.
4. Table of latitudes.
5. Table of chronometer errors.
6. Table of meteorological observations and barometer heights, Captain Raynolds' route, 1859.

7. Table of meteorological observations and barometer heights, Lieutenant Maynadier's route, 1859.
8. Table of meteorological observations and barometer heights, Captain Raynolds' route, 1860.
9. Table of meteorological observations and barometer heights, Lieutenant Maynadier's route, 1860.
10. Meteorological observations at Deer creek (winter quarters.)
11. Meteorological observations at Fort Pierre.
12. Report on geology by Dr. F. V. Hayden.
13. Report on fossil plants by Professor J. S. Newberry.
14. Report on birds by Dr. Elliott Coues.
15. Report on mammals.
16. Catalogue of plants by Dr. George Engleman.
17. Report on carices by Professor Chester Dewey.
18. List of mosses and liverworts by Professor Sullivan.
19. List of shells by Professor Binney.

Very respectfully, your obedient servant,

A. A. HUMPHREYS,
Chief of Engineers, Major General.

Hon. E. M. STANTON,
Secretary of War.

OFFICE UNITED STATES LAKE SURVEY,
Detroit, July 1, 1867.

GENERAL: I have the honor to submit herewith my report of the exploration of the "head waters of the Yellowstone and Missouri rivers, and of the mountains in which they rise."

In presenting this report I deem it proper to give a short statement of the circumstances under which it has been prepared.

The expedition returned to Omaha in October, 1860. After discharging the employés, and settling the accounts of the party, I repaired to Washington with a portion of my assistants, and commenced the preparation of the report. Good progress had been made, and I had expected to have it ready for the following session of Congress, when the breaking out of the rebellion scattered my assistants, seriously interfering with my work.

On the 1st of July, 1861, I reported that, if my services were needed elsewhere, the preparation of the report could be suspended with no other injury than that necessarily incident to delay. On the 10th of that month I was ordered to join the army in the field, and shortly after all work was suspended.

In the summer of 1862 I was prevented by severe and protracted illness from continuing on duty in the field, and in that condition applied for authority to resume the report, which was granted, "provided it did not interfere with the medical treatment I was undergoing." My physician would not consent to my attempting the work.

In January, 1863, while yet an invalid, I was again, at my own request, ordered on duty with the army, and another application was made for authority to resume the report. This time, in connection with my other duties, my request was granted, but my other duties prevented any considerable progress being made.

In April, 1864, my health not being yet restored, I was ordered to this place as "superintendent of the survey of the north and northwest lakes, and light-house engineer for the 10th and 11th districts," comprising the entire lake region. Each of these duties was, at the time and has been continually since, much more extensive and complicated than before the war, when the superintendence of the lake survey, or of a single light-house district, was considered ample duty for one officer.

With triple duty on my hands, and instructions that forbade my devoting any time to the report that interfered with my other duties; without assistants who were engaged on the expedition, or who were familiar with such duty, I trust that it will not be considered strange that the presentation of the report has been delayed, or that I should be ready to admit its many and great imperfections.

Very respectfully, your obedient servant,

W. F. RAYNOLDS,
Lieut. Col. Engineers, and Bvt. Brig. General.

Brevet Major General A. A. HUMPHREYS,
Chief of Engineers U. S. Army, Washington, D. C.

REPORT OF BREVET COLONEL W. F. RAYNOLDS, U. S. A., CORPS OF ENGINEERS, ON THE EXPLORATION OF THE YELLOWSTONE AND MISSOURI RIVERS, IN 1859-'60.

Table of contents.

OFFICE LAKE SURVEY, *Detroit*, 1867.

SIR: After spending the greater part of the previous winter on duty at the southern part of Florida, on the 6th of April, 1859, I was summoned by telegram to Washington, where I received the first intimation that it was the intention of the department to assign to me the important duty of exploring the extensive, and then almost unknown, country drained by the Upper Missouri and Yellowstone rivers. My entire want of previous preparation for this duty is offered as an explanation of the many deficiencies that I am conscious exist in the performance of the duty assigned to me.

*Not Printed.

The following are the instructions under which the exploration was made:

"WAR DEPARTMENT, OFFICE EXPLORATIONS AND SURVEYS,
" *Washington, April* 13, 1859.

"SIR: Under clauses of the military appropriation acts, providing for 'surveys for military defences, geographical explorations and reconnoissances for military purposes,' I am directed by the Secretary of War to instruct you to organize an expedition for the exploration of the region of country through which flow the principal tributaries of the Yellowstone river, and of the mountains in which they, and the Gallatin and Madison forks of the Missouri, have their source.

"The objects of this exploration are to ascertain, as far as practicable, everything relating to the numbers, habits and disposition of the Indians inhabiting the country, its agricultural and mineralogical resources, its climate and the influences that govern it, the navigability of its streams, its topographical features, and the facilities or obstacles which the latter present to the construction of rail or common roads, either to meet the wants of military operations or those of emigration through, or settlement in, the country.

"Particular attention should be given to determining the most direct and feasible routes:

"1. From the neighborhood of Fort Laramie to the Yellowstone, in the direction of Fort Union, on the Missouri.

"2. From the neighborhood of Fort Laramie northwesterly, along the base of the Big Horn mountains, towards Fort Benton and the Bitter Root valley.

"3. From the Yellowstone to the South pass, and to ascertaining the practicability of a route from the sources of Wind river to those of the Missouri.

"To accomplish these objects most effectually the expedition should proceed by the Missouri river to Fort Pierre. Here a large number of the Dakotas will be assembled to receive their annuities, and overtures should be made to obtain their assent to your proceeding to the source of Powder river by the Shayenne and its north fork, by which a new route leading west from the Missouri river would be examined. To aid you in accomplishing this object, the clothing, *et cetera*, to be given to the Dakotas by the government, under the treaty made with them by General Harney, will be turned over to you by the Indian Bureau for distribution.

"From the source of Powder river the expedition should proceed down that stream to its mouth; thence along the Yellowstone to the mouth of Tongue river, up which a detachment should be sent to its source. The remainder of the party should continue on the Yellowstone to the mouth of Big Horn river, and ascend the latter stream to the point where it leaves the mountains. Here the two divisions of the party should be united. The approach of winter may require the expedition to pass that season in this neighborhood, or if time suffices, the expedition may ascend the Big Horn river to Wind river, where a favorable wintering place can be found.

"The next season should be spent in examining the mountain region about the sources of the Yellowstone and Missouri, to ascertain the character of the routes leading south and west from the navigable parts of those rivers. On returning one party should descend the Missouri, using skin boats to Fort Benton, where a Mackinac boat should be in readiness. The other portion should descend the Yellowstone, in skin boats, to its mouth, where it should join the party with the Mackinac boat, and all proceed to the settlements. With a pack train it would not, perhaps, be practicable to carry more than three months' full supply of provisions, but the abundance of game in much of this region renders it unnecessary to provide the usual quantity of bread and bacon.

"The following places are convenient as depots, and you should make your arrangements accordingly, viz: The Platte Bridge, Fort Laramie, and the

American Fur Company's posts, Fort Alexander Sarpy, Fort Benton, and Fort Union. If the Dakotas should withhold their consent to the expedition proceeding up the valley of the Shayenne, and you should not deem it advisable to make that examination without their consent, the expedition will proceed to Fort Clark or Fort Union, and move to the Yellowstone near the mouth of Powder river.

"You will use your own judgment in modifying the plan proposed in the event of any unforeseen circumstances or physical obstacles preventing an adherence to it.

"You will endeavor by all the means in your power to conciliate and gain the friendship of the different Indian tribes you may meet, and will assure them of the good will of the government, and of its protection in all their rights. You are authorized to purchase Indian goods to be used in compensating the Indians for their services when required, and for purchasing from them such articles as you may need. By thus securing their friendly co-operation you will not only be relieved from danger of interruption, but be enabled to obtain from them much valuable information which would be withheld if you were obliged to enter their country in a hostile attitude.

"To aid you in the discharge of these duties, you are authorized to employ eight assistants as topographers, geologist and naturalist, astronomer, meteorologist, physician, &c., at an average salary not exceeding $125 per month, and to pay their actual travelling expenses to and from the field of operations, and to subsist them while in the field. You will procure your assistants, employés, equipment, supplies, &c., at those points which seem to ensure the most economical and effective organization for the party. The sum of $60,000 will be set aside from the appropriations to defray the expenses of the expedition, which amount your expenditures must not exceed.

"The colonel of topographical engineers will be directed to supply you with such instruments as you may require on your requisition.

"The commanding general of the Department of the West will be directed to detail an escort of 30 picked men of the infantry, under the command of a lieutenant, who will report to you for duty.

"Transportation for the provision and equipage of the escort, their subsistence and their necessary ammunition, will be furnished respectively by the quartermasters', commissary, and ordnance departments.

"The quartermasters', commissary, medical, and ordnance departments will be directed to furnish, as far as practicable, all necessary transportation, provisions, arms, and supplies, those required for the civil employés to be paid for at cost prices at the place of delivery, from the appropriation for the expedition.

"All necessary transportation, provisions, arms, and supplies which you cannot obtain from those departments, and all minor instruments, books, and drawing materials, will be purchased out of the appropriation for the exploration.

"You will communicate with the department through this office, to which you will make the reports and returns required by regulations of an officer of engineers in charge of a work or operation, and such other reports, transmitted as often as the means of communication will allow, as will keep the department apprised of your various movements, and the progress of the expedition under your charge. On the completion of your field duty you will return, with your assistants to Washington, and prepare the maps and reports necessary to a full exposition of the results of the expedition.

"Very respectfully, your obedient servant,

"A. A. HUMPHREYS,

"*Captain Topographical Engineers in charge.*

"Captain W. F. RAYNOLDS,

"*Corps Topographical Engineers, Washington.*"

The district that I was thus ordered to explore is bounded on the north by the British possessions, on the east by the Missouri river, on the south by the Niobrara and the Platte, and on the west by the dividing ridge of the Rocky mountains, thus extending from the 43° to 49° of north latitude, and from the 100th to the 113th meridian of longitude west of Greenwich. Its dimensions are thus 650 miles east and west measurement, and nearly 400 north and south, while its area is about 250,000 square miles, nearly one-fourth larger than all of France, or than the kingdoms of Spain and Portugal, and more than double the area of Great Britain. Previous explorations in this region were confined almost exclusively to the immediate vicinity of the great rivers, or penetrated only to the borders of the district named. Lewis and Clarke in 1804'-5-'6 ascended the Missouri, crossed the continent, and returned by the Yellowstone. I can testify to the wonderful accuracy of their descriptions of localities, but their geographical positions are not always reliable. Nicollet in 1839 reached Fort Pierre. His investigations and determinations of positions were such as characterize all the labors of that eminent savant. Governor Stevens in 1852, in his railroad expedition, confined his explorations mainly to the Missouri river, or to the country north of that stream, above the mouth of the Yellowstone. Lieutenant Warren, topographical engineers, explored the Black Hills in 1855, and ascended the Yellowstone, as far as the mouth of Powder river, in 1856, determining accurately his positions and adding greatly to previous knowledge of these localities. "Bonneville's Adventures" and "Astoria," two of Irving's delightful sketches, are accounts of adventures, many of which were located in this district, but it is difficult to trace the routes travelled, and no reliable data are given for geographical positions. Several other expeditions were conducted along the Missouri, mainly with the view of determining the geological features; but none of these added much to our geographical knowledge. The fur companies in their dealings with the Indians have for years had their agents travelling in all parts of this country, but their journeyings have had no scientific character or value. All preliminary information in regard to the interior of this vast region was thus exceedingly vague and unsatisfactory.

The district is naturally divided in a marked manner into three great sections. Of these the eastern is drained by several streams having a general easterly course and emptying into the Missouri. The middle division comprises the entire drainage of the Yellowstone, whose main branches all possess a northerly course. The third division, includes the drainage of the southern and eastern bankof the Missouri, above the Yellowstone. Aside from these general features, which suggest themselves at a glance at the map, there are some minor topographical facts of interest that can be stated.

About latitude 38°, near the Spanish peaks, the main-dividing crest of the continent takes a westerly trend, and from this point branches off an outlying chain running nearly north and south. This, as it gradually diverges from the range, forms the eastern boundary of the "parks," in which the Arkansas and the Platte have their sources. Near latitude 41° the main crest trends still more rapidly to the westward, enclosing between it and the outlying range a wide and comparatively level tract, known as the "Laramie plains," which may be regarded as a fourth "park." In this series of "parks" the most striking feature is the northerly course of all the streams. The south fork of the Platte rises in the South park, and runs nearly north for more than 100 miles before it turns suddenly to the east. The Middle park is drained by the head-waters of the Colorado, which also have a northerly course of about 50 miles before leaving it. The North park is drained by the north fork of the Platte, and this stream flows in a northerly course for 150 miles and, passing through the Laramie plains, unites with the Sweetwater, after which it assumes the general easterly course of the Platte. These same general features of topography obtain on an enlarged scale north of the Platte. The outlying spur, indeed, loses its great elevation and becomes rather a divided than a mountain range, but it continues in a northerly course, striking the Missouri river near the mouth of the Yellowstone in latitude 48°, and still affects the course of the rivers and the formation of the country. The great divergence of the main-divide to the northwest makes the distance here between it and this outlying ridge very great, and the clearly defined parks are found along the base of the former; of these there are three, namely, the valleys of the upper Big Horn, of the upper Yellowstone, and of the three forks of the Missouri, which are basins surrounded by mountain ridges, with the streams all tending northward. Between these minor parks and the outlier are the great valleys of the Yellowstone and the Upper Missouri.

The course of the outlier in its southern part is marked by lofty peaks, (among which may be mentioned Pike's, Long's, and Laramie,) but north of the Platte the Little Missouri buttes form its most prominent landmarks, and it soon sinks, as stated above, to a mere prairie ridge, although at the mouth of the Yellowstone it is so prominent that it attracted the attention of the earliest travellers in that country. Eastward of this ridge the country to the Missouri is (as far as we explored it) the high, broken prairie of the west, presenting no serious obstacles to travel; and the Black Hills lying eastward of and contiguous to the outlier, and rising to a height of from 2,000 to 3,000 feet above the general level, was the only marked instance of upheaval we encountered in this immense plain. South of this great tract visited by the expedition are found the valleys of the Kansas and Arkansas rivers, with their tributaries, having a generally easterly course, similar to that which characterizes the Platte after leaving the mountains.

RIVERS—TRIBUTARIES OF THE MISSOURI.

North of the Platte, the principal streams flowing eastward are the White, Niobrara, Shayenne, Moreau, Palanata or Grand, Cannon Ball, and Heart rivers. Of these, the White and Niobrara, receiving their supply of water from the outliers of the Black Hills and the high lands north of the Platte, are large streams, and always contribute considerable water to the Missouri.

The Shayenne is much the most important tributary between the Platte and Yellowstone. It is formed by two main branches which entirely surround and drain the Black Hills, and as it receives its water from the numerous mountain streams of this district, its supply is much more constant and reliable than that of any of the other rivers to the north. Its valley below the forks is from half to three-quarters of a mile in width of alluvial soil, and covered with a heavy growth of bottom grass. Beautiful cotton-wood groves fringe its banks throughout its whole length. This portion of the river receives several tributaries, but all are prairie streams, and consequently contain little water during a great portion of the year. The river-bed is mainly quicksand, and great care is consequently requisite in finding fords. The bluffs bordering the valley below the forks are bold, and in most instances access to the river bottom from the neighboring plains is difficult if not impracticable.

Wherever the bluffs have been subjected to the action of water they present the stratified clay formation of the "bad lands." Above the forks the bluffs are found close to the stream, and the valley becomes narrower. The tributaries are clear, and constant mountain creeks flowing through beautiful valleys. The whole region of the Black Hills is unquestionably destined at no distant date to afford homes for a thriving population. The mountains will furnish a sufficient supply of pine lumber for ordinary uses, and, although timber is very scarce in the region as a whole, yet the Black Hills will fully supply this great deficiency in the district immediately adjoining.

The Moreau or Owl, the Grand or Pell, the Cannon Ball, and the Heart rivers occur in the order named, and are mere prairie streams of unusual length. In the dry season they contribute little water to the Missouri, but their beds indicate that, at certain seasons, they are formidable torrents. The banks of these streams are lined with a narrow fringe of cotton-woods.

Beyond these, and yet east of the outlying ridge, are two important rivers—the Knife and the Chan-cho-ka, or Little Missouri—flowing to the northeast, instead of to the east, as was the case with the others. The Little Missouri rises in the Black Hills, whence it receives a constant and considerable supply of water, and its length is over 200 miles. This stream having more timber upon its banks than its neighbors, is called by the Indians "Chan-cho-ka," or Thick Timbered river. The title, however, is only comparative, and should not create the impression that the valley would be elsewhere considered heavily timbered.

THE YELLOWSTONE AND ITS TRIBUTARIES.

The foregoing complete the catalogue of the larger streams east of the outlier explored partially or completely by the expedition. Upon crossing the outlier the great valley of the Yellowstone is at once reached. The tributaries of this river—the Powder, the Tongue, the Rosebud, the Big Horn, Pryor's, and Clark's forks—all flow to the north until they reach the Yellowstone. Further west the same is true with reference to the Yellowstone itself, which near its source flows for more than 100 miles to the northward before changing its course to the east.

The first stream west of the ridge is Powder river, (which derives its name from the sulphurous vapors rising from burning beds of lignite in its vicinity,) of which the Little Powder is the main tributary from the east. The latter rises near Pumpkin Butte, flows through the "bad lands" for over 100 miles, and joins the main stream in latitude 45° 28′. This stream, when crossed by us in July, 1859, was almost dry. Its valley is wide, and contains the usual growth of cotton-wood. Clear fork is the principal western tributary of the Powder, and leaves the Big Horn mountains, in which it takes its rise, a dashing mountain torrent. Upon its banks is found considerable pine, which the excellent water-power of the stream will in time convert into lumber for the use of the coming settlers. Crazy Woman's fork and Willow creek are less important tributaries of the Powder, finding their sources in or near the mountains, and emptying into the main stream above Clear fork. The Powder itself rises in the Big Horn mountains, about latitude 43° 25′, flows northeast about 60 miles, then turns to the north, and empties into the Yellowstone in latitude 46° 42′. Its valley (which is barren and yields but little grass and an abundance of artemisia) averages a mile in width throughout its entire length, until within 50 miles from its mouth, it becomes narrower and the bluffs more ragged and broken. Travelling in it is greatly impeded by deep and almost impassable ravines which cross it at nearly right angles, and are concealed by the sage until their very edge is reached. These gullies are caused by the action of the water upon the light soil, and are among the most disagreeable features of the country. The bed of the river is mainly a treacherous quicksand, and great care is necessary in selecting fords. The depth of the water is not, however, such as to offer any obstruction, except during freshets. The bluffs bordering the valley are throughout the much-dreaded and barren "bad lands," and this stream must ever remain of little or no value to the country.

Tongue river rises in the Big Horn mountains, and is in some respects an improvement upon the Powder. Its valley is narrower, but contains less sage and more grass. The stream flows in the main over a gravel or stony bottom, and thus presents no especial obstructions to crossing. The river bottom is less torn up by gullies, and the bluffs are not as rugged and impassable. Yet the Tongue river valley presents few attractions to the settler. The soil is light, and the timber chiefly cottonwood, and scarce—disadvantages that will for years seriously affect its prospects for settlement and development.

The third tributary of the Yellowstone is the Rosebud, which rises in the Chetish or Wolf mountains, and, during our journey in August, 1859, contained no running water. Its valley is narrow, and resembles that of the Tongue. Near its source, however, are some open valleys, that by contrast appear attractive.

The Big Horn, which is next reached, is the main tributary of the Yellowstone. It is formed by the junction of the Popo-Azie and Wind rivers, both of which are considerable and noted streams. Thirty miles below the point of junction the river enters the mountains, passing through a cañon 20 miles in length, after which it flows among broken and barren hills, occasionally interspersed with small level valleys. During this part of its course, which is nearly 100 miles in extent, it receives several tributaries, of which the chief are No Wood and No Water creeks on the east, and Gray Bull and Stinking rivers upon the west. This part of the country, as will be seen from the detailed statements of Lieutenant Maynadier's explorations, is repelling in all its characteristics, and can only be traversed with the greatest difficulty. Below the mouth of the Stinking, the Big Horn again enters the Big Horn mountains, and passes through a second cañon of 25 miles in length, emerging in latitude 45° 10′. The peculiar topography of this region, whereby the same river flowing to the north cañons twice through the same mountain range, is well set forth and made plain in the rough language of the guide Bridger, who said: "The Big Horn mountains are just the shape of a horseshoe, and the Big Horn river cuts through both sides, dividing the heel from the toe." The lower cañon must present a series of views of great magnificence. The gorge cannot be less than 3,000 feet in depth, and whether the banks are sloping or perpendicular, the scenery must be grand in the extreme. Bridger, who claims to have once passed through on a raft, declares that for mingled sublimity and beauty this cañon is unequalled by any that he has ever seen. Below this the Big Horn flows some 10° east of north for about 70 miles to its junction with the Yellowstone. The valley is open, and from two to five miles in width, being bounded on either side by high rolling prairie hills. Near the Yellowstone it is crossed by a high spur of the Chetish mountains, on the top of which is found a stunted and straggling growth of pines. The soil improves as you ascend towards the mountains, and near the lower cañon is very fertile, and covered with as heavy and luxuriant a crop of grass as could be found upon the continent. For 30 miles above its mouth the Big Horn flows upon the east side of its valley, but shifts to the other about half the distance to the mountains. The expedition forded the Big Horn without trouble about a mile and a half above its mouth, or about half a mile below the junction of Tullock's creek, and again about 35 miles above. These fords were well marked by Indian trails leading to them, and are the principal if not only crossings, as repeated attempts made at other points by naturalists, hunters, and other members of the party uniformly failed, the depth of water and rapidity of the current deterring the most daring. At these fords the water was only from two to two and a half feet in depth. The river bed, throughout its entire course below the mountains, partakes of the general character of the Yellowstone and Missouri, the stream being crooked and badly cut up by islands and sandbars. Of the tributaries of the Big. Horn below the mountains those upon the west were not visited by us, nor are they of much importance. Of those upon the east the first is Tullock's creek, which empties into the main stream about two miles above the Yellowstone. It rises in the Chetish mountains, and flows through a timbered valley about 50 miles in length, so wide that it was mistaken at first for that of the Big Horn or Yellowstone. The stream itself, however, contains but little water, and this in October, 1859, was found only in pools. The second of the eastern branches is the Little Horn, or, taking a literal translation of the Indian name, the "Little Big Horn." This empties into the main stream about 30 miles above Tullock's creek, and flows through a wide bottom towards the north, its length being 60 or 70 miles. Upon its upper tributaries several good camping grounds are found near the base of the mountains.

Of the rivers that unite to form the Big Horn, the Popo-Azie is a short stream, formed by the union of several branches which rise in the southern part of the Wind River chain and to the northward of the South pass. These do not unite until near the junction of the Popo-Azie with Wind river. Its drainage is entirely from the mountains and the supply of water is therefore quite constant. Wind river rises near the northwestern extremity of the Wind River range and flows to the southeast parallel with those mountains and between them and the Big Horn range. Its course is such that a glance at the map leads to an inquiry why it does not flow into, and form a continuation of, the Platte, instead of abruptly changing its course and discharging its water through the Big Horn into the Yellowstone.

This is at once solved by an inspection of the profile of our route between those streams, by which the point of junction of Wind river and the Popo-Azie is shown to be 200 feet below the level of the Platte at the Red buttes. Wind river is rapid and filled with boulders, and its valley is narrow and unproductive. The mountains upon either side are bold and lofty, and present a constant succession of striking landscapes. At the sources of the stream is a lofty basaltic ridge, rising from 12,000 to 13,000 feet above the ocean, stretching across the head of the valley, and connecting the dividing crest of the Rocky mountains with the Big Horn range. Near this point and on the dividing crest, in latitude 43° 28′, a peak rises 13,750 feet above the ocean level, (as determined by angle of elevation taken from route,) which may justly be considered as the topographical centre of North America, the rain which falls upon its sides being drained into the Gulf of Mexico through the Mississippi, the Gulf of California through the Colorado, and the Pacific ocean through the Columbia. I have designated this mountain on the maps as " Union peak."

West of the Big Horn, the other tributaries of the Yellowstone are Pryor's river, Clark's fork, the Big Rosebud, and Beaver river. These streams are comparatively short and small, find their sources in the mountains, and flow to the north.

Beyond these is the valley of the upper Yellowstone, which is, as yet, a *terra incognita*. My expedition passed entirely around, but could not penetrate it. My intention was to enter it from the head of Wind river, but the basaltic ridge previously spoken of intercepted our route and prohibited the attempt. After this obstacle had thus forced us over on the western slope of the Rocky mountains, an effort was made to recross and reach the district in question; but, although it was June, the immense body of snow baffled all our exertions, and we were compelled to content ourselves with listening to marvellous tales of burning plains, immense lakes, and boiling springs, without being able to verify these wonders. I know of but two white men who claim to have ever visited this part of the Yellowstone valley—James Bridger and Robert Meldrum. The narratives of both these men are very remarkable, and Bridger, in one of his recitals, described an immense boiling spring that is a perfect counterpart of the Geysers of Iceland. As he is uneducated, and had probably never heard of the existence of such natural marvels elsewhere, I have little doubt that he spoke of that which he had actually seen. The burning plains described by these men may be volcanic, or more probably burning beds of lignite, similar to those on Powder river, which are known to be in a state of ignition. Bridger also insisted that immediately west of the point at which we made our final effort to penetrate this singular valley, there is a stream of considerable size, which divides and flows down either side of the water-shed, thus discharging its waters into both the Atlantic and Pacific oceans. Having seen this phenomenon on a small scale in the highlands of Maine, where a rivulet discharges a portion of its waters into the Atlantic and the remainder into the St. Lawrence, I am prepared to concede that Bridger's "Two Ocean river" *may* be a verity. Had our attempt to enter this district been made a month later in the season, the snow would have mainly disappeared, and there would have been no insurmountable obstacles to overcome. I cannot doubt, therefore, that at no very distant day the mysteries of this region will be fully revealed, and though small in extent, I regard the valley of the upper Yellowstone as the most interesting unexplored district in our widely expanded country.

The general course of the Yellowstone itself, after leaving the mountains, is a little north of east through four and a half degrees of longitude, and then northeast to its junction with the Missouri. Throughout its entire length it flows through a wide, open valley, bounded by high, rolling hills.

This valley has long been the home of countless herds of Buffalo and consequently the favorite hunting ground of the Indians.

When my party first reached the bluff overlooking the Yellowstone, the sight was one which, in a few years, will have passed away forever. I estimated that about 15 miles in length of the wide valley was in view. The entire tract of 40 or 50 square miles was covered with buffalo as thickly as in former days, in the west, (when cattle were driven to an eastern market,) a pasture field would be, which was intended only to furnish subsistence to a large drove for a single night. I will not venture an estimate of their probable numbers.

And here I would remark, that the wholesale destruction of the buffalo is a matter that should receive the attention of the proper authorities. It is due first and mainly to the fact that the skin of the *female* is alone valuable for robes. The skin of the male, over three years old, is never used for that purpose, the hair on the hind quarters being not longer than that on a horse, while, on the fore quarters, it has a length of from four to six inches. The skin is also too thick and heavy to be used for anything but lodge coverings, while the flesh is coarse and unpalatable, and is never used for food when any other can be had. The result is that the females are always singled out by the hunter, and consequently the males in a herd always exceed the females, in the proportion of not less than ten to one.

Another, but far less important, cause of their rapid extinction is the immense number of wolves in the country, which destroy the young. The only remedy that would have the slightest effect in the case would be a prohibition of the trade of buffalo robes and a premium upon wolf skins. I fear it is too late for even this remedy, and notwithstanding the immense herds that are yet to be found, I think it is more than probable that another generation will witness almost the entire extinction of this noble animal.

THE UPPER MISSOURI AND ITS TRIBUTARIES.

Beyond the upper Yellowstone, and immediately at the foot of the main-divide of the Rocky mountains, lies the valley of the Upper Missouri and of the Three Forks. The Missouri is formed by the junction, in latitude 45° 56′, of the Gallatin, Madison, and Jefferson rivers, streams which take their rise in the Rocky mountains and have a general northerly course. Their order, in relative importance, is the reverse of that in which they are named above, the Gallatin being the least and the Jefferson the greatest, although the difference in size is not marked. The soil in the valley of the Three Forks is good, the grass fine, and the streams are all bordered by fringes of trees that add great beauty to the landscape. The neighboring mountains are well timbered, and will, therefore, furnish an abundance of lumber for the future settlers, and there is no part of the field of our exploration that on the whole presents greater natural advantages than this. Standing upon the bluff north of the junction of the three rivers, and looking to the south, the eye rests upon a charming picture of level and fertile valleys, environed by gently-sloping and grass-clad hills, and divided, to appearance, into immense parks by the hedge-like fringes of trees lining the river banks. In the distance snowy ranges of mountains fill the horizon upon all sides, and furnish the delightful landscape with a pure and appropriate setting. Below the Three Forks the Missouri flows nearly north for two and a quarter degrees of latitude, passing through the gate of the mountains and over the Great Falls, and then changes its course to nearly due east, keeping this general direction through eight degrees of longitude, ultimately bending to the southeast and mingling its waters with those of the Mississippi on their way to the Gulf of Mexico. The tributaries of this great river, between the Platte and the Yellowstone, have been already described. Of the branches between the Three Forks and the Yellowstone I can speak but briefly. Of those flowing from the north and west the chief are the Sun, the Teton, Maria's river, and Milk river. The two latter are large and important rivers; but none of these were visited by my expedition. Of those which flow from the south the principal are Smith's river, the Muscleshell, and Big Dry creek.

Smith's river is a mountain stream, flowing through a narrow valley, which would not be capable of supporting a large population. Its passage through the mountain gorge is marked by numerous scenes of striking and romantic beauty.

The Judith rises in the Judith mountains and flows northward into the Missouri. Near its head there is a small tract of fertile country, but, as we approach the Missouri, the river becomes less important, and at the mouth there is but little water in dry seasons within its banks.

Some little doubt has arisen as to the identity of the Muscleshell. Lieutenant Mullan, of the artillery, in 1852 reached it in a journey to the southeast from Fort Benton. He describes it as a stream from two to four feet deep, and with a rapid current, and judged from its banks that, at high water, it was 120 yards in width. This so much exceeded previously conceived ideas of its size, that Lieutenant Warren concluded that Lieutenant Mullan had reached the Yellowstone. Lieutenant Mullins, of the dragoons, who commanded my escort, however, crossed the Muscleshell some 50 miles below where Lieutenant Mullan saw it, and found only a stream of 30 or 40 yards in width. The day before Lieutenant Mullins reached its banks I passed its mouth and found there no running water. I think, therefore, there can be no reasonable doubt that Lieutenant Mullan was correct in saying that he had reached the Muscleshell, and that after leaving the mountains the stream gradually sinks in the earth, growing less in size and importance as it approaches the Missouri. The evidences at its mouth, however, prove that at times it must be a mighty torrent draining a vast area of country.

Of the Big Dry but little is known, aside from the general fact that in the wet season it is a pretentious river and at other times but little else than a dry channel.

NAVIGABLE STREAMS.

The Missouri has been navigated to Fort Benton, and doubtless boats can ascend the short distance from that point to the foot of the Great Falls, but this has only been accomplished during high water, and the first steamer that reached Fort Benton, was warped over several of the rapids above the mouth of the Yellowstone. Lieutenant Maynadier, in his report on the Yellowstone, expresses the confident conviction that at no distant day boats will ascend that stream to the mountains. The attempt has not yet been made, and it is hazardous to predict that science cannot overcome any obstacles that may be presented, but when the tables of altitudes, prepared from barometric measurements, are examined the showing is far from favorable to the realization of Lieutenant

Maynadier's hopes. The Yellowstone, at the point at which Lieutenant Maynadier struck it, below the mouth of Shield's river, is about 200 feet higher than the Missouri at the Three Forks, and 1,700 feet higher than the Missouri at Fort Benton. Shield's river is but little further than Fort Benton from the point of junction of the Yellowstone and Missouri, and as the profile shows a nearly uniform descent in the Yellowstone, it is evident that the fall of the latter is 1,700 feet greater than that of the former in a nearly equal distance. Considering the difficulties encountered from the current of the Missouri, I cannot but think that the navigation of a stream whose waters possess such a greatly accumulated velocity is at least problematical.

When I was upon the Big Horn I was impressed with the conviction that that stream could be navigated by boats of proper construction as far as the lower cañon, or about 80 miles from its mouth, but an examination of the barometric heights shows a fall in this distance of 620 feet, which must create a current of great power. Hence I can readily understand how Lieutenant Maynadier failed to appreciate the constant and rapid descent of the Yellowstone, and I conclude that the objections to the navigability of that stream are equally valid with reference to the Big Horn.

RAILROAD AND WAGON ROAD ROUTES.

The country between the outlier and the Missouri is the high, broken prairie of the west, and but little difficulty will be found, as far as regards grade, in crossing it either with wagon or railroads in any direction.

The district between the Yellowstone and Missouri from Fort Union, in latitude 48°, as far south as 46° 30′, is believed to be very broken, and, from the nature of the soil, it will offer great difficulties to the construction of a permanent roadway.

The broad valley of the Yellowstone affords peculiar facilities for a railroad, and it is, moreover, the most direct route to the important region about the Three Forks, with all its agricultural and mineral wealth.

The only serious obstacle that would be encountered in this entire distance is the ridge between the waters of the Gallatin and those of the Yellowstone, and, as this is shown to be only about 1,700 feet in height, it is believed it could be crossed without great difficulty, especially as the approaches upon either side are shown by profiles of our route to be of easy grade.

The valley of the Yellowstone can be reached with comparative facility near its mouth, or near the junction of the Powder, but between these points the country lying to the east is represented, by all who have passed over it, as broken, barren, and impracticable.

At the eastern base of the Big Horn mountains there is a belt of country some 20 miles in width that is peculiarly suitable for a wagon road, and which I doubt not will become the great line of travel into the valley of the Three Forks.* Being immediately at the base of the mountains, this strip is watered by the numerous streams which rise in the hills but soon disappear in the open country below, while the upheaval of the mountain crest is so uniform in direction that a comparatively straight road can be laid out close to their foot without encountering grades that are seriously objectionable. I travelled through this region with heavily loaded wagons in the fall of 1859 without embarrassment.

The valley of the Big Horn, from latitude 43° 30′ to latitude 45° 10′ north, is surrounded on all sides by mountain ridges, and presents but few agricultural advantages, The geological structure of the mountains, however, would lead us to expect valuable mineral deposits in the ridges. This region is totally unfit for either rail or wagon roads.

---

*NOTE FOR 1867.—The recent developments of this country have opened this route by the foot of the Big Horn range, and forts are now established along the entire line.

Between the Yellowstone and Missouri the country is mainly broken and unattractive. Lieutenant Mullins, in his journey from Fort Benton to Fort Union, followed as closely as possible the crest of the divide between the waters of these rivers. I quote from his report this language: "The country passed over in my route, with the exception of that portion in and near the Judith mountains, and lying contiguous to the streams forming the drainage of the same, is worthless. Although it is a much nearer route from Fort Union to Fort Benton, than that on the other side of the river, I think the latter far preferable for military purposes. A railroad could be constructed along my route at comparatively slight cost, as there are no great elevations to overcome." North of the Missouri the country is open as soon as the stream is left, and but little difficulty will be found in traversing it in almost any direction. The usual route for the traders between Fort Benton and Fort Union is on this side of the Missouri, and partially in the valley of Milk river.

My route in 1860 ran near the base of the dividing ridge of the Rocky mountains from the vicinity of the South Pass to Henry's lake, a distance of about 200 miles, keeping on the eastern slope to the head of Wind river and subsequently on the western. The summit of the ridge is lofty throughout, and I do not believe it will ever be thought expedient to cross it by rail between the points named.

The valley of the Three Forks offers every facility for transit, the open country bordering upon the Gallatin, the Madison, and the Jefferson presenting an agreeable contrast to the surrounding rugged mountains. Low pass, near Henry's lake, through which I entered this valley, is as favorable, as regards elevation, as any point can be for crossing the dividing crest of the mountains. It is 1,500 feet lower than the South pass, and without any prolonging of the route, rails can be laid from the waters of the Madison to those of Henry's fork of the Columbia, through this pass, not using a grade of over 50 feet to the mile.

MINERAL PRODUCTS.

Very decided evidences of the existence of gold were discovered both in the valley of the Madison and in the Big Horn mountains, and we found some indications of its presence also in the Black Hills, between the forks of the Shayenne. The very nature of the case, however, forbade that an extensive or thorough search for the precious metals should be made by an expedition such as I conducted through this country. The party was composed in the main of irresponsible adventurers, who recognized no moral obligation resting upon them. They were all furnished with arms and ammunition, while we were abundantly supplied with picks and shovels, and carried with us a partial stock of provisions. Thus the whole outfit differed in no essential respect from that which would be required if the object of the expedition had only been prospecting for gold. The powder would serve for blasting and the picks and shovels were amply sufficient for the primitive mining of the gold pioneer, while the arms would be equally useful for defence and in purveying for the commissariat. It is thus evident that if gold had been discovered in any considerable quantity the party would have at once disregarded all the authority and entreaties of the officers in charge and have been converted into a band of gold miners, leaving the former the disagreeable option of joining them in their abandonment of duty, or of returning across the plains alone, through innumerable perils. It was for these reasons that the search for gold was at all times discouraged, yet still it was often difficult to restrain the disposition to "prospect," and there were moments when it was feared that some of the party would defy all restraint.

The lignite beds found so frequently upon the Powder, Platte, and Yellowstone, are not coal, though often mistaken for it, but are not entirely valueless as fuel. The troops formerly stationed near Platte Bridge used some of the best variety for that purpose, and it was found quite serviceable.

AGRICULTURAL PROSPECTS.

Probably over three-fourths of the country over which the explorations of my party extended possesses a soil that, other conditions being favorable, would render a generous return for the labors of the husbandman. The most marked and peculiar feature of the entire region is the absence of trees. Apart from the mountains it is only upon the immediate banks of the streams that timber is to be found, and even under these circumstances it is confined to a narrow belt, very rarely extending 200 yards from the water's edge. In small ravines near the summits of certain ridges there are occasionally found a few bushes or vines, but these are so rare that their presence is always deemed a fact worthy of special mention. In the mountain districts considerable timber is found which may meet the chief needs of the country, but a very small portion of it only would be deemed valuable in a lumber region. Considering the nature of the country, however, the timber in the mountains is an inestimable blessing, and it will be the source of innumerable benefits.

The bunch and buffalo grasses of the plains are highly nutritious, and afford sustenance to immense herds of buffalo. They are of quick growth, ripen rapidly, and by early summer are as perfectly cured as possible. Standing in this condition throughout the winter, animals find excellent grazing during the entire year without human aid. The quantity of grass yielded on any given area of ground is not proportionately large, and thus the extent of territory ranged over by animals wintering on the plains far exceeds that which would be amply sufficient to furnish them with subsistence in more favorable regions, but, nevertheless, it is a great grazing country, and can support in the aggregate vast herds of cattle.

The question, "Why are these vast plains destitute of timber?" is often asked and variously answered. The most popular explanation is the annual recurrence of immense fires, whence the conclusion is drawn that if those fires could be avoided, trees would at once spring up in abundance.

Those who advocate this theory add as a corollary, that if trees once cover the country, rain will become more abundant. Sufficient data have not as yet been obtained for a final and full discussion of this subject, and theory is yet to be substituted by facts. I nevertheless believe that the well-known hypothesis of Professor Gayot—that the ocean is the great source of the supply of moisture for all continents, the water absorbed by the atmosphere being precipitated in rain by coming in contact with the colder currents of air, and that therefore it naturally follows, (all other things being equal,) that the interior of all large bodies of land must be comparatively destitute of moisture by reason of remoteness from the source of supply—is sustained in every respect by the meteorology of this region. Mountain ranges intercepting the upper currents of air would cause the moisture in them to be precipitated, and hence the mountain sides remote from the ocean would be much more abundantly supplied with rain than the level tracts in the same vicinity. While travelling from the Missouri river westward, over the plains, in 1859, we scarcely saw a drop of rain until we reached the Black Hills, where we encountered several hard showers. Between the Black Hills and the Big Horn mountains we were again on the plains, and without rain. Along the base of the latter range we found frequent showers and an abundance of clear, beautiful water. The same remarks apply to our explorations in 1860. During a large portion of the early part of the season we were in the mountainous districts, and frequently drenched by heavy showers. During the latter half of the season, while remote from the mountains, but little rain was encountered. It is a source of extreme regret to me that the importance of this question of the amount of rain-fall in the country was not fully impressed upon my mind at the commencement of the expedition that I might have placed a more competent observer at Fort Pierre, and one who would have given proper attention to this subject, as meterological observations made at that post would, if carefully kept, have helped greatly to settle many doubtful points. The rains were all noted, it is true, but the amount of the fall was not accurately measured. I have examined these notes carefully, and, from the imperfect data they embody, estimate the annual fall of rain and melted snow at less than 20 inches. General Humphreys, in his report on the physics and hydraulics of the Mississippi river, gives us the result of one year and eleven months' observations at this point, a mean annual fall of rain of 13.8 inches, and in the same report the mean annual fall at Fort Laramie is given at 16.6 inches, and at Fort Benton 13.1 inches. These data all point to the conclusion that the annual fall of rain in this entire region is not probably more than 15 inches. The immediate banks of the water courses would feel this lack of moisture the least. Hence it is here we find the only trees that grow upon the plains proper. In the heads of ravines we naturally expect springs, and in such localities a few bushes are occasionally found. Copious rains always prevail in mountain ranges, and in them trees abound. From all these facts I am forced to conclude that the converse of the usually accepted theory is correct, or that the absence of forests is due to lack of moisture, instead of the latter being a result of the former fact. I suggest that the importance of this matter is such as to justify a thorough investigation. Careful and reliable data of the amount of rain-fall will alone determine the productiveness of the vast region between the Missouri and the Rocky mountains.

INDIAN TRIBES.

The principal Indian tribes inhabiting the explored region are the Dakotas, or Sioux, and the Absaroukas, or Crows. The Dakotas are by far the most numerous and powerful. This tribe is a confederacy of ten bands, speaking the same language, but separately organized under their own chiefs. These subdivisions are so decided that it is not uncommon for some of the bands to be engaged in a war in which others do not take part, although they never war upon each other. They occupy the country on both sides of the Missouri from the mouth of the Yellowstone to Fort Randall, and from Powder river, on the west, to Minnesota river, on the east. Some efforts have been made to introduce Christianity and civilization among the Dakotas of Minnesota, and their language has been reduced to writing and a dictionary thereof published. West of the Missouri the missionary has not yet visited them, and they know nothing of civilization save as it is presented in rather a doubtful phase by the traders. The bands differ materially in their disposition towards the whites. Those to the south or near the Platte seem disposed to be peaceable, while those in the north are fierce, ill-tempered, and warlike. I am not surprised at the horrible atrocities committed by those savages since I visited them, and I am impressed with the conviction that there can be no permanent peace with them until the policy of the government shall be radically changed. Some restrictions must be imposed upon the sale of arms and ammunition. The agents must not be permitted to deal with the Indians entirely through the traders, and to be dependent upon them for protection, guides, transportation, interpreters, &c., &c. Moreover, when depredations are committed by the Indians, and it becomes necessary to chastise them, treaties should not be subsequently negotiated in which their future quiet is purchased by large presents, as was the case in the Harney treaty of 1857, which I consummated at Fort Pierre, as this is simply offering a premium for future outrages, and lessens the savage's appreciation of the power and majesty of the government. In these and many minor respects sweeping reforms are vitally necessary in our Indian policy.

The Absaroukas, or Crows, occupy the country west of Powder river, as far as the valley of the Three Forks of the Missouri, on both sides of the Yellowstone. They have had little or no intercourse with the whites save traders. They are divided into three bands—the mountain, lower, and middle—together, numbering about 3,000 souls. They have never had trouble with the whites, and are disposed to be peaceable. They occupy the best buffalo ground in the west, but are jealous of intrusion; and while they expressed a willingness that I should pass through their country, were careful to add that they could not consent to my remaining. As game becomes scarce the territory they claim as their own is constantly encroached upon by surrounding tribes, and this fact leads to frequent wars. The Crows, though few in number, are noted warriors, and thus far have been able to maintain their independence and defend their territory. At the time of my visit, however, they evidently feared the effect of this constant pressure, and expressed a dread of being ultimately overpowered. Though they have seen little of civilized life, they have learned all its vices. Nothing was safe that they could steal, and their licentiousness was beyond conception. The Crows made (I think) just complaint that their annuities were not delivered to them in their own country, but were taken, in 1860, up the Platte, where they were expected to receive them, being thus compelled to pass through the country of the Sioux, their most formidable enemies—an evidence of gross stupidity and carelessness, or something worse, on the part of those who were responsible for this occurrence.

MISCELLANEOUS.

The report, which is herewith submitted, of Professor F. V. Hayden, now of the University of Pennsylvania, upon the geology of this country, will be found to contain all information upon that branch up to date. Professor Hayden accompanied the expedition, and he has made the geology of the northwest his special study for years, having visited portions of it, not only in company with government explorations, but at his personal expense. His opportunities have therefore been greater than those of any other person for treating this important subject.

The meteorological records of the expedition are also submitted, and it is believed they will furnish important data for judging of the climatic condition of the country.

The botanical specimens collected were placed in the hands of Dr. George Engleman, of St. Louis, whose report will be found herewith.

The zoological specimens were forwarded to Professor S. F. Baird, of the Smithsonian Institution, and the report of this gentleman thereon is likewise submitted.

The fossil plants have been examined by Professor J. S. Newberry, the fossil vertebratæ by Professor Leidy, the unios by by Isaac Lea, of Philadelphia, the carices by Professor Chester Dewey, of Rochester, New York, and the mosses by Professor Sullivan, of Columbus, Ohio. The reports and descriptive catalogues prepared by each of these gentlemen upon their respective topics are appended.

A map of the country passed over by the expedition was prepared in 1861, and forwarded to the department in April, 1864. The recent mining developments caused so great a demand for this map, that the department decided upon its publication. The original having thus passed out of my hands, I, as a part of the report, annex hereto a lithographed copy received from the bureau. My daily journal, and the reports of Lieutenant H. E. Maynadier, Lieutenant John Mullins, Mr. J. Hudson Snowden, and Mr. J. D. Hutton, submitted herewith, embody all the details of the incidents of the expedition.

It is but justice that in closing I should express my thanks to every member of the expedition for the satisfactory manner in which I was aided by them in the performance of the duties committed to my charge.

Respectfully submitted:

W. F. RAYNOLDS,
Brevet Colonel U. S. Army, Major of Engineers.

Brevet Maj. Gen. A. A. HUMPHREYS,
Chief of Engineers, U. S. Army, Washington, D. C.

Journal of Captain W. F. Raynolds, United States army, Corps of Engineers.

CHAPTER I.

PRELIMINARY—FROM FORT PIERRE TO FORT SARPY.

After receiving my instructions I remained in Washington until the 25th of April, engaged in organizing my party, procuring instruments, and arranging the other preliminaries of the expedition.

Fisrt. Lieutenant H. E. Maynadier was assigned to duty with me, and, as contemplated by my instructions, the party was organized for operation in two divisions.

The services of the following persons were procured as assistants, viz: J. D. Hutton, as topographer and assistant artist; J. H. Snowden, as topographer; H. C. Fillebrown, as meteorologist and assistant astronomer; Antoin Schonborn, as meteorologist and artist; Dr. F. V. Hayden, as naturalist and surgeon; Dr. M. C. Hines, as surgeon and assistant naturalist; George Wallace, as time-keeper and computer.

After engaging the services of these gentlemen, and having completed the organization of my party, I received verbal orders from Hon. John B. Floyd, Secretary of War, to employ and take with me the following persons, (without any special duty being assigned to them,) viz: W. D. Stuart, of Virginia; J. M. Lee, of Virginia; P. C. Warring, of Virginia; Wainwright Heileman, of Virginia; George H. Trook, of the District of Columbia; J. P. A. Vincent, of Illinois; Calvin G. Wilson, of Illinois.

These gentlemen were subsequently assigned as assistants in the various branches, and helped to lighten the labors of the expedition.

Private business detained me a few days in Ohio, and I arrived at St. Louis on May 6.

After perfecting my preliminary arrangements in St. Louis, I repaired to Fort Leavenworth, and St. Joseph, Missouri, to complete the outfit, and joined the steamer conveying the party up the river at St. Joseph on June 4.

The party embarked at St. Louis May 28, upon the steamers Spread Eagle and Chippewa, owned by Messrs P. Chouteau, jr., & Co., and employed in their Indian traffic on the Upper Missouri.

Their cargoes consisted of the annual shipment of goods for the American Fur Company; the annuities for the Indians of the Upper Missouri and Blackfeet agencies; the articles destined for the Dakota, or Sioux Indians, under the treaty negotiated by General Harney, which had been entrusted to me for distribution; all our outfit, including animals, provisions, and camp equipage, and also a large amount of supplies designed for Lieutenant Mullan's wagon road expedition.

The boats were thus heavily laden, and were able to travel only during the day, and, above Sioux City, they were compelled to halt also each day to procure their supply of fuel.

Above Sioux City we found the Yancton Sioux at their old camping ground under their chief, Smutty Bear. Upon our arrival they visited the steamers in full costume, and received the usual feast of coffee and hard bread. This is the band that recently sold their lands and are now concentrated upon a reservation and commencing to learn the arts of civilization. Their agent not being with us, we only exchanged friendly greetings, and after a brief halt resumed our progress up the river.

June 13.—We reached Fort Randall, the highest point occupied by United States troops. The post was under command of Captain Lovell, 2d infantry, and garrisoned by four companies of that regiment.

At this point I was joined by Lieutenant Caleb Smith, 2d infantry, with 30 men who were detailed as my escort. Lieutenant Smith was acting as officer of the day when we arrived, but having been relieved embarked his command upon the steamers during the night, so that we were able to depart early the following morning.

June 18.—We arrived at Fort Pierre about noon. We found the principal chiefs embraced in the Harney treaty awaiting our arrival, although but few of the warriors were present. This is accounted for by the scarcity of game near Fort Pierre and the uncertainty of the time of our arrival, as it would be manifestly impossible for a large body of Indians to subsist long in the vicinity of this point.

The Dakotas are, and have long been, the most formidable Indians in this region, and before leaving Washington I had been informed by the Secretary of War, and also by the Commissioner of Indian Affairs, that I might expect trouble from them.

In 1857 their depredations along the Platte had resulted in the despatch of General Harney to that frontier with a suitable force, followed by the severe chastisement of the marauders. Subsequently General Harney negotiated a treaty with them, in which it was stipulated that they should keep the peace while the United States agreed to donate a large amount of supplies, clothing, arms, &c. The latter had been entrusted to me to deliver under the provisions of the treaty.

The tribe is divided into ten distinct bands, and inhabits the country upon each side of the Missouri from the Niobrara to the Yellowstone. One band, the Yanctons, as I have before stated, has made a treaty with the government and gone upon a reservation. The remaining nine contend that such treaty was negotiated without their consent, and deny the right of the Yanctons to sell their lands without the permission of all.

I had been informed that this treaty was the chief cause of the prevalent dissatisfaction, and also that they believed the goods to be given them to be intended to purchase their lands. It was therefore a matter of primary importance that I should at once ascertain their disposition and intentions.

Upon the landing of the steamer I requested that the chiefs would come on board, within an hour, for " a talk ;" and all present, to the number of about 50, soon appeared, decked in full court dress, with feathers and paint in profusion. I was assisted in this council by Colonel Vaughn, former agent for these Indians, and at the time agent for the Blackfeet of the Upper Missouri, and by Major Schoonover, the successor of Colonel Vaughn in this agency.

I opened the council by informing them that I was glad to meet them ; that they had waited long for the goods promised by General Harney, which would have been given them last fall had not the river frozen up ; and that these goods were entirely distinct from their regular annuities, which would be delivered by their agent, who was present. I impressed upon them the fact that my business was simply to carry out the terms of the Harney treaty, and then discharge other duties that had been assigned me by the President. I also sought to make them clearly realize the distinction between the duties with which I was charged and those of their agent, and carefully avoided giving them any intimation of my knowledge of their reported disaffection, or affording them any grounds for even an idea that under any circumstances the right to pass through their country would be relinquished. I closed by inviting them to speak freely. They then asked to be allowed until the next day to deliberate, and promised that they would then give me an answer.

Upon meeting in council the following morning, I suggested to the chiefs that as I had an interpreter in whom I could confide, it was desirable that they should select one in whom they would also be willing to trust.

Thereupon they selected Jean Lefrombois, the interpreter of the trading house. All things being then in readiness, Bear Rib, the head chief of the Unkpapa band, spoke as follows:

MY BROTHER: To whom does this land belong? I believe it belongs to me. Look at me and at this ground. Which do you think is the oldest? The ground, and on it I was born. I have no instruction; I give my own ideas. The land was born before us; I do not know how many years; it is much older than I.

Here we are. We are nine nations, (or bands.) Here are our principal men gathered together. When you tell us anything we wish to say "yes," (that is consent,) to what we like, and you will do the same. There are none of the Yanctons here. Where are they? It is said I have a father, (the agent,) and when he tells me anything I say "yes;" and when I ask him anything, I want him to say "yes."

I call you my brother. What you told me yesterday I believe is true, and I slept satisfied last night. The Yanctons below us are poor people. I don't know where their land is. I pity them. These lower Yanctons I know did own a piece of land, but they sold it long ago. I do not know where they got any more. Since I have been born I do not know who owns two, three, four or more pieces of land. When I get land it is all in one piece, and we were born and still live on it. These Yanctons, we took pity on them. They have no land. We lent them what they had to grow corn on it. We gave them a thousand horses to keep that land for us, but I never told them to steal it and go and sell it. I call you my brother, and I want you to take pity on me, and if any one steals anything from me I want the privilege ot calling for it. If those men, who did it secretly, had asked me to make a treaty for its sale, I should not have consented.

We who are here all understand each other, but I do not agree that they should steal the land and sell it. If the white people want my land, and I should give it to them, where should I stay? I have no place else to go. To-day I talk very good, say good words, and why do they not report them to my great father? What I say to-day I assume will go to my great father?

My brother, what I tell you I tell my father (agent) also. He takes my words and puts them into the water, and makes other reports of what words I send to my great father. I believe there are poor people below who put other words in the place of those I say. My brother, look at me; you do not find me poor, but when this ground is gone then I will be poor indeed.

My brother, I will speak no bad words. What I say I will tell you as a good friend; and what I tell you I wish you to say "yes" to in the same way. When my great father sends white people to this country I do not strike them, but help them, and act as their friend. I know this: if I should go below and have no money, the whites would not let me go.

Everything our great father sends to tell me I know is for our good, and I always listen to him. One thing I am thinking about, and I am going to tell you. General Harney has been here and made ten chiefs. What he said I have not forgotten. General Harney told us that no whites were going to travel through this country; but I see wagons landed and you wish to go through. For my own part I am willing, as you are sent by the great father. I always listen to the whites. I am an Indian, and not bad. What I think is good. I hope you will take pity on me, and that the white people below will keep away.

I hear that a reservation has been kept for the Yanctons below. I will speak again on this subject. If you were to ask me for a piece of land I would not give it. I cannot spare it, and I like it very much. All this country on each side of this river belongs to me. I know that from the Mississippi to this river the country all belongs to us, and that we have traveled from the Yellowstone to the Platte. All this country, as I have said, is ours, and if you, my brother, should ask me for it I would not give it to you, for I like it and I hope you will listen to me.

Two Bears, head chief of the Yanctonais, followed in a long speech in the same strain, asking many questions in regard to the Yancton treaty, to which I replied as best I could, finding my data in a copy of the treaty in possession of Major Schoonover. He closed by earnestly appealing to me not to go through their country.

To this I replied that one of the stipulations of the Harney treaty was that persons travelling by authority should not be molested, and that it was only upon condition that they would carry out that agreement that I should give them the promised goods, thus claiming the privilege of transit as a right and not as a favor. I also told them I could only obey my instructions, and that I had no orders with reference to talking about the Yancton treaty. Their language I would report, but I could do nothing more.

The "talk" continued throughout the day, others of the chiefs speaking, and all dwelling on the Yancton treaty and their unwillingness that I should pass through their country, urging that I should go around by the Yellowstone. Finding, however, that I was firm upon this latter point, they then inquired if the tribes would be held responsible if some of the young men, whom the chiefs could not restrain, should give me trouble.

I replied that the President would undoubtedly hold the entire nation responsible if I should be molested, adding that I was fully able to defend myself, if necessary, and that I should certainly do so I also declared that even if I was entirely alone I was unquestionably entitled to the right of transit through their country, and if I was attacked the President would send soldiers and wipe the entire nation from existence. After further conference, without satisfactory results, I declared I should talk no longer, and demanded an immediate answer to the simple question: Would they take the goods and guarantee my safe passage through their territory, as stipulated in the Harney treaty, or should I keep the former and force my way through? The presentation of this alternative was sufficient, and they replied, "you can go." I then demanded that they should furnish the expedition a competent guide, and stated my readiness to deliver to them their goods. They replied that their people were not present, and therefore they would not be able to remove the latter. It was then arranged that I should deliver them, with the understanding that they should be stored at this point until the chiefs could assemble their people for their removal. All questions being thus amicably settled, the council closed with the shaking of hands.

Shortly after the close of this conference I visited the trading-house, where the chiefs were lodged in a large apartment specially devoted to their accommodation. I found myself "behind the scenes" and in the midst of the revelations usually attending such investigations.

The Indians were lounging about the room literally *au naturel*. They had discarded their gaudy vestments and barbaric trappings, and with these their glory had departed. A filthy cloth about the loins, a worn buffalo robe, or a greasy blanket, constituted the only covering to their nakedness. They were lying about on the floor in all conceivable postures, their whole air and appearance indicating ignorance and indolence, while the inevitable pipe was being passed from hand to hand. Dirt and degradation were the inseparable accompaniments of this scene, which produced an ineffaceable impression upon my mind, banishing all ideas of dignity in the Indian character, and leaving a vividly realizing sense of the fact that the red men are savages.

It having been decided that we should leave the river at this point, our equipment was landed hastily from the steamer, and we pitched our tents upon the bank about dark. Sentinels were posted, and thus we quietly passed our first night in camp.

From June 20 to June 28, we remained at Fort Pierre, delivering the goods to the Indians, purchasing such articles for our outfit as were needed and obtainable, loading our wagons, and perfecting the other arrangements for our journey. I had hoped to obtain horses from the Indians, but they were so perverse that nothing could be procured from them, save through the medium of the regular traders. Whether this was the unbiased and deliberate action of the Indians, or the result of the influence of the traders, I am not prepared to say. It is certain, however, that it operated exclusively for the benefit of the traders, from whom we were compelled to make all indispensable purchases, paying such prices as they were pleased to demand.

On the 23d of June we were visited by a party of some 40 warriors of the Brulé Sioux, under their sub-chief, the Medicine Cap, or as he is generally known, the Frog. This chief seemed to exercise much greater authority over his warriors than is usual, and he is one of the finest representatives of the Indian race I have met. About 35 years of age, straight as an arrow, over six feet in height, possessed of striking features, a keen black eye, and an expressive face, he is physically one of nature's noblemen. I was near the trading-house at the time of his arrival. He ordered his men not to come in but to seat themselves on the outside at some distance and wait for him. These orders were obeyed as quietly and promptly as if by a body of well-trained troops. He then entered the trading-house, accompanied by three of the old men of his band, and I followed. After a prolonged conversation I extended to him an invitation to visit my camp, which he readily accepted. Accordingly early in the afternoon my sentinels reported the approach of a body of Indians from the direction of the trading-house. They proved to be the Brulés, but the Frog was not in the number. They came to our lines but did not attempt to cross, and instead, quietly took seats upon the grass just beyond the limits of our encampment. After the lapse of an hour the chief, accompanied by the old men of his band and an interpreter, was discovered approaching from the trading-house. He walked directly to my tent and apologized for the delay by explaining that he had been in search of an interpreter, knowing that the visit would be useless unless he could talk. I expressed my pleasure at seeing him and also my admiration at the discipline he maintained in his band.

He replied that they were good people; their hearts were good to the whites, and he had tried to restrain the Indians and keep peace with the whites. He added that he had with him but a small party of men, who had come to trade, having left their families and lodges behind them, as they wished to return as soon as possible; they could not bring their lodges for the reason that it required too many horses to carry the poles.

At this I remarked that a white man had improved upon their lodges and made much money by it, (alluding to the Sibley tent,) and pointed to one that was pitched near by. He looked at it, and observing how perfectly smooth it was replied, "It must have a great many poles." I answered, "No; only one." With a start of surprise he exclaimed, "Let me go and see it." He examined it carefully, but when he saw the single pole standing on an iron tripod for a base, with the iron ring and chain at the top, he remarked, sorrowfully, "Ah! that is iron; we cannot have it." I asked, "Why, cannot that be made of wood?" After examining it carefully he replied, "I think it can; I have a man in my tribe I think can make one. He can make an excellent axe helve, and I think he can make that; I will have him try."

The interest and eagerness for improvement exhibited by this Indian was wholly in contradiction to the usually received opinion that they are indifferent or lack curiosity. I should not be surprised to learn that he had extemporized Sibley tents for his band. I also showed him the goods I had left for the Brulés, with which he seemed much pleased, saying they would come with their head chief and get them. Before parting I made him a small present from my limited stock of Indian goods, with which he was greatly delighted.

Tuesday, June 28.—All of our arrangements having been perfected, we broke camp early this morning. The multiplicity of little things demanding attention, the fact that our animals were unused to work, the inexperience of our drivers, and many minor causes, produced innumerable delays, however, so that although we were up at 4 a. m., 9 o'clock had arrived before the train was in motion. All things considered, our start was a success, and we had far less trouble than was anticipated with refractory mules and similar annoyances.

My original intention was to ascend the Missouri to the mouth of the Shayenne, and thence push up the valley of that stream, but from the representations of the traders and Indians I was satisfied that travel by this route would be arduous if not impracticable, and as it was essential that our animals should become fully accustomed to work before attempting difficult roads, I determined to follow the ordinary course of the traders to the Shayenne.

We started directly west, following the road to Fort Laramie. At the distance of about a mile from camp we reached the bluffs, at the foot of which were a number of Indian graves, the bodies being either enclosed in boxes, many of which were not more than four feet in length, although containing the remains of adults, or else wrapped in skins or blankets and laid upon scaffolds of poles from four to six feet in height. Some of the bodies were rolled in scarlet blankets and flags, and other votive offerings of cloth or ornaments decorated all the scaffolds. The scene was well calculated to remind us that we had left civilization and were now among savages.

Through a convenient ravine, a long gradual slope of about two miles brought us without difficulty to the summit of the bluffs, where we entered upon a wide table-land so nearly level that the eye could not detect the course of the drainage.

Passing some four miles over this high prairie, we reached the descent to the valley of Willow creek, a tributary to the Wakpa Shicha, or Bad river, or, as called by the traders, the Teton. The declivity was abrupt, and in descending it the awkwardness of one of the drivers resulted in the inversion of the relative positions of his cart, its contents, and himself. No serious damage resulted, however, and we soon reached the bed of Willow creek, and encamped after a day's march of eight and a half miles.

This point is the traders' usual camping ground for the first night after leaving Fort Pierre, the rule being a short march for the first day. We found here but a scanty supply of poor water, stagnant in pools in the bed of the stream. Fuel is also scarce, the timber being limited to a few cottonwoods and willows. The grass is tolerably good. The valley of the stream is narrow with high hills on each side. We were accompanied to camp by one of the employés of the trading post, and the afternoon was occupied in writing final adieu to friends, to be sent back to Fort Pierre, and there await the return of the steamers from the mouth of the Yellowstone.

Wednesday, June 29.—We left camp at 6½ o'clock, a. m., crossing Willow creek and climbing a long and steep ascent before again reaching the table-land. Our day's march was over high and somewhat broken country, the ground being parched and dry, and the whole landscape characterized by the sombre tints of autumn. The general avidity was occasionally relieved by narrow strips of green verdure marking the course of the drainage during the melting of snow or in wet weather. Now should be the commencement of harvest, but no crops would ripen here for lack of moisture.

Our route lay along the divide between branches of the Teton river, having Willow creek upon the right for the first seven or eight miles. About ten miles from camp we crossed the bed of Frozen Man's creek, a small prairie drain now dry. Its valley promises tolerable grass but no wood. We encamped after a march of 15 miles on Water Holes creek, where, as the name indicates, a small supply of water was found standing in pools. The pasturage was passable, but our suppers were cooked with fuel brought from our previous encampment on Willow creek. During the day we did not see a stick of wood large enough for a riding switch.

Thursday, June 30.—This morning we lost one of our Indian horses. During the night he slipped his halter, and not being accustomed to the herd, wandered off and, by his wildness, defied all efforts at recapture. When last seen he was travelling towards Fort Laramie at a rate of speed that justified the expectation of his early arrival at that post.

Since leaving Fort Pierre we have been following the Fort Laramie road, but this morning, about two miles from camp, abandoned it, diverging to the north and crossing the ridge separating the waters of the Teton from those of the Shayenne. The country is high but not broken, offering no special obstructions to the passage of wagons.

We encamped at night near the head of a small tributary of the Shayenne, which the guide calls Hermaphrodite creek. Its water was also found in stagnant pools, and was quite warm, although not unpalatable. The distance travelled to-day was 19¾ miles. The night was cloudy, a fact which prevented astronomical observations.

Friday, July 1.—We left camp this morning at 5½ o'clock, the character of the country traversed being unchanged. To our right the valley of the Shayenne could be seen in the distance, the neighboring bluffs presenting a rugged and forbidding appearance.

Six miles from camp we crossed the bed of another stream, Dry Wood creek by name, now consisting only of a series of water holes, and resembling in its general characteristics those previously described.

At about 10 miles distance from the starting point of the day, we entered upon a high plateau stretching out five or six miles and ending at the bluffs of the Shayenne. Here we found our first serious obstructions. The descent was very abrupt, and at one point it was found necessary to attach ropes to our wagons and carts, and, having them thus steadied, to lower them down by hand. A little labor will, however, render the road perfectly practicable.

Upon reaching the river bottom we crossed the mouth of Plum creek, an insignificant stream, in whose passage we experienced more trouble from mud than water, and encamped about a mile beyond in a grove of cottonwood trees, upon the banks of the Shayenne, which, at this point, is muddy and rapid, resembling the Missouri upon a diminished scale. It is the first running water we have seen since leaving the Missouri, a distance of 63 miles.

In the country travelled by us thus far, there is not suitable timber sufficient to construct a single log cabin 15 feet square, and if half a dozen settlers were to locate upon it they would exhaust the entire stock of fuel before the first winter had elapsed, with the imminent danger of meeting death by freezing. It is practicable, however, for ordinary frontier travel at the proper season, although the scarcity of wood and water and the quality of the grass would forbid attempts of this nature upon any extended scale. That the country is totally unfit for agricultural purposes appears to me unquestionable.

Saturday, July 2.—I determined to spend the day in the valley of the Shayenne, and explore this stream above and below the point at which we had reached it. In order that no time should be lost, however, we struck our tents and crossing the river encamped about three miles above our previous position.

Difficulty was experienced in fording the Shayenne, its bed being little else than a quicksand. At the point ultimately selected the water was but two and a half feet deep, just touching the body of the carts but doing no harm. By rapid driving all the teams crossed in safety excepting one cart, which sunk in the sand, thus compelling us to unload it. The chronometers I directed to be carried over by hand, thereby nearly losing one, the horse of its bearer, Mr. Fillebrown, sinking in the quicksand, but he, having the presence of mind to dismount, came over with his burden in safety.

The valley of the Shayenne is about a mile in width, with a fringe of cottonwood trees bordering the stream. The soil is good, the surface being covered with a heavy growth of long grass. The trees are short, gnarled, and very much scattered, presenting the general appearance of old orchards, and there is no difficulty in passing through in any direction.

Our camp is in one of those open groves, and the refreshing grass and grateful shade is in striking contrast with our previous encampments. The bluffs bordering the river are about 500 feet in height, being in most places impassable for wagons, and are covered with the bunch grass of the prairie.

Before leaving camp this morning I directed Mr. Hutton to descend the river, as far as compatible with a return in the evening, sketching its course and ascertaining its general character. Mr. Snowden also received the same instructions as to explorations up stream, and each gentleman was accompanied by an attendant.

Both returned promptly, and Mr. Hutton reported that the valley below remained of the same character as at our crossing, the bluffs, however, becoming more broken and impracticable. Mr. Snowden reported that above the river impinged frequently upon the bluffs on either side, so that it would be impossible to follow the valley without making frequent crossings. This determined me to leave the river and proceed along the bluffs on the north side—a course in accordance with the advice of our Indian guide.

The day has been very sultry, the thermometer standing at 100° in the shade; the difference between the wet and dry bulbs being 30°. The exposure to wind and sun is telling upon the faces and lips of the party, totally unaccustomed thereto, but, in other respects, the continued good health of all is remarkable.

Sunday, July 3.—We remained in camp to-day, believing this to be my duty to my Maker, my country, and the party. I have determined that nothing but absolute necessity shall induce me to move camp on the Sabbath, recognizing as I do that the solemn command for its observance is as binding upon the plains as elsewhere. Consequently nothing save the necessary guard duty was required of any of the party.

After dinner I invited all who were willing to attend a short religious service, consisting of the reading of a portion of Scripture, and of a short sermon, and closing with prayer. I am glad to be able to say the service was well attended.

Towards night a heavy gale arose, requiring all hands to turn out and fasten down their tents. After dark a bright light was observed in the prairie to the north of us, which Bridger interpreted as indicating that the Indians are watching our movements.

Monday, July 6.—We had not the time to show our patriotism by remaining in camp to-day, and therefore concluded to do so by marching. We left camp before 6 o'clock, and passing up the valley a short distance, availed ourselves of a convenient ravine to climb the hills upon the north side of the river. The ascent was long and tedious, but most of the teams reached the summit without doubling, and we then started along the divide between the Shayenne and Cherry creek, which soon became very narrow, until about six miles from camp, the river turned more to the southwest, our route continuing along the divide nearly west.

The day was intensely hot, the thermometer standing at 107° in the shade, and our sufferings were extreme. No tree nor shrub afforded shelter from the beating rays of the sun, while a brisk breeze from the southwest, sweeping over the parched and heated soil, struck us like a blast from a furnace. Both men and animals were almost overcome by fatigue and great thirst, the only water upon the route being one or two small pools that were found to be far too salty for use. All who could be spared from the train scattered over the country in pursuit of water, and ultimately, after a terrible march of 19 miles, a pool was found that could at least be swallowed, although the taste resembled that of a weak solution of Epsom salts. Here we determined to encamp, and gladly sought shelter beneath the wagons and carts from the blazing sun.

Before leaving the steamers the party had been presented by Mr. Chouteau with a basket of champagne, which had been kept with special reference to the celebration of the national birthday. After camping, therefore, it was brought forth, and although warmer than is generally desirable, our thirst and exhaustion rendered it very enjoyable and refreshing. As to myself, the heat and labors of the day brought on a high fever, and I laid down with the reflection that this was a Fourth of July not soon to be forgotten.

Tuesday, July 5.—A change of wind in the night brought an agreeable change of temperature, and morning found me well and ready for an early start. Two miles from camp we found a pool of fresh water, with which our canteens were filled. Two or three miles further other pools were found, all being in the beds of small streams which drain into the Shayenne. Our day's march was over a gently rolling country, through which several herds of antelope were roaming, being the first game that has been seen. The hills are covered with grass, but it is parched and dry, and only in the valleys is there any relief from the universally brown appearance of the landscape. The soil is good, and if irrigation were possible, would yield bountifully; but, judging from the present season, the want of moisture is beyond remedy.

The valley of the Shayenne has been visible upon the left most of the time since we abandoned it, so that it can be traced with considerable accuracy. The hills by the river are very broken, and we have kept near the divide for the purpose of finding good travelling. Our Indian guide states that Cherry creek lies but a short distance to the north. Owing to the hardships of yesterday I did not attempt a long march to-day, but halted on a small branch of the Shayenne, after travelling 12½ miles. We found water again in holes and the grass tolerably good, but wood as usual is scarce.

Wednesday, July 6.—The stream upon which we were encamped last night is called by our Indian guide Painted Wood creek, a title for which the only possible excuse is the presence of so little wood of any description.

We have been travelling for some days upon an old Indian trail, which has materially aided us. Soon after leaving camp this morning, however, we discovered that this was carrying us too far to the north, and we therefore abandoned it, continuing nearly due west and keeping near the upper part of the drainage into the Shayenne, the streams all running to the southeast into that river. The country continues unchanged—a high rolling prairie, with no distinctive characteristic from that previously described.

I despatched Mr. Hutton to locate the forks of the Shayenne, but he returned at night without succeeding, reporting that the country in the immediate vicinity of the river is very broken, being impassable on horseback in most places, so that he had not the time to penetrate as far as would be necessary and return at night, as he had been instructed. Another attempt will be made to-morrow.

Here the river bluffs are visible apparently about ten miles to our left, and the country in the distance does not threaten any difficulty in its crossing, but it is only by close inspection that its true character can be determined. Cherry creek can be seen three or four miles to our right, and our Indian guide states that there is running water in it only in the wet season. Its valley is level and open, and contains but little timber. As the soil here is excellent, I question if the scarcity of timber is not due entirely to the absence of moisture.

Our camp is upon another branch of the Shayenne, and water is still only found in holes, while wood also continues very scarce. After getting into camp I attempted some computations, but found the weather too hot for mental labor, the thermometer standing at 104° in the shade.

Thursday, July 7.—An early start was effected this morning with the intention of a long day's march. We travelled for three miles up a gentle slope, reaching the divide between the Shayenne and Owl Feather creek, the tributary of Cherry creek, which we have seen on our right for the past two days. Six miles from camp we reached the creek itself, and found it in a wide open valley, with its banks lined by trees, presenting a prospect beautiful in itself, and especially pleasing from its variety. The water in this stream is also standing in pools, but is abundant. The relics of a large encampment prove this to be a favorite resort of the Indians, and the "signs" also indicate the recent presence of buffaloes.

Twelve miles from camp, Owl Feather creek bent to the northwest, and we left it advancing still westward. By a long and gradual slope, we again ascended the divide between it and the Shayenne, the summit being the highest point yet reached. From it we had our first view of the Black Hills. Behind the entire line of our day's march was visible, and in the north could be seen the far remote buttes about the sources of the Moreau. Nothing, however, save the Black Hills, towards which we were advancing, was visible that threatened to intercept our march, the neighboring country resembling that we had already crossed without noteworthy difficulty.

We descended a short distance from the summit of the ridge, and encamped upon another tributary of the Shayenne. I immediately ordered a well to be dug in the bed of the stream, and at a depth of three feet found water of the temperature of 54° Fahr., which was an immense improvement upon any we have tasted since being deprived of the ice-water of the steamers. Water for our animals was found as usual in holes, but wood at this camp was still very scarce. The grass was tolerably fair.

There has been more gravel noticeable in the soil passed over to-day than heretofore, and occasional outcroppings of an inferior sandstone show decided geological changes, indicating that we are approaching the upheaval of the Black Hills.

Mr. Hutton spent the day away from the train in locating the forks of the Shayenne, his efforts being crowned with success. He reports the country near the river as generally impassable, even on horseback, so that a march up the river bank would have been impossible. Clouds obscured the sky at night, and prevented observations.

Friday, July 8.—We left camp at 5 a. m., and, about four miles out, crossed a branch of the stream upon which we had been encamped. Water, in holes here, enabled us to refresh our animals, and we then pushed on through a fine level country, crossing several small drains emptying into the Shayenne.

The road presented no obstacles whatever for 11 miles, when we reached the bed of "Thick-timbered creek," the descent to which was steep, although not very difficult. This creek takes its name from a few cottonwoods, elms, &c., in its valley, the presence of a little timber being a rarity sufficient to justify such a recognition of the fact. After a further march, we encamped on Iriquois creek, a tributary of the Shayenne, whose water is very salt, and totally unfit for drinking. We found some that was better by digging, but even this augmented rather than allayed thirst. Nevertheless, as we had already travelled over 16 miles, and the thermometer now stood at 110° Fahr. in the shade, there was no remedy.

We have now been out 10 travelling days, and are 140 miles from Fort Pierre. The whole country traversed is entirely unfit for the residence of whites, although the soil, aside from its lack of moisture, might be pronounced good.

A few antelope are the only living things we have met in this desolate tract, but buffaloes have evidently been here, and may return at more favorable seasons of the year. Six bulls were seen to-day in the distance, as we drove into camp, being our first sight of these famous "lords of the prairie." We are now approaching the Black Hills, however, and will soon have them around us in abundance.

The stream upon which we are encamped now has water only in holes, but the marks along the valley prove unmistakably that at times it is deep and probably impassable. The banks are abrupt, but a crossing was found without difficulty. To-morrow we hope to reach the north fork of the Shayenne, and once more see running water.

As yet we have met no Indians, nor any indications of their presence here for months, although the fires burning around us nightly show that they are watching our movements. Our Indian guide, who was furnished at Fort Pierre by the chiefs in council, has been very efficient, perpetually watching for good roads, and, since he has learned the requirements of our wagons, rarely mistaking. I have furnished him a mule, and he now seems extremely happy and talks of accompanying us through the entire trip. His felicity is probably explained by the fact that he has been abundantly fed; a full stomach constituting the Indian idea of the acme of all human happiness.

Dark clouds at night prevented astronomical observations, and seem to promise rain, a most acceptable boon, if it shall cool the heated air.

Saturday, July 9.—We left camp at 5 a. m., and after about four miles march came upon a small pool of water which had been fresh, but now gave irrefutable evidence that at least one buffalo was in this region, the color and flavor of the barn being unmistakable. This fact, however, did not prevent its being used freely, nor the taking away of a supply in our canteens—anything that will not create thirst being acceptable.

The country is here very level, considering our proximity to the Shayenne, and an occasional turn to avoid a hill or gully was all that was required till we approached the river, when the abruptness of the descent necessitated considerable search to find a suitable road for our wagons. We were successful, however, and by noon crossed the stream, and pitched our tents in a grove of young cottonwoods on its banks.

The river here is a clear, beautiful stream, about 30 yards in width and two feet deep, flowing over a stony or gravel bottom. The banks are steep and of loose sand, rendering care necessary in the selection of the points at which we entered and emerged from the stream in our fording, but this was the only difficulty encountered.

Our camp is on a gentle slope on the southwest side of the river, above the mouth of Bear Butte creek, with a row of cottonwoods between us and the water, and the spot is far more inviting than any we have found since commencing our life under canvas. Timber here is still scarce, and all that is visible could be easily transplanted into a plot of a quarter of an acre. Very little can be found that is fit for fuel, and none that could be used for building purposes. The scarcity of timber is, in fact, one of the most salient features of the country. From the Missouri to this point, a distance of 155 miles, we have scarcely seen trees enough, on the average, to furnish shade for a single person in each square mile traversed—certainly not, if we except those in the valley of the Shayenne.

The thermometer for the past week has ranged from 100° to 110° Fahr., and yet our marches have averaged 15 miles per day. This evening we have had quite a storm, accompanied with rain, which it is to be hoped will cool the air.

Sunday, July 10.—We remained in camp to-day, in accordance with my previously expressed determination. The rain last night failed to cool the air, as the thermometer this afternoon stands at 100°. This evening a storm seems to be impending in the northwest.

Monday, July 11.—We left camp at 5 o'clock and 20 minutes a. m., and travelled westward near the divide between Bear Butte creek and Cottonwood creek, the river bearing off to the north. Our route laid over a fine level country, crossing no streams, the drainage tending towards Bear Butte creek, and the ridge upon the right being somewhat broken.

The day was very fine, the thermometer not rising above 80° Fahr., and the men and animals being in excellent condition, after the rest of yesterday, we made rapid progress. After travelling 13 miles I ordered the train to incline to the left for water, which we found in the north fork of Bear Butte creek, where we encamped, after having marched 16.8 miles. We had scarcely pitched our tents before we were visited by a heavy rain, coming from the west out of the Black Hills.

After dinner, as the storm seemed to be over, a large party started for the summit of Bear butte, which was not a mile from our camp. Before reaching it, however, they were drenched by another shower. This hill is very steep and the ascent difficult, a large part of the path laying over rock debris, which, on the steep slope, furnished only a very treacherous footing. The butte is composed of trap, and its upper portions are mainly destitute of vegetation. On the summit are a few stunted pines. Its height is about 4,500 feet above the level of the sea, or 1,500 above our camp, and the top was reached by the party in an hour. This peak is detached from the main group of the Black Hills, and, being at some distance from them, forms a prominent landmark, as is evident from the fact that it has been plainly discernible by us since the 7th.

Rain fell most of the afternoon, but before sundown the sky was illuminated in the west, and a beautiful rainbow spanned the butte in front of our camp. The mountain was nearly in the centre of the arch, clothed in delicate purple tints, the contrast with the dark clouds in the back-ground forming a scene of singular and great beauty.

Since dark the rain has been falling steadily, and the prospect now seems gloomy for a march to-morrow. Some of our recruits are just experiencing the first discomforts of camp life.

Tuesday, July 12.—The morning was dark and cloudy, but we left camp before 6 o'clock, a. m., travelling over a comparatively level road, and our course bearing a little north of west. Eight and a half miles from camp we reached Cottonwood creek, in the valley of which we found a few stunted oaks, the first thus far seen. There is a small bottom at the point we crossed the creek, but hills narrow upon the stream just above. All the grass upon the creek had been recently burned, and to the south among the hills the smoke was still rising. This creek is about three feet wide, and flows over a gravel bed.

Ascending the hills to the west by a long but easy slope, we travelled over a flat divide for two miles, and descended by another gentle declivity to the east fork of Crooked, or Roman-nosed creek, passing which we continued on to the west fork of the same stream. Having crossed the burnt district we found grass again upon the west bank, and encamped here, having travelled 15½ miles. We have been all day skirting the Black Hills, lying upon our left and rising in a succession of dark ridges, while on our right is an extended prairie view, varied by several marked isolated hills. We are now encamped on a little mountain brook, with an abundant supply of fresh water, wood, and excellent grass. The soil in these valleys is good, and the country much more habitable than the plains.

Wednesday, July 13.—We left camp at 5½ o'clock, passing down the valley of the stream upon which we had encamped for a mile and a half, and then, crossing a ridge of low hills, we entered, at the distance of four and a half miles, a small ravine and creek that gave us considerable trouble, as we were compelled to cut down the steep banks, which were 15 feet in height on each side, and could not spare the time requisite to make a good road.

Leaving this stream our route bore off to the left, crossing through a gap a spur of the mountain, eight miles from our morning camp. The road in this gap was rocky and uneven, making hard work for the animals. Two miles further on, after an easy march, we came to a fine running stream, 15 or 20 feet wide and a foot deep, crossing our route at right angles. Our Indian guide called it Mi-ni Lu-sa, or Running Water. Half a mile beyond we came upon a small brook flowing through a muddy bottom, the Indian name being Kle-kle-wak-pa-la, or Miry creek. It was not more than 10 feet wide, but as the first of the party entered it I discovered that their animals sank far into the mud. I therefore drove off in quest of a better ford, the Indian guide seating himself quietly upon the bank as I did so.

After a prolonged but unsuccessful search I returned, when the interpreter said, "the guide declares that you may look, but you can find no better crossing than this." A thorough investigation convinced me that this was true, and we soon reached the opposite bank without especial trouble. This is but one of many instances in which our guide has manifested a perfect and minute knowledge of the country, that has been invaluable to the expedition.

After a march of about two miles further we encamped on a stream, which, from its color, was unanimously called Red Earth creek, the banks opposite and above being a bright red, and the earth tinging the water. Our Indian calls it Wo-ke-o-ke-lo-ka-wak-pa, or the river that heads in a basin or springs. It is 30 or 40 feet wide, and four or five feet deep. At the suggestion of the guide, some of the party commenced angling and caught a few fish of the mullet species, and also one or two catfish weighing from one to three pounds each.

The grass at this camp is good, and wood and water abundant. Our road to-day was the first that could be called bad, yet the picks and shovels were brought into requisition but twice, and the march of 13 miles was accomplished in seven hours. With the exception of the scarcity of good water and of timber east of the Shayenne, there are no obstacles in this country to the passage of troops. A very few trains, however, would consume the entire stock of fuel to be found at many of our camping places.

Thursday, July 14—We left camp at 5½ a. m., but before going three miles were compelled to cross two streams, which occasioned some trouble. One was a dashing mountain torrent, eight feet wide and as many inches in depth; its source being a spring which formed a pool of the area of a quarter of an acre, a mile to our left in the prairie. This pool gave the name to a neighboring itte, called by Lieutenant Warren Crow peak, but by our Indian Basin butte.

A mile or two further we crossed Red Earth creek, (Wo-ke-o-ke-lo-ka,) after considerable detention, resulting from the fact that we were compelled to cut down the banks on each side to make a passable road for our wagons. So great were these delays that, upon reaching the opposite bank, we found that we had averaged only a mile in an hour since leaving camp. Still, notwithstanding these hindrances to our small party, the obstructions would cease to be formidable before the the pioneer force of a large body, and would cause little or no delay.

After passing Red Earth creek our route inclined to the right, towards the ridge we had crossed, and we then continued in a northerly direction towards the north fork of the Shayenne. After advancing nine miles from our previous camp our line of march had inclined so much to the right that we were travelling considerably east of north.

Here we crossed a small stream running to the eastward, on the left of which was a high, rocky ridge, to whose summit I rode. It proved to be the last outlier of the Black Hills. To the north stretched out a broken prairie as far as the eye could pierce, while in the south lay the Black Hills, and in the distance the peak of Bear butte bounded the landscape. The ridge upon which I stood was formed of an inferior soft sandstone, and it continued to about a mile below the point at which we had crossed the stream.

Our Indian having declared that after leaving this point we should find no more water until we reached the north fork of the Shayenne, I determined to encamp near the end of the bluff.

As we were pitching our tents, however, it was discovered that neither was there any water here, the stream having suddenly disappeared in the sand. I determined to risk digging rather than turn back, and was fortunately successful. This incident affords an excellent illustration of the nature of streams in this region; and it is not safe to follow down their beds in pursuit of water, the supply being generally greatest in the vicinity of their sources.

Wood is abundant at this camp, the valley containing a large grove of ash, elms, and oaks. The grass is also excellent. The country travelled to-day has been broken, the rocky formation jutting out in denuded peaks upon all sides.

The valleys contain good soil, which would amply repay cultivation. Upon the sides of the bluffs a few scattered pines flourish; and in the valleys the timber consists of ash, elm, and oak, the trees, however, being universally too small for building purposes.

Friday, July 15.—We left camp at 5 a. m., our course bearing about north-northwest. At the outset the country before us appeared to be a slightly undulating prairie; but after advancing six or eight miles, and upon approaching the river, we found it to be crossed by a number of rather formidable ravines, commencing in several adjacent low pine hills, and filled with scrub oak, cherry, plum, and other underbrush. They were all crossed, however, without serious delay, and in a few miles further we ascended a ridge upon our right and looked down upon the north fork of the Shayenne.

The descent to the river was 150 feet in height, but not difficult. The valley is a mile in width, rocky and covered with cactus. We crossed the stream and encamped on the left bank amid rather poor pasturage, wood, however, being abundant. The river is muddy from recent rains, and contains about two-thirds of the volume of water which we found in its banks at the mouth of Bear Butte creek. I was anxious to follow up the valley from this point, but the Indian guide pronounces it impossible, and declares the only feasible route to lay along the ridge on the left bank. His knowledge of the country has been proven to be so accurate, and is so serviceable, that I shall not reject his advice.

I had to-day the first opportunity of testing my Maynard rifle, hitting a deer at a distance of over 300 yards. The weapon is a capital one, when in order, but it has been found difficult on the plains to give it the required attention.

Saturday, July 16.—We started at 5 a. m., and leaving the river ascended the ridge to the northeast of the camp. It was quite steep towards the summit, the slope of clay and rock being covered with stunted oaks and pines. This ridge is 400 feet above the stream, and our route lay along its crest to the northwest. We adhered so closely to the divide that during the entire day's march the land sloped from us upon both sides; but finally we turned to the left, descending again to the river (which was distant from our course about one and a half mile) for the purpose of encamping. We shall, of course, be compelled to-morrow to retrace our steps, as the river bottom is impracticable for teams.

We passed to-day over the most barren and desolate region yet seen, and a few scattered tufts of grass, with large quantities of artemesia, constituted the only vegetation. About five miles from our last night's encampment, shale slate was found cropping out near the top of the ridge, and in close vicinity were seen large quantities of iron pyrites, imparting to the whole surface of the hill a blackened and burnt appearance. Some of our Frenchmen called it "*terre brulé*," a not inappropriate name.

A few stunted pines were visible on the neighboring ridges, and "signs" of buffalo are abundant; but the latter seem to have gone to more favored regions, as the short and thin grass on these hills would furnish only miserable pasturage. Even upon the river bank it is quite poor, and the general desolation of the scene is extreme. Civilized life could find no home in this region, and if the savage desires its continued possession, I can see no present reason for its disputing.

We have not yet met any Indians, nor any indications of their recent presence. The site of our camp is, however, marked by the remains of an immense Indian lodge, the frame of which consists of large poles, over thirty feet in length. Close by is also a high post, around which a perfect circle of buffalo skulls has been arranged.

Sunday, July 17.—We passed the day in camp, holding the usual religious services.

Monday, July 18.—Starting about 5 o'clock in the morning we retraced our steps to the top of the ridge traveled on Saturday. The ascent was long and steep, the summit being 350 feet above the camp. We followed the ridge for five or six miles, it gradually becoming narrow and crooked, and constantly increasing in height until ultimately we found ourselves upon a bluff from which we enjoyed a commanding view of the adjacent country.

Before us lay the valley of two rivers: that of the Chan-cho-ka-wah-pa, or Thick-wooded river, more commonly known as the Little Missouri, whose course could be traced far off to the northeast, where it was finally lost to sight behind the whitish bluffs that filled the northern horizon—on its way it was joined by two considerable branches rising to the north; in another direction stretched the valley of the north fork of the Shayenne, which, at a point two miles from our previous camp, has suddenly deflected to the southwest, and was flowing from that direction.

Between the rivers lay a broad plain, so apparently level that only the test of the barometer revealed a slight slope upwards towards the Little Missouri. The centre of this tract, which was about ten miles in diameter, was marked by a small pool without visible outlet. Far in the distance, up the valley of the Sahyenne, the eye also noted the singular peak of Bear Lodge, rising like an enormous tower, and, from its resemblance to an Indian lodge, suggesting the origin of its title. Both the Shayenne and Little Missouri are sizable streams at this point. Notwithstanding their present proximity, however, the Little Missouri empties into the Missouri in latitude 47° 15′, and the Shayenne in latitude 44° 40′, the river distance between their mouths being over 600 miles.

Descending from the bluff and crossing the plain, which was found to be covered with cactus, we reached the Little Missouri after a six-miles' march, and followed it up one or two miles until it became necessary to cross its bed, when, as that would plainly require much labor, we pitched our tents upon the right bank, having travelled 15 miles. Wood and water is sufficient for camping purposes, but grass is scarce at this point.

In the evening we were the victims of an alarm. A cry was raised, followed by a rush of the animals about 10 o'clock p. m., but the alertness of my men prevented a stampede, and it was found on investigation that the caving in of a portion of the river bank had originated the disturbance. No damage resulted and quiet was soon restored.

Tuesday, July 19.—The point for crossing having been selected last night, work was commenced at 4 o'clock this morning with pick and shovel. It required two hours of hard labor to level the banks sufficiently for our vehicles, and it was not until half-past 6 that the train was in motion.

After passing the stream, we continued up the valley on its left bank, over a level plain, clumps of sage constituting the only vegetation on its naked surface. The whole plain was cut up by gullies from one to three feet in depth, hidden by the sage until they were reached, rendering travel very difficult. We were compelled to send several of the party in advance to reconnoiter, and, while our progress was slow, the wear and tear upon both animals and men was excessive, and neither can long withstand such severe trials. But little work with pick and shovel was required, however, passable crossings having been found for all save one of the ravines.

About 1 o'clock we were glad to encamp after a march of 13 miles. Our camp is again on the Little Missouri, the grass in the bottom affording tolerable pasturage for our animals.

A party of five started early this morning for Bear Lodge, but they returned late in the afternoon, without any positive conviction that they had even seen it. They secured, however, the entire benefit of two or three heavy showers that we had observed passing to our left, but which did not visit us. They represent the country between our route and the Shayenne as rugged in the extreme, so that it is evident that we have passed as near that river as is possible, unless a road can be found in its valley—a contingency they were not able to settle, and I do not deem probable.

Our camp adjoins a deep gully that requires digging down before it can be crossed, and our wearied men are now engaged upon this work. Dark clouds at night prevented observations.

Wednesday, July 20.—The valley up which we travelled yesterday is bounded on our right by hills covered with stunted pines, and this morning we turned to the west and pushed across this ridge, which separates two of the branches of the Little Missouri. The streams are not more than six miles apart, and the hill between, although rising to the height of only 250 feet above our camp, severely tasked our mules in the ascent.

The valley into which we subsequently entered was even more desolate and barren than that left, and no grass could be found, except in the immediate neighborhood of the stream, and even there it is scarce. We are now in the buffalo region, and small herds are to be seen in all directions. Their presence may explain some of the prevalent barrenness, as they consume all the grass in their paths.

We continued up the valley of the second fork of the Little Missouri for over six miles, and, finding a point in which the grass looked more promising than elsewhere, encamped after a march of 13 miles. Lieutenant Maynadier and our hunter started off this afternoon in quest of buffalo, and after a long and hard ride reached camp three hours after the train, bringing a supply of meat. Bridger and some of the soldiers also went out after encamping, and returned having killed three cows each. We are therefore abundantly supplied with choice bits of this celebrated game, and roast ribs and hump are the order of the day in camp.

Mr. Hutton and our Sioux interpreter, Zephyr Rencontre, made a second attempt to-day to reach Bear Lodge. They returned to camp about 3 p. m. and report having found it, and that it is, as I had supposed, an isolated rock upon the bank of the river, striking only from the fact that it rises in a valley, and from our point of vision, on the morning of the 18th, it was not brought in contrast with the surrounding heights; but by no means forming a prominent landmark when viewed from the north.

We have been in sight all day of two very high peaks which must be those called the Little Missouri buttes by Lieutenant Warren, although he speaks of having seen three from his point of view on Inyan Kara peak. They are by far the loftiest points in sight, if indeed they do not surpass the peaks of the Black Hills.

About an hour after the train was in motion, our Indian guide was missing and has not been since seen. When last noticed he was looking for a point at which to cross a gully, and having found one uttered his usual cry of "wash-te," (good,) and then sought shelter from a slight shower under a neighboring pine. He remained there until all the train had passed, and then quietly slipped away. Mr. Hutton reports having seen signal fires near Bear Lodge, and the probability is that he has gone to join his tribe. I cannot believe that he meditates mischief, but think he is afraid to remain with us longer, as we are now nearly out of the Sioux country, and will soon be among the Crows. He has spoken repeatedly along the route of accompanying us through the entire trip, but his courage has probably failed with the prospect of meeting the hereditary enemies of his tribe.

His services have been of the greatest value; his minute knowledge of the country having excellently qualified him for his important duties, while his invariable good humor and honest face had made him a universal favorite with all the party, and had given foundation for the hope that he was an exception to the usual rule as to Indian honesty. He has, however, testified to his thorough training as a savage, by taking with him the mule, saddle and bridle, that I had furnished him. The important nature of the assistance he has rendered us will far more than compensate for the value of the stolen property; but his method of collecting his pay was peculiarly Indian, and hardly to be justified by civilized law or the code of natural honesty.

Although it is certain that the Indians are watching our movements, and, doubtless, our guide has joined them, I cannot yet believe that they intend hostilities; but, for reasons of prudence, and to guard against possibilities, I have ordered the guard to be doubled.

Thursday, July 21.—The night passed quietly and we did not start until about 6 o'clock. Our route lay up the fork of the Little Missouri, some little distance from the stream, that we might avoid the numberless gullies and the inevitable sage, whose perpetual recurrence rendered our line of march very devious.

We crossed several tributaries of the Little Missouri, now dry, one being distinguished by a little timber upon its banks. Barren sage and cactus plains and naked hills describe the country through which we have passed to-day, the latter having been apparently once covered with grass, since eaten off by the buffaloes, which have been to-day seen in large numbers upon all sides. Some of these animals came very boldly up to the train, and, in one or two instances, with very ludicrous results.

Three large bulls charged down upon us at one point in the march, to the great alarm of one of the escort, who dropped his gun, and, raising his hands, exclaimed, in all the accents of mortal terror, "Elephants! elephants! my God! I did not know that there were elephants in this country!" On another occasion, as a band was passing close by the train, one of the teams started in full pursuit, and was with great difficulty checked. It was probably the first buffalo chase on record with a six-mule team.

As we approached the head of the stream we commenced looking for water and a camp, and a spring was ultimately found that flowed after cleaning out, and by digging we obtained the luxury of pure and cool water of the temperature of 50°. Another attempt at digging at a distance of 30 feet brought water, however, from a different strata, the temperature being 10° higher, or 60°.

We are now within a mile or two of the drainage of Powder river, and as soon as we shall have passed the crest before us will be out of the Sioux or Dakota country. The fires still continue in the distance; but no Indians have made their appearance, and their promise to permit us to pass through unmolested has been unbroken. Except for purposes of communication with our Indian guide the interpreter has been useless. My American guide, Bridger, is now on familiar ground and appears to be entireiy at home in this country. I therefore anticipate no difficulty in dispensing with the services of our fugitive Indian.

The grass at this camp is tolerable, indeed would be abundant if it were not for buffalo visits. Of wood there is also no lack.

Friday, July 22.—Our route this morning was nearly west and directly up the valley in which we were encamped. Numerous ravines entered it upon both sides, all being more or less wooded. Taking advantage of a convenient spur, we ascended to the summit of the ridge by a long and gradual slope of about two and a half miles from camp, and from the point thus reached looked down upon the valley of Powder river.

The view unfolded before us was grand, though uninviting from the appearance of desolation and the hardships threatened in our future marches. Rugged, chalk-like hills stretched off to the distant horizon, barren and forbidding, the surface of the interlying valleys being variegated with clumps of trees, denoting the occasional presence of water-courses, hardly worthy to be dignified with the name of streams. The gorges of the ridge upon which we stood, however, were filled with pines, many over two feet in diameter, that would excellently answer for building purposes and the other uses of lumber. The ridge at the point of our crossing is 4,288 feet above the sea level, while the elevation on each side is considerably higher. This seems to be a continuation of the Black Hills and of the great outlier of the Rocky mountains, which further south forms the eastern boundary of "the parks." No evidence of upheaval can be observed however, nor are there any reasons for calling this elevation a mountain, yet it forms one of the great topographical features of the country, and upon many of the old maps it appears as the Black mountains.

Our route, after running along this spur for a mile or two, turned down an abrupt winding hill to a lower spur, between two of the small branches of Little Powder river. We followed this crest over an exceedingly bad road, which, in many places, was not of sufficient width to permit the passage of a single wagon for about six miles, when we were compelled to abandon it and descend to the valley on our left. There we expected to find water, but the bed of the stream was perfectly dry, and an attempt to supply the deficiency by digging also failed. We were commencing to contemplate the pleasant prospect of passing the night thirsty, when word was brought that some of the party had found water upon the north side of the ridge. There being no certainty of its presence ahead, and the guide confessing his ignorance as to where any could be found, I concluded to retrace our steps something over a mile across the ridge to a point at which it was known to exist.

The spur, along the summit of which we had been travelling and which we now crossed, is as perfect a specimen of "bad lands" as can be found in the country. It is almost wholly devoid of vegetation. Its sides have been washed into deep and impassable ravines by fierce rains, and with the numerous spurs of similar characteristics that radiate from it upon all sides it presents a phase of desolation peculiar to this region.

The entire district is totally unfit for the home of the white man, and indeed it seems to have been deserted by the Indians. Animal life has not entirely forsaken it, however; for, among the scattered pines in the heads of the ravines, several grizzly bears have been started by the party, and scattered bands of buffalo have been seen roaming among the barren hills in the distance, as if in search of food.

We encamped about 3 p. m., having marched 15 miles. The water is salt, and so impregnated with buffalo urine as to be scarcely usable. Grass is very scarce, but there is a fair supply of fuel.

Saturday, July 23.—Our route to-day was directly down the branches of Little Powder river upon which we had been encamped. Our guide Bridger favored following the bank of the stream, but it was ascertained to be impracticable, as we found ourselves to be in a perfect labyrinth of gullies, whose crossing would necessitate an immense amount of labor with the pick and shovel, attended, of course, with serious delay.

We, therefore, again ascended the ridge, although this was a divergence of two miles from our direct path, and, with many short turns and much difficult climbing, ultimately reached its summit, where a passable road was found, bearing generally in the right direction. We followed this till, coming to a valley that was apparently practicable, we descended it, only to find it wholly impassable. We then crossed the ridge, between the valley of our camp fork and the Little Powder, and with great trouble descended into the valley of the latter, where a ride of half a mile across the bottom brought us to the stream itself. It is now small and insignificant, being not over five feet wide and two or three inches in depth; but its bed, 100 yards in width, with banks 15 or 20 feet in height, shows that, at times, it is a large river, while the driftwood above its banks proves its occasional great depth.

The valley is from half a mile to two miles in width, and a fringe of cottonwood trees gives it an appearance more inviting than a closer examination justifies.

We encamped upon its west side, in a grove of cottonwoods. The grass is very scarce, the buffaloes having recently consumed very thoroughly such little as there naturally would be, and we are compelled to give our animals a wide stretch of grazing to satisfy their wants. The arduous work of the week has told upon them and they plainly show the need of rest and nourishing food. Indeed we all shall rejoice at the welcome quiet of the sabbath.

Sunday, July 24.—The day was spent in camp with the customary religious services, which, I am glad to be able to say, were better attended than previously.

Monday, July 25.—On leaving camp this morning we travelled almost due north down the valley of the Little Powder, which we found to be a mile or more in width, the stream keeping in a remarkably crooked channel, necessitating its crossing five times in the first five miles and 10 in the day's march.

A fine growth of cottonwood is found on its banks, but the greater portion of the valley is a mere sage plain, with little or no grass. The river is now very low, and in many places the water is only standing in pools. The bluffs bounding the valley are barren and present a chalk-like appearance, and it is only upon their summits that grass could at any time grow, and even this has been now consumed by the buffaloes, which have been far more numerously visible to-day than heretofore.

At a few low points we found a coarse grass that the buffaloes had rejected, but our mules ate it with avidity. The supply was not sufficient, however, and the deficiency was met, both last night and to-night, by hewing down cottonwood trees and allowing the animals to feed upon the bark. This they did with apparent relish, and the branches were peeled as thoroughly as it could have been done by hand. This is an expedient that is frequently resorted to by the Indians when the grass fails or is covered by snow; and Bridger asserts that, in cases of necessity, animals can be subsisted upon this bark through an entire winter.

Tuesday, July 26.—I this morning gave directions for the command to continue its march down the stream, while I, with two companions, ascended the high grounds upon the left of the route, to obtain a more extended view of the surrounding country, and if possible see the valley of the main Powder river. The hills were rugged and bare, rising to the height of about 500 feet above the level of the stream. From their summit the Powder was in plain sight, at a distance not exceeding four miles.

The landscape before us was wide in extent, but characterized by forbidding desolation. The valleys of the Powder and its branch were marked by narrow and sinuous belts of green, but these, with here and there a solitary pine of stunted growth, constituted all the verdure that relieved the monotony of barrenness. Naked brown hills rose upon all sides, broken into irregular peaks, and with their sides torn into deep and impassable gullies by the mountain torrents—a petrified representation of an angry sea in all the fury of a storm.

At scattered points herds of buffalo were feeding upon the scanty brown grass that had struggled into existence upon the more gentle slopes of the hills, and on one of the neighboring peaks a magnificent bull had stationed himself as if on the outlook, his motionless form standing out in clear and bold relief against the distant sky. If he was searching for more promising pasture grounds in the vicinity, his instinct or his vision must have been indeed keen to have reached satisfactory results. The scarcity of grass is indeed becoming serious, and it is only in rare spots that we can find sufficient pasturage to herd our mules. The soil is also poor, and I doubt if a single section of land in sight would produce sufficient to furnish an ordinary family with a respectable meal.

The descent from the hill was difficult even upon horseback, and I only reached the train after it had stopped on the main river and had commenced preparations to dig down the banks for a crossing. As this would consume considerable time, and the grass was better upon this than the opposite side, I ordered a halt for the night. We were enabled to obtain a meridian altitude of the sun, which gave us for our latitude 45° 27′ 51″. Dark clouds and a threatening storm prevented observations at night.

During the afternoon several frightened buffaloes charged through camp and were shot by the party. The river at this point is about 80 yards wide, and about two feet deep. The bed is a quicksand, making it necessary to be very cautious in crossing, and both above and below our camp the stream is divided by islands and bars into several channels.

Wednesday, July 27.—The river banks having been sufficiently cut down to enable our teams to reach the water, we were ready to resume our forward movement at 5½ o'clock this morning. Before starting we thought the river had fallen considerably, but on entering the stream it was found that the bed had been deepened by the shifting of the sand banks in the current, and it was thus deeper than when first reached last night. The work of cutting down the banks thus proved almost useless, for by the time half of the teams had crossed it became necessary to seek another ford, which was ultimately found about half a mile above. By 7 o'clock we were all safely on the left bank. Our route lay now down the valley of Powder river, which was covered with large sage bushes, through which we were compelled to break a road. After travelling thus about six miles we reached a point at which the stream flowed against a cut bank, and a deep gully rendered it necessary that we should either cross the stream, or abandon it and ascend the hills. The river bed being a mere quick sand, and it having been demonstrated by trial that it could not be crossed even on horseback, we were compelled to accept the latter alternative. After a long and hard pull over lands washed and badly cut up by rains, we reached a fine open plain, sloping almost imperceptibly to a stream, distant some six or eight miles. We passed easily and rapidly along the crest separating this stream from Powder river, the hills between our course and the river valley being so abrupt as to prevent our descending into the latter again, until we had marched nearly eight miles. When we did finally regain the valley it was found to be filled with buffalo, and although the party was greatly fatigued with the arduous labors of the day, a general chase commenced, resulting in the increase of our stock of provisions by a bountiful supply of fresh meat. One large band charged directly upon the train and were only turned by a well-directed volley. The grass on the river surpassed our expectations in its quality, thus indicating that the buffalo have been in the valley but a short time. Their lowing is heard all about our camp this evening.

While upon the hill to-day, and as I was riding rapidly in advance of the train with the view of finding a route by which we could return to the valley, I lost a much valued seal, and as this mishap occurred near the source of the branch we had discovered by leaving the river, I named the creek after the motto of the seal. My hard gallop near the head of "Mizpah" creek will not be easily forgotten. The distance travelled to-day was 19½ miles, and we reached camp at 3 p. m.

Thursday, July 28.—We made no effort for an early start this morning, as our mules had suffered severely in the labors of yesterday and needed rest. We left camp, however, about 6½ o'clock, continuing down the river and keeping in a wide open plain upon the left bank. Several ravines intercepted our course, making considerable detours necessary, but with one exception all were crossed without using the pick and shovel. At 11½ o'clock we hurried towards the river to find a camping ground, but owing to the scarcity of grass our search was continued till after 1, when a halt was ordered, and as the prospect appeared to be growing worse rather than improving we pitched our tents for the night. This scarcity of grass has become the leading feature in the country, and can, of course, be partially explained by the presence of the buffalo in such large numbers. These animals have thoroughly consumed such poor pasturage as the valley affords, and as a result our mules fare badly. The prevalent desolation shows no signs of abatement. The eye grows weary with the constant sight of barren hills and blue sage.

The buffaloes are very poor and their meat tough and unpalatable, but the supply is abundant, and their chase affords capital sport for the party. Antelope in bands of from five to ten are also seen almost every hour, and my great surprise is that the game succeeds in finding in this desert sufficient food to sustain life. The presence of these animals in such large numbers in this barren region is explained by the fact that this valley is a species of neutral ground between the Sioux and the Crows and other bands nearer the mountains, or, more correctly speaking, the common war ground visited only by war parties, who never disturb the game, as they would thereby give notice to their enemies of their presence. For this reason the buffalo remain here undisturbed, and indeed would seem to make the valley a place of refuge.

This afternoon a buffalo calf chased by wolves sought safety in camp, but was killed before the reason of its unexpected visit had been ascertained. The day has been very sultry, and the thermometer at 2 p. m. stood at 100°, but before sundown a smart shower passed over us from the northwest, which, with the wind, brought a most grateful and refreshing change of temperature. We travelled to-day 15½ miles. Since leaving Fort Pierre have marched 373 miles.

Friday, July 29.—We left camp about the usual hour, and after a march of about a mile reached a deep and impassable gully. An attempt to cross the river failed, its bed proving to be mud and quicksand, and we were compelled to diverge towards the hills, ultimately succeeding in crossing the gully with considerable difficulty. Two miles further on a second of three obstructions was encountered, and two hours were consumed in cutting down the banks. The depth of this gully was, by measurement, 37 feet, and the slope, after the cutting down, 24°.

With all our labor it was found impossible, with our small force, to construct a decent road, and we were enabled to haul but one wagon across with a ten-mule team. I was satisfied that it was wiser, upon all considerations, to make a circuit of ten miles rather than so task our jaded animals. I therefore ordered the escort wagons which were the lightest and whose teams were in the best order, to cross the gully under command of Lieutenant Smith, and directed him to push on to the river bank and encamp. The rest of the train, under Lieutenant Maynadier, advanced to a point where the ravine became more level, and then by a detour of three or four miles effected an actual advance of as many rods, reaching camp an hour and a half after Lieutenant Smith.

I drove to the summit of the neighboring hills, but found no change in the barrenness of the prospect. We encamped in the best grass found in the valley of Powder river. The total distance travelled was only 10½ miles, but it has been the most trying and vexatious day's march yet made, and a few such would seriously dispirit the entire party. Clouds at night prevented observations.

Saturday, July 30.—We continued our route down the river, along a level road, the chief obstruction being found in the interminable sage, which vastly augments the labor of the teams. One or two gullies crossed the route, but were passed without difficulty. About ten miles from camp we crossed the river over the first good ford yet found, the bottom being gravel, and the approaching slope easy. A small creek emptying into the Powder from the east required care in crossing, however, as the bed was miry, but after its passage we again reached the river bank and encamped, having travelled 13½ miles.

The valley of the stream is continually becoming more narrow, and Bridger declares that it will be impossible to follow it much further. The bluffs also commence to look very formidable, and as I hope to have the Yellowstone explored next season, I have almost determined to accept Bridger's advice, and strike across the country for Fort Sarpy, the Fur Company's trading-house on the Yellowstone; by so doing we shall obtain some knowledge of the regions back from the river, which cannot be procured by simply following the Powder to its mouth, and then ascending the valley of the Yellowstone. We shall also thus avoid twice travelling over a portion of our route.

We have tolerably good grass in this camp, which our mules greatly need; wood and water is, of course, abundant.

Sunday, July 31.—The day was spent in camp with the customary religious observances. I find that the entire party eagerly anticipate throughout the week the welcome rest of the Sabbath, and upon Monday morning our labors are resumed with renewed vigor, an illustration of the physical advantages of this heaven-appointed day of rest.

Monday, August 1.—Our route to-day was still down the valley of Powder river, along its right bank. The road has not been bad, being crossed by only two or three not very formidable gullies. About ten miles from camp we recrossed the river at a tolerably good ford; the bed of the stream having a stony bottom, and fewer quicksands than we had found higher up.

The valley is becoming still narrower and more barren. We passed little or no grass, and as early as 11 o'clock I decided to halt upon the first tolerable pasturage and recruit our animals. The hills are, as usual, desolate and forbidding in appearance, while the valley is but little more inviting, though over both numerous small bands of buffalo are roaming. After a march of 15¼ miles, we encamped for the night, the grass being still scanty and of very poor quality.

After reaching camp, Bridger started in search of a route across the hills towards Tongue river. We are now within 40 or 50 miles of the mouth of the Powder, and the character of the stream cannot change materially in that distance, and its further exploration is comparatively useless. It is, moreover, absolutely essential that we should, as soon as possible, enter a region better provided with grass for the benefit of our animals, and I hope to do so by crossing the hills.

We know that the valley of Mizpah creek, the head of which we saw on the 27th, is not far to the west of us, and our first object will be to reach and pass it. As matters now stand, we shall be compelled either to abbreviate our marches very materially or our animals will soon be entirely broken down. Bridger returned late at night after a six-hours' ride and makes a rather discouraging report, but thinks we will be able to succeed in at least crossing the Mizpah. From that point we shall be compelled to make a second examination to ascertain the most feasible route to Tongue river.

Tuesday, August 2.—I left camp before the train in company with the guide, with the purpose of looking for a route to the Mizpah. A liberal use of the pick and shovel made one that was practicable to the top of the ridge, and from that point a broad, open valley lay before us, and a march of only six miles brought us to the banks of the creek.

The valley of the Mizpah is little, if any, less than that of the Powder, and the border of cottonwood trees gives it all the appearance of a considerable stream, but at present it is nothing but a beautiful clear-running brook. From the marks of the driftwood on the banks it is evident, however, that at times it is not less than 20 feet deep and 400 yards in width, and, as we saw its source some 30 miles above this point, and know that there it is 200 feet above Powder river, its fall must be such as to give it an almost irresistible current.

The summit of the ridge over which we passed is about as perfect a specimen, on rather a small scale, of "bad lands" as any yet seen. It is entirely destitute of vegetation, and the strata in the washed hillsides are beautifully variegated, exhibiting all colors from the jet black of a lignite seam, through the red and yellow of burnt material, to an almost perfectly white clay, all arranged with the regularity of masonry, and presenting an appearance of peculiar and rare beauty.

Our camp is in a pleasant valley, but surrounded on all sides by these "bad land" hills. Had we come down the valley of the Mizpah from the point at which we touched it on the 27th ultimo to this point, we would probably have found better travelling, and better grass, and have decidedly shortened the distance.

Wednesday, August 3.—After encamping yesterday the guide and both the topographers started in advance to ascertain the best route by which to leave the valley. They went in different directions, but all agreed upon a single road as the only one that would prove feasible. This morning we therefore ascended the stream for about two miles to the selected point, thence turning directly west, up a small branch of the Mizpah, towards the dividing ridge, which lay between us and Tongue river. The road was almost impracticable, and the constant labor of every available man was required to enable us to make any progress whatever. We halted several times with the view of finding a better route, but repeated disappointments testified to the excellence of the original judgment of our guide and the topographers. The ascent was not specially steep, but a series of gullies crossed the path, of which every one was necessarily dug down before it could be passed. Contrary to expectations, however, we ultimately accomplished a march of nine miles and encamped at a point within about one and a half mile of the summit. Water was obtained by digging, and sage and buffalo chips furnished fuel. The grass on the hills was scarce but excellent in quality. Beyond camp much work is necessary to render the road passable, and all hands are industriously engaged this afternoon in the manufacture of a western highway.

After the halt I rode in advance some four or five miles, passing the summit, and obtaining a view of the country about Tongue river. It differs but little from that over which we have just passed, but the valley of the river appears far more inviting than that of the Powder, and I trust we have left behind us the worst of the washed lands.

Thursday, August 4—Starting this morning at about 6 o'clock, we passed over the divide between Powder and Tongue rivers. The summit was reached in a march of about an hour, the road being but a slight improvement upon that of yesterday, but as these difficulties seemed nearly at an end we all felt animated with renewed vigor. Upon reaching the ridge we followed its crest for a mile or more towards the north, and then struck off on a spur leading directly towards Tongue river.

Here our hopes of good travelling reached an untimely end, and progress only augmented our toil and darkened our prospects. We were soon again among the "bad lands," whose acquaintance we had formed upon the Powder, and this amalgamation of sterile clay and stone, washed into gullies and totally devoid of vegetable life, surrounded us upon all sides. The steepness of the descent also rendered it impossible for us to abandon the ridge and enter the valley, until, after a long march, we reached a deep gorge badly torn up by irregular ravines. By arduous labor with the spade, however, we made a road over its rough surface, and finally reached the plain, and headed for a belt of timber in the distance indicating the presence of a water-course. Our progress was delayed by other gullies, so that we did not reach the stream and encamp until about 2 o'clock p. m.

We found water in abundance standing in pools, but of poor quality. The grass was scanty and miserable, and it was only after a long search, that we found pasturage of any description for our tired beasts. A further advance, however, was clearly impossible. We therefore remained here after a laborious march of eight hours, the distance travelled being 13½ miles.

The work to-day has been the most arduous by far yet imposed upon the expedition, and I should have pronounced the road travelled impracticable, if it had not been actually passed over.

Friday, August 5.—The stream upon which we are encamped is called by Bridger Pumpkin creek, taking its name from a species of wild gourd that is said to be found upon its banks. Its bed is some 30 or 40 yards wide, and in the wet season would be impassable. The stream is not of great length, but empties into Tongue river some six or eight miles below this point. Our route this morning lay down its valley, crossing the creek every few hundred yards, as its course is very crooked, and the nature of the country prevents our leaving its banks. The soil is sandy and the strength of our mules has consequently been much overtasked.

After a march of this character for six miles, we passed over a low ridge to Tongue river, which at first resembled a mere tributary of Pumpkin creek. Its valley is no wider, and at this point there is but little timber, and, as the water was wholly invisible, the creek apparently was the larger. Upon a closer approach, however, Tongue river was found to be a fine rapid stream, from 70 to 100 yards in width and 13 inches deep, flowing over a gravelly bottom. Its water is clear and for the season very cold.

Upon reaching its banks, we looked in vain for grass for our animals. The little that was found proved totally insufficient, and we therefore encamped in a grove of young cottonwoods, and supplied the deficiency in pasturage by our previous expedient of lopping off and feeding to the mules and horses the young and succulent boughs.

The point of junction of Tongue river and the Yellowstone was pointed out by Bridger to-day as we passed along, and, as it is not more than 12 or 15 miles distant, the Yellowstone cannot be correctly located upon our maps by about 15 miles. Bridger now advises that we travel up Tongue river some distance, before crossing to the west, for the purpose of avoiding the bluffs on the Yellowstone. This is not in accordance with my pre-conceived plan, but I shall accept his advice out of deference to his remarkable knowledge of the country.

After encamping, some of the party succeeded in catching several very fine cat-fish over 18 inches long, furnishing an agreeable variety in our monotonous bill of fare.

A rather novel hunting adventure also afforded us considerable amusement. A drove of buffalo were feeding in the vicinity, and a bull of unusual size was discovered a little distance from camp. Nearly a score of men started to bring down the game. By great caution they crept up within range, and a volley felled the brute to the ground. The entire party rushed up in hot haste to the supposed carcass, when the animal slowly raised up on its fore feet and, with threatening head, commenced approaching them, dragging along the ground its hind quarters, which had been paralyzed by a ball grazing the spine. The spectacle was at first appalling, and all the hunters promptly took to their heels to avoid the dreaded charge they supposed to be imminent. A few minutes revealed, however, the ridiculousness of their situation, and vengeance was speedily wreaked upon the buffalo by his prompt despatching and butchering.

Saturday, August 6.—Our march to-day has been short and easy, and we advanced only about five and a half miles up the level valley of Tongue river. The stream is very sinuous, and we were compelled to cross it three times, but in so doing found no especial difficulty. It is entirely free from quicksands and was not deep enough to embarrass fording. Its valley is much narrower than that of Powder river, but the adjacent hills are less "washed" and barren. Timber is scarcer, and grass decidedly more abundant, the latter fact being chiefly explained by the presence of the buffalo in fewer numbers.

Our camp is in a fine grove of cottonwoods, with an excellent growth of grass beneath them, which, with the rest of to-morrow, will, I trust, recuperate our animals, whose condition has become so reduced that short marches have latterly been an absolute necessity.

This afternoon has been intensely warm, the thermometer standing at 106° Fahr. in the shade, and the difference between the wet and dry bulb being 37°. This latter is more remarkable when it is considered that we are in a grove of quite large trees and on the immediate banks of one of the most considerable streams in this country. Is not this dryness of the climate the cause of the great scarcity of vegetation in this region, and is not this the leading fact to be considered in forming an estimate of its agricultural character? If the present extreme drought is regular and prevails each season, the scarcity of trees is sufficiently explained, and the impossibility of the soil, however good, repaying cultivation fairly demonstrated. An examination of the soil itself in many places reveals no sufficient reason for the scarcity of timber, which is found only on the banks of water-courses, and in ravines near the summits of the highest hills, where moisture is most abundant, and we must therefore seek other causes. Are they not found in the dryness that so universally prevails elsewhere?

Sunday, August 7.—The day was spent in camp with the usual service, the firing of three shots from a revolver answering for the church bell of civilization. The atmosphere to-day was remarkably clear, and the temperature delightful, a high northwest wind last night having cooled the air. At 7½ o'clock this morning the themometer marked 60°, but it was colder in the night and must have been 10° lower. The change from yesterday is most refreshing.

This afternoon was marked by a curious optical illusion. About 3 o'clock it was reported to me that two Indians had been discovered upon the brow of a neighboring hill looking down upon our camp. The use of our best glasses apparently justified this opinion, as two forms were distinctly visible upon a ridge, distant about a mile and a half, one standing and the other in a recumbent posture.

We concluded they were Crows, and, as this tribe is friendly, it was determined to bring them into camp and have a "talk," and a party started for that purpose. The fact that we had seen no human faces save our own since leaving Fort Pierre was an additional and powerful inducement. The absolute motionlessness of the figures aroused my suspicions, however, and I resorted to one of Troughton and Simms's large astronomical telescopes, and by use of the most powerful terrestrial eye-piece, studied the supposed strangers very carefully.

The resemblance to human beings was still striking, but it was plainly evident that they were only curiously shaped rocks, to which the afternoon light had imparted an additionally strange appearance. This opinion was soon verified upon the return of the disgusted party that had visited the hill, and failed to discover their mistake until they had almost reached its summit.

Monday, August 8.—Our march to-day was also short and still up the valley of Tongue river towards the point from which we shall strike across the country to the Rosebud. The valley here is very narrow, and Bridger calls it the cañon of Tongue river. Twice we have been compelled to abandon it and cross spurs of hills against which it flows, but above this point the river bottom is wider and looks more inviting.

The hills we have passed are very broken, and would probably have proved impassable had we attempted to leave the river valley. The road was tolerably good, the sage constituting the chief obstruction, and the descent of the first spur crossed being steep, necessitating considerable work with the pick. The river we passed three times to-day without much difficulty, and our camp is now upon its left bank.

The sickness of one of our teamsters, occasioned by bathing and exposure to the sun, constitutes our first case of decided illness, and this is not serious. The health of the party has thus far been unusually excellent.

A magnificent buck elk was shot just after encamping, being the first of that species of game yet seen. His horns were about four feet long and still in the velvet. The flesh is not considered as great a delicacy as that of the buffalo, but it is a change, and of course agreeable.

The night was beautifully clear, and well improved in the matter of astronomical observations.

Tuesday, August 9.—We this morning left Tongue river and started across the hills to the westward, passing up the valley of a dry creek, leaving the river near our camp. We found the road a vast improvement upon that previously traversed. The ascent was gradual, and brought us to the foot of a long, crooked spur, up which we passed without much trouble, but with hard pulling.

Near the summit we found a few stunted pines, out of which, as I was riding in advance of the train, I started an enormous grizzly bear with her cubs. After reaching the summit we travelled for some five miles over a high, undulating prairie, which drained into the Yellowstone, and from thence over rolling hills covered with pines. The ravines upon each side of us were impassable, and the selection of the road proved Bridger's excellence as a guide. To the right of our course lay a range of beautifully rose-tinted hills, their summits crowned with pine and forming a marked feature in the landscape.

All the ravines in this part of our route were dry, and search was made in vain for water. We were, therefore, compelled to continue on across a ridge separating us from another branch of the Yellowstone. We then found the country entirely changed, its surface being more level and destitute of timber. Two or three miles beyond the crest of the ridge a spring was found that promised, by cleaning out, a sufficient supply of water, and we therefore halted, after a march of 18½ miles.

Grass at this camp is scanty, and wood still scarcer, consisting only of small pines obtained from the sides of the distant hill. The difficult ascent from the valley to-day exhausted our mules at the outset, and rendered the day's march one of the most severe of the expedition. The country traversed has been worthless for agricultural purposes, and the pines are small and of no utility save for fuel. From the last ridge crossed we obtained our first view of the Wolf or Chetish mountain in the distance.

Wednesday, August 10.—After the train started from camp this morning I ascended a rugged butte in the vicinity, from which a view was obtained of both the Yellowstone and the Rosebud. Desolation still characterized the landscape. Naked hills were its salient features, the barrenness being only relieved by scattered pines upon rocky spurs on the left, and stunted cottonwoods and occasional strips of verdure in the river valleys. The hills were generally of a dull brownish yellow, but here and there formations broke to the surface, of chalky white, or tinted with a delicate vermillion, while jagged rocks cropped out upon many of the most abrupt slopes.

Our course lay to the west, the broken country upon the right rendering a detour necessary to the southward. During the first half of the march we passed over a high, rolling plateau, destitute of grass or water, but affording an excellent road. We then entered with much difficulty a ravine draining into the Rosebud, and thus reached the valley of a dry fork, down which we passed to the Rosebud itself, where we encamped upon a small spot of salt grass scarcely large enough for the picketing of our mules; the scarcity of pasturage still continuing in this region.

The Rosebud shows evidences of being occasionally an important stream, but now contains no running water whatever, its bed being a mere succession of stagnant pools, which, from the fact that the water is several feet below the general level, are very difficult of access. The entire river bottom is covered with sage, and a scattered growth of cottonwood upon its banks completes the picture. The distant hills in the south in which the stream finds its source are plainly visible, and a marked gap in them apparently denotes an easy road in that direction.

After reaching the camp, Bridger examined the country to the west for several miles, and reports a good road for that distance, but seems uncertain as to its continuance. If our vague information relative to the position of Fort Sarpy is correct we should reach that post this week.

Thursday, August 11.—Our route to-day lay directly over the hills to the westward, and nearly parallel with the course of the Yellowstone. The first three or four miles was one continued ascent, and then our course was intercepted by the head of a wide valley of the old washed lands. With great labor we reached the main ridge bounding the valley of the Rosebud, upon which we found a good, although hilly and crooked, road, tending nearly in the right direction.

Upon each side were steep gorges filled with stunted pines, with here and there a cottonwood or cherry bush. At 11 o'clock I sent out parties to look for water, but none could be found. The search proving unsuccessful, I rode in advance of the train until I came in sight of a valley containing the almost unfailing indications of water. I then ordered the train to descend into it by continuing along the circuitous but easy route on the spur, while I took a shorter path with the view of selecting a camping ground.

To my great disappointment I found the valley entirely devoid of grass and water, although filled with sage, cottonwood, and willow. I examined the bed of the stream very thoroughly in both directions without success, and climbed a bluff to obtain a more extended view of the neighboring country. To my astonishment the train was not in sight, and I therefore drove hastily back to ascertain the cause of its disappearance. I found it encamped but a short distance back, upon (probably) the only pool of water in the valley, which had been accidentally found in the course of the long detour, and I had entirely missed. The men had wisely gone into camp without waiting for orders.

I am becoming very anxious to reach Fort Sarpy and the Yellowstone, as our mules are rapidly breaking down, and I assume that there we shall obtain better pasturage. If good grass can be found to-morrow I shall halt over Saturday and Sunday, and devote the time to procuring more definite knowledge of our exact locality. Bridger calls the stream we are now upon, Emmel's fork.

Friday, August 12.—We this morning moved to the southwest out of the valley of Emmel's fork, and with hard pulling ascended the hills to the west, upon whose summits we found comparatively good travelling. Our course was still to the south of west till we reached a wide and deep valley which intercepted our path, and was so marked that it was at first thought to be that of the Yellowstone, but from its location and bearing it was soon evident to all that it was only the main fork of the stream upon which we had encamped last night.

The country upon the opposite side of the valley was very rough and uninviting, and it was therefore determined not to cross it, but to turn northward to the Yellowstone. Avoiding the breaks in the bluff we found an excellent road to the point at which the two forks unite. It was here indispensable that we should descend to the level of the stream, and finally this was effected with the greatest trouble and labor, only arduous exertions and the most watchful care bringing the wagons safely down the steep hillside and over the formidable rocks. Our progress in the valley was also difficult, and we went into camp at the first water reached.

The western fork, down which we have travelled for the last five miles of our day's march, evidently heads in the Wolf mountains, which have been in sight for the past few days, and it must drain a large area of country. I was surprised to find that the water in its bed is confined to a few pools, and is of the poorest quality. The valley is from one to two miles wide and distinguished by a considerable growth of cottonwood. Sage is abundant but the grass is rather poor.

Dr. Hayden has been for one or two days impatiently anxious to examine the geology of the range of Wolf mountains, visible at a distance of 20 miles in the southwest. I had promised him the opportunity, but to-day he disappeared without orders or permission, and at night has not rejoined the train. The distance of the journey undoubtedly explains the latter fact, and as his party consists of four men they are doubtless able to defend and take care of themselves.

Saturday, August 13.—Dr. Hayden and party not having returned, I determined not to move camp to-day, but await them in my present position, improving the delay by sending out an expedition to seek the Yellowstone. An additional advantage resulting from this course will be that it will give our animals the benefit of two days' rest. The Yellowstone party, consisting of one of my topographers, Mr. Hutton, with the guide and interpreter, mounted on our three best horses, left camp at an early hour this morning, going northward.

Dr. Hayden and his companions returned about the middle of the afternoon. The ride, which they expected to be about 10 miles, proved to be over 20, and they had undergone many hardships, as their jaded appearance testified. As I had supposed, they had visited the Wolf mountains to gratify the impatience of the geologist. I improved this incident to issue an order forbidding any one to be absent from the train over night without explicit permission, deeming this to be indispensable to the safety of the party, and feeling justified in so doing by the serious responsibility for so many lives resting upon me.

In the afternoon the party returned from the Yellowstone, having reached it by travelling some 12 miles. Their report of the road is by no means favorable, and, far worse, they have seen no indications of the passage up of the boats with our provisions. We have now, however, the advantage of knowing our location, with the power of determining our future actions accordingly. Years have elapsed since our guide passed through this special region, and he has forgotten some of the minutiæ, though he seems perfectly familiar with its general features. We are all totally ignorant of the site of the Sarpy trading-house, as it has only been built within the last few years, and since any of the expedition visited this country.

Sunday, August 14.—We passed the day in camp as usual, and held the customary religious services. With these two days of rest I hope we shall have no further trouble with our beasts, as they have recruited wonderfully.

Large fires are visible in the Wolf mountains this afternoon, probably the signals of Indians who are undoubtedly watching our movements, although they have not yet showed themselves. The day has been exceedingly warm, the thermometer standing at 108° Fahr., the difference between the wet and dry bulbs being 40°. A high northwest wind this afternoon gives promise of more agreeable weather. Last night, however, I was cold under two blankets, and the change is most remarkable between the day and night temperatures.

Monday, August 15.—We left camp at 6½ o'clock, our course bearing down the valley of Emmel's fork, upon which we had encamped. The stream is very crooked, winding from bluff to bluff upon either side, and thus rendering its passage necessary almost every half mile. The lowness of the water made the crossing of the bed a comparatively easy matter, but we were compelled to dig down the banks upon each occasion, and this greatly retarded our progress.

After a march in this fashion down the valley about half way to the Yellowstone, the bed of the creek became so miry that its further crossing was impossible, and we therefore climbed with much difficulty the spur of hills upon our left and, crossing it, descended thence to the valley of the Yellowstone, a small ravine, materially facilitating the latter portion of the march.

From the summit of the hill we obtained our first view of the Yellowstone valley itself, of which over 50 square miles was visible, literally black with buffalo, grazing in an enormous herd whose numbers defy computation, but must be estimated by hundreds of thousands. We found the distance from the foot of the hills to the water about three miles, three-fourths of the intervening country consisting of a barren plain elevated about 100 feet above the water, covered doubtless at times with grass, but now cropped as closely as any village common and presenting an appearance of extreme barrenness.

A short and abrupt descent of a few feet leads from the terrace, upon which we are encamped, to the water's edge. The bank is covered with a rich growth of weeds and salt grass, which, fortunately for us, the buffalo do not relish but our mules devour with avidity. Large cottonwood trees also border the stream, so that we can say, what we have not been able to say for a long time, wood, water, and grass are abundant. The distance travelled to-day is 16.4 miles, and the total, since leaving Fort Pierre, 546 miles.

There are no evidences of the passage of the boats at this point, and as we are in some doubt as to whether we are above or below the station for which they are bound, (Fort Sarpy,) I have organized two small parties, the first to ascend the valley as far as the mouth of the Big Horn, and the second to descend until they obtain some information of the whereabouts of our supplies or their own provisions fail.

Both parties will take with them supplies for six days, and the first will be under the charge of Lieutenant Maynadier, the second under Mr. Snowden. Should these parties return without tidings of the boats, we shall have to adopt the Indian method of "making meat," and start for Fort Laramie with the expectation of subsisting on meat diet. Fortunately, buffalo are abundant and there is no danger of starvation at present.

Tuesday, August 16.—Lieutenant Maynadier and Mr. Snowden started with their parties this morning by 7 o'clock, that of Lieutenant Maynadier numbering seven and that of Mr. Snowden six persons. These are considered sufficiently strong, as we are now in the country of the Crow Indians, and they are not regarded as hostile. Moreover, our animals are in such poor condition that it is very desirable to use them as little as possible.

As I hope to have an opportunity of sending down the river by Major Schoonover, agent for the Crows, who is to come up in the boats with their annuities, I have set all hands at work making copies of notes and repacking all articles that we wish to be relieved of, such as geological and other specimens, in order that we may reduce our baggage to the smallest possible compass. I also wish to have a field map completed to send back, that in case of accident some record of the work accomplished may be preserved.

This is the first actual halt made since leaving Fort Pierre, so that, for lack of opportunity, we are materially behind in this class of work. All our wagons and carts are emptied, their contents are being thoroughly overhauled, and invoices are being made of the stock on hand. We have work of this description sufficient to occupy all the party for several days, so that our halt is beneficial for other reasons than the rest afforded the animals.

Wednesday, August 17.—We remained in camp awaiting the return of the exploring parties and busily plotting, computing, copying notes, repacking supplies, &c., &c.

Two Crow Indians came into camp about 3 p. m., being the first human beings outside of the party seen for 50 days. They report having passed Lieutenant Maynadier and his party this morning, and state that the boat with our supplies was at the mouth of Tongue river 15 days since, in which case it should have reached this point by this time. Their village of 100 lodges is two days' march behind them, and they have come down to receive their annuities.

These Indians are of much lighter color than the Sioux, and have a less savage and repulsive expression. They are well formed and of medium height. In their costume the most striking feature is a cap made of *par fleche*, or prepared buffalo hide, consisting of a large visor shading the eyes, with the addition of a band of the same material encircling the head, the upper edge of which is cut into points, imparting a decidedly regal appearance. It is entirely crownless, however, and thus affords no protection whatever to the head. They are well mounted, and armed with both gun and bow and arrows. They do not present a very formidable appearance, but have the reputation of being as good warriors as any tribe in this region.

Thursday, August 18.—We are still in camp and employed as yesterday. Lieutenant Maynadier and party returned about noon. They report that Fort Sarpy is only about nine miles above camp and in this bottom. The party ascended the river some 20 miles above the trading-house, and reached a bluff impassable even on horseback, at which point it will be necessary either to cross the stream or leave it and make a detour through the hills. Lieutenant Maynadier reports that it is useless to attempt to reach the mouth of the Big Horn by the valley upon this side. As it is possible that Mr. Snowden's party may have passed the boats without seeing them, I have engaged the Indians, who are yet with us, to go down the river, and carry a letter to Mr. Meldrum, the agent of the American Fur Company, who is expected up in them.

Our hunter finds no difficulty in abundantly supplying us with meat, and in a short time to-day killed seven buffaloes. Men with carts were sent out to bring in the choice pieces.

Friday, August 19.—The Indians left camp early this morning for the boat. About 10 a. m. a band of 30 or 40 savages were seen coming up the river and proved to be Crows, headed by "Two Face," a sub-chief, who rode into camp in full court costume, announcing his name by the expressive procedure of touching his face and holding up two fingers. He calmly took temporary possession of the largest tent, making himself completely at home. He had supposed that it was my quarters, judging from its size that it belonged to the commander, a mistake that I was in no haste to correct. He soon discovered his error, however, and transferred his hospitality (the only term for his general appropriation of things) to my tent. From him I learned that his band had left the boat the day previous and that Mr. Snowden and his party were close at hand.

The latter arrived about noon bringing with him, Major Schoonover, the Indian agent. Mr. Snowden met the boats 41 miles below, (by land,) and reported that it would require five or six days for them to reach our camp. He also brought a request from Mr. Meldrum that I would send him the assistance of a number of men and animals, a request I shall gladly comply with, as I am very anxious to shorten my stay here as greatly as possible.

Major Schoonover reports that during the journey up a small war party of Sioux obtained possession of the horses belonging to the boats and were induced to return them only with great difficulty and under circumstances that were at one time seriously threatening. This outrage was the more aggravated from the fact that Major Schoonover is also the agent for the Sioux, and thus they were robbing their own agent.

The reputation of this tribe for principle is poor, even among savages, and they will plunder friend or foe alike if immunity is certain. The Sioux also informed Major Schoonover that a band of 350 picked warriors had started to intercept and attack my expedition. If the story is true, their courage failed, for their distant signal fires have been the only evidences of their neighborhood.

Our party, however, is formidable in numbers and excellently armed, and the latter fact I impressed upon the Sioux chiefs at Fort Pierre by affording them occular demonstration of the improved quality of our fire-arms. While I do not overrate our own strength in frontier warfare, I entertain no apprehensions of Indian hostilities, for the savages are too cowardly to attack where there is a prospect of a resistance so determined and so effective. The story told Major Schoonover was probably a mere piece of Indian bravado.

Saturday, August 20.—Lieutenant Maynadier left camp this morning with four men and twelve mules to meet the boats and hasten their difficult ascent up the river, and I hope that by this means we shall gain a day or two in the date of our departure.

Letter-writing to distant friends and families has occupied the energies of all, and the mail will be carried down the river by Major Schoonover in a batteau as far as Sioux City, reaching there, the nearest frontier post-office, at a distance of 1,500 miles from our camp, a fact that illustrates the marvellous extent of the great system in the west and our remoteness from civilization. The letters will probably reach their destinations about midwinter.

Sunday, August 21.—We passed this Sabbath as its predecessors, in camp, and with religious services.

The Indian messengers sent to the boats returned during the day with a note from Mr. Meldrum, stating that he was ten miles below the mouth of the Rosebud and would reach this point in seven days from the date of his letter, (the 19th.) I hope that the assistance sent him will materially shorten this interval, as the delay is greatly to be regretted from the fact that we shall now be troubled to reach winter quarters before cold weather. The nights are already becoming uncomfortably chilly.

Monday, August 22.—The Crows are encamped in large numbers a mile or two up the river and in close vicinity to camp, and are becoming very troublesome. Like all Indians, they are importunate beggars, and about camp they take constant and the most disagreeable liberties, thronging into our tents, rolling their filthy bodies up in our blankets, and prying into everything accessible. Their personal uncleanliness is disgusting and their bodies are covered with vermin. They have no ideas of chastity, and greater general degradation could be with difficulty imagined. The men take pride in appearing in all the tawdry finery they can obtain. The common dress is woollen clothing, such as pantaloons, shirts, and hats, purchased from the traders, blankets (which are plenty) and buffalo skins forming the outer covering.

The full state dress, used by the chiefs and great warriors on extraordinary occasions, is quite imposing, consisting of moccasins ornamented with beads, leggings of skins, embroidered also with beads and porcupine quills dyed the most brilliant colors, and a large outer covering somewhat resembling the Mexican *serapa*, but made of skin and richly decorated. Ermine skins are highly prized by them, and almost invariably the *serapa* is fringed with them. Vermillion is freely used as a war paint, and it is not uncommon to see the entire face as brilliant as the best Chinese pigment can make it.

The chief of the lower band, Two Bears, wore moccasins consisting of the paws of a grizzly bear, with the claws and horny portion of the foot preserved.

Eagle feathers are used to ornament the head, and a Crow glories in his long hair, which is worn straight down the back, frequently reaching to the knees. This is filled with gum, forming a compact mass, and is generally dotted over with white spots of paint.

Only in cases of extreme grief—mourning for friends, &c.—is the hair ever cut. A more senseless display of grief, common among them, is to gash the forehead and allow the blood to flow over the face, remaining there until worn off by time or obliterated by dirt.

As among all savages, the women are the mere slaves of the men, doing all the menial service. A case in point caused considerable amusement in our party. A young Indian, almost a mere lad, with a stout and fine looking squaw wife, has pitched his lodge a short distance from camp, upon the opposite side of a small branch of the river. In all their visits to camp the wife carries her liege-lord upon her shoulders through the water with the most obsequious devotion.

The Crows are fairer than the Sioux, many of the mountain band being sallow and hardly a shade darker than whites who undergo similar exposure. This fact was so marked that the first seen were supposed to be half-breeds, but we were assured that they were of pure Indian descent.

Tuesday, August 23.—Soon after dinner to-day Lieutenant Maynadier returned to camp, and with him came Mr. Robert Meldrum, the agent of the Fur Company, who is in charge of the long-expected boats, which are still some

20 miles below. It has been found almost impossible to navigate the Yellowstone, the water being too low, although the vessels, which are batteaux, draw only 18 inches. At Mr. Meldrum's suggestion I shall send down a number of the wagons to-morrow to receive part of the freight and thus lighten the load.

The afternoon and evening was spent in conversation with Mr. Meldrum, obtaining information from him with reference to the most feasible routes before us and the peculiarities of life among the Indians. He is undoubtedly the best living authority in regard to the Crows, outside of the tribe, having spent over 30 years in their country, during that time visiting the regions of civilization but once, and on that occasion spending only 19 days in St. Louis. He has long lived among these Indians, assuming their dress and habits, and by his skill and success in leading their war parties has acquired distinction, rising to the second post of authority in the tribe. He of course speaks their language perfectly, and says that it has become more natural to him than his mother tongue. I noted the alacrity with which he ceased speaking English whenever an opportunity offered.

The Indians were so troublesome about camp to-day that I posted a double guard at night for the purpose of freeing us from the annoyance of their visits.

Wednesday, August 24.—Six wagons started this morning for the boats under the wagon master, accompanied by a guard, with Mr. Meldrum acting as guide.

The Crows are still swarming about camp, although they have not been quite as troublesome as for a few days past. The men do not seem dishonest, and Mr. Meldrum says that we need not distrust them, but added that the women and children would steal everything possible, and it has therefore been found necessary to keep a rather strict watch upon all portable articles.

Our mules and the beasts of the Indians have thoroughly consumed the grass in this vicinity, and it will be soon necessary to find new pasturage. Our animals are immensely improved in condition by the rest and nourishing food obtained during our halt.

Thursday, August 25.—The wagons that were sent to meet the boats returned this evening with full loads, and there are now hopes that we shall be able to resume our march from this point in a few days. The day was chiefly spent writing and computing. The Indians, save two or three lodges, all left to-day and ascended the river to Fort Sarpy, where they will await the arrival of the boats with their annuities.

Friday, August 26.—The long-expected boats came up this evening, but our supplies are so confused with those of the Fur Company and of the Indian agent, that it will be necessary to unload the cargoes entirely, and I have therefore concluded to have them push directly on to the fort where we will join them on Monday.

The afternoon and evening were spent in obtaining information in regard to the country between the Yellowstone and the Platte. I had a skeleton map prepared showing those points with which we are acquainted, and Mr. Meldrum has filled in the leading features from memory. The information thus obtained will be of the greatest value, as it will enable a separate party to reach the head of Powder river, a matter of much importance as I cannot obtain a second guide, and propose exploring two routes from this point. As we shall pass through the country we shall have an opportunity of verifying Mr. Meldrum's statements and testing the accuracy of his topographical knowledge.

High winds prevailed at night and the sky was obscured by scattered clouds, but not sufficiently to prevent observations.

Saturday, August 27.—The entire day was consumed in preparations for the resumption of our journey, and especially in arranging for the division of the expedition into two parties for separate explorations.

Sunday, August 28.—The Sabbath was spent quietly in camp, and in the evening the northern sky was illuminated by an aurora borealis of unrivalled splendor. It was preceded by a dull reddish light just over the northwestern horizon, and more immediately heralded by brilliant streaks, flashing irregularly up the northern heavens. In a short time this became continuous, and between 9 and 10 o'clock so vivid that the north star was entirely obscured and distinct shadows were cast. From 11 o'clock till midnight the grandeur of the celestial display surpassed all attempts at description. Vast sheets of glowing light rose successively to the zenith in irregular pulsations, while the illumination filled the entire arch of the heavens, and the horizon of the northwest was marked with all the gorgeous coloring of sunset. Shortly after midnight its brilliancy began to pale, breaking the spell that had enchained the party during a spectacle of such unwonted magnificence.

Monday, August 29.—We struck our tents and resumed our march early in the morning. An accident to one of the escort teamsters, who was thrown from his horse and struck by one of the wagon wheels in the head, receiving a severe scalp wound, delayed us some time, as, after his injuries had received proper attention from Dr. Hines, we were compelled to empty one of the spring wagons carrying the instruments, and thus extemporize an ambulance. For this reason we did not reach Fort Sarpy until after 10 o'clock, having traversed during our 10-mile march the wide open valley of the Yellowstone, differing in no essential respect from that in which we have been encamped for the past two weeks.

We found the trading-house situated in the timber on what during high water would be an island, a channel, now dry, passing to the south of it. The "fort" is an enclosure about 100 feet square, of upright cottonwood logs 15 feet high, the outer wall also forming the exterior of a row of log cabins which are occupied as dwelling houses, store houses, shops, and stables. The roofs of these structures are nearly flat, and formed of timber covered to the depth of about a foot with dirt, thus making an excellent parapet for purposes of defence, the preparations for resistance to possible attacks being further perfected by loopholes in the upper part of the outer row of logs. The entrance is through a heavy gate which is always carefully closed at night. No flanking arrangements whatever exist, and the "fort" is thus a decidedly primitive affair. It is amply sufficient, however, to protect its inmates against the schemes and the martial science of the Indians.

We found that the boats had but just arrived, and everything was still in confusion, while the agent of the Fur Company had promptly commenced traffic with the savages, considerately allowing our matters to take care of themselves. I found assembled at this point the two largest of the three bands into which the Crows are divided, and I therefore determined to improve the opportunity by holding a council to-morrow and explaining to them the purposes of my visit to their country. The necessary notifications have been accordingly sent to the various chiefs.

CHAPTER II.

FROM FORT SARPY TO WINTER QUARTERS.

Tuesday, August 30.—The entire morning was consumed in endeavoring to bring to a focus our arrangements for the Indian council. An annoying delay, however, resulted from a cause that would be hardly admissible in ordinary diplomatic conferences. The horse of the head chief was missing, supposed to have been stolen by the Blackfeet, and the entire energies of the tribe were devoted to the recovery of the animal or discovery of the robbers, to the exclusion of all other business, however important. Search ultimately discovered the animal in a neighboring wood, whither he had strayed, and at 1 o'clock the council convened for the discussion of such secondary questions as the relations of the Crows and the President.

I told them I had come among them by order of the President, not to do harm, but that I might ascertain their condition, and return and report. I was not a trader, nor did I come among them as their agent. Many years had passed since any one had been through their country in the way that I was then going, for no other object than to see them and the country. The President was in the habit of sending out persons to visit all parts of his country, both among the whites and Indians, and this was my entire errand.

I should do no harm, would endeavor not to drive off the buffalo, and would only kill what was absolutely necessary for my party to eat. I also expressed my gratification at the fact that, although I had been among them for some days, property had not been molested, and added that I hoped we would continue constantly friends. I then invited them to reply, and volunteered to take their messages, if they desired to send any, to the President.

Red Bear, the head chief, was sitting upon one side of the circle, and did not seem inclined to answer at first. I subsequently ascertained that his reluctance was occasioned by the fact that he had come down from the mountains without his court dress, and disliked to appear save in his paraphernalia. The urging of Two Bears, the chief of the lower band, and second chief of the tribe, prevailed at last, however, and he came forward, dressed in semi-civilized style, with pants, shirt, and hat, and said, with a quiet and dignified air:

BROTHER: We are glad to see you. We are glad to hear from the Great Father. The Absaroukas (the true or Indian name of the Crows) have always been the friend of the whites, and have always treated them well; we have never killed a white man. We are perfectly willing you should pass through our country. You can do so without being molested. Should you, however, wish to stop in the country and build houses, we should object to your doing so. We are a small tribe. You see here the most of us. We have enemies on all sides, the Sioux on the east, the Blackfeet on the west, and they are making war on us all the time. We want to be let alone, and we want our Great Father to protect us.

I replied that I would tell the President their wishes, but they must make peace and not always be at war. They are, indeed, a small band compared with their neighbors, but are famous warriors, and, according to common report, seldom fail to hold their own with any of the tribes unless greatly outnumbered. Their numerical inferiority will, however, undoubtedly result in their ultimate extermination in the interminable war waged among hostile tribes in this region.

I was very favorably impressed by the dignified, quiet manner of this chief. His whole deportment was so in contrast with the bluster of the Sioux orators we met at Fort Pierre that it was remarked by all. The Sioux were loud and rapid talkers, gesticulating most vehemently. Red Bear, on the contrary, stood quietly within three or four feet of me, with his hands clasped in front of him, and looking me steadily in the eye, spoke as calmly and quietly as was possible. Mr. Meldrum acted as interpreter, and there was an additional advantage in his being able to express the chief's ideas in better English than was possible by the half-breed interpreters at Fort Pierre. Indeed, Red Bear, the chief of the Crows, and the Frog, sub-chief of the Brulé band of Sioux, were the only Indians I met who inspired me with the slightest admiration, or who in any degree came up to imaginary standard of Indian character we are apt to get from reading popular romances of Indian life.

The "talk" ended by the distribution of a few presents from my limited stock, and the setting forth of the usual "feast," consisting of coffee and hard bread, which proved highly satisfactory.

After the close of the "talk" I succeeded in procuring, through the traders, (who shrewdly prevent the Indians from dealing directly with us, and thus realize large profits for themselves from both parties,) seven ordinary horses—an addition to my stock of animals greatly needed. The balance of the day was consumed in perfecting arrangements for the resumption of the march.

A newly arrived party of Crows reported to-day that a large band of "80 camp fires" of Sioux had lately attacked and killed a small band of 11 Crows. "Eighty camp-fires" indicates a body of several hundred warriors, and this is probably the party who are reported as having designed to attack us. If this is the fact, they must have crossed our track, and, of course, ascertained our whereabouts, and their refraining from troubling our expedition is evidence that the savage understands at least the principle embraced in the adage of civilization, that discretion is the better part of valor.

Wednesday, August 31.—Some complications in the settlement of the provision account occasioned an unexpected delay this morning, and it was not until 10 o'clock that we finally left Fort Sarpy, around which, as we moved off, all Indians were collected receiving their annuities from Major Schoonover.

We pushed up the valley of the Yellowstone for nine miles over a barren, dusty plain, with scarcely the semblance of vegetation upon it, the soil resembling the dry bed of a stream, and the dust raised by the train filling the air. Turning to the left, up a small valley which looked as unpromising as any that could be imagined, we continued our journey three miles further, when we found a living spring and a tolerable supply of grass. The water was far from the best, but still was palatable, and we therefore encamped.

The Yellowstone, for 10 or 15 miles above Fort Sarpy, flows entirely on the north side of the valley, having a wide plain on its right bank. The timber is confined entirely to the river's edge and is not very abundant.

Thursday, September 1.—Our route this morning bore up the valley of the stream upon which we had encamped, and the travelling was detestable, although our previous experience has reconciled us to the worst roads and given confidence in our power to overcome all obstacles. The great obstruction to-day was sand, in which our newly laden wagons sank deeply and seriously tried the power of our animals. One of our teams stalled and, falling behind, caused a delay of an hour or more.

We continued up the stream to the point at which it forked, and thence up the western fork, the valley of which soon becoming too narrow compelled us to cross the bed of the intervening stream, causing considerable labor, and to take to the hills.

At this point I drove ahead with Bridger, and from a convenient ridge obtained a view of the country before us. The prospect was decidedly inauspicious, the whole surface of the adjacent hills being cut up into steep gorges, and the chances for passable roads appearing to steadily decrease. Under such circumstances, I ordered a search for water with a view to encamping, and ultimately an oozing spring was found in a neighboring valley, which by digging yielded enough for the men but left none for the animals. Bridger, however, was more successful, and found an abundance of water in a valley some two miles distant, to which the herd were driven.

Bridger reports that our route to-morrow will be into and down the valley of Tullock's fork, a branch of the Big Horn, which we are approaching, and as I propose that Lieutenant Maynadier shall go up that stream, I gave him his orders that he may make his arrangement to leave us when we strike the creek. The grass at our camp to-night is tolerably good.

Friday, September 2.—The road this morning continued up the valley in which we had encamped, thence along the ridge for about a mile, and then turned down a small creek that flows into O'Fallen's or Tullock's fork of the Big Horn. We reached the latter stream at about noon after a march of seven miles.

At this point Lieutenant Maynadier and party separated from us, ascending the fork, while we continued down to the Big Horn, arriving at that river after a further advance of seven miles, and pitching our tents upon its right bank. The division of the party was a necessary step, and we separated in excellent spirits and with mutual and fervent good wishes.

The road to-day has been very poor, and until we reached the valley of Tullock's creek the hills were so steep that it was barely possible to cross them. West of the ridge gully after gully intercepted our progress, and at times we were forced into the bed of the streams, where the sand or stones formed serious obstacles. These circumstances, added to the delay occasioned by the separation of the parties, made the day a very laborious one, and we were in the saddle between nine and ten hours, although the distance travelled was less than 15 miles.

One of our horses escaped this morning, and was pursued by Mr. Wilson and one of the men, who have not as yet returned. In all probability they were compelled to return to Fort Sarpy, in which case they will have over 50 miles to travel, and cannot get back before to-morrow afternoon.

Dark clouds have filled the sky in the northeast all day, and a cold north wind blowing this evening rendered a fire necessary for comfort, and eventually culminated in a storm, which has prevented observations and caused serious personal discomfort.

Saturday, September 3.—The storm of last night had not abated this morning and did not cease until 10 a. m., leaving then a mud in which locomotion with loaded wagons is impossible. This fact and the non-arrival of Mr. Wilson led me not to move camp.

Mr. Wilson ultimately returned about 3 o'clock in the afternoon, bringing with him the missing horse which he had found at Fort Sarpy. He passed last night in the Indian village as the guest of Red Bear, the head chief. He reports that the whole village of 130 lodges is upon our trail, and that they propose accompanying us to the head of Powder river.

This is decidedly overdoing the matter of amicable relations. A single guide would be of invaluable service, but the continual company of 500 savages of all ages and both sexes, devoid of any strict ideas of property, expecting to be allowed free access to our stores, and with a general friendship for our portable articles rather than for our persons, can hardly be esteemed one of the leading advantages to be derived from amity with the aborigines. They have not shown themselves as yet, however, and I am in hopes that their usual lack of veracity will not fail in this instance, and that they will break the promise made Mr. Wilson, which, in this case, as far as we are concerned, is more to be honored in the breach than the observance.

The guide states that the best route up the valley of the Big Horn will lie for some distance at least on the west side of the river. Search has therefore been made during the day for a good crossing, and one has been found above camp which will answer, although rather deep.

Our escort being now reduced to 14 men, one-half having been detailed for duty with Lieutenant Maynadier, we have not the force to post a guard of soldiers every night. I have therefore been obliged to make a detail from my teamsters and packers, and to use my assistants as officers of the guard. The chilly nights do not tend to render this service one of the luxuries of frontier life.

Sunday, September 4.—I had desired to improve the first clear sky afforded for astronomical observations, to determine the position of our present camp and also of the mouth of the Big Horn river, but failed in this last night. The air this morning was quite cold, the thermometer standing at 34°.

After our usual religious services, I finally succeeded in getting morning and afternoon observations for time, and circummeridian observations of the sun for latitude, which will be enough to give the position of the camp with tolerable accuracy.

Monday, September 5.—Some of the party having discovered a good ford below camp, our route this morning ran down the stream that we might take advantage of it. The ford proved to be excellent, and will be of importance when the valley of the Yellowstone becomes a route for emigrants. It is mid-way between Tullock's or O'Fallen's creek and the junction of the Big Horn with the Yellowstone, and probably three quarters of a mile or a mile above the latter point. In going from the east to the west side of the river the route inclines well up the stream, and at the present stage of the river we found the water not over the axletrees of our wagons. In fifteen minutes from the time the first team entered the water the last was on the opposite bank, having passed over a firm, stony bottom. Some little clearing was required upon the west bank, and then the train moved rapidly up the valley.

About ten miles from the ford a bend of the river compelled us to cross a ridge of hills for a mile or two, both the ascent and descent being accomplished with difficulty by reason of the steepness of the slope and the heavy loads in our wagons, but still the obstacles were slight compared with others previously overcome.

After again reaching the valley, search was at once commenced for a camping ground, but the scarcity of grass compelled us to travel three or four miles further before halting. We at last selected a spot upon the river, furnishing on the low ground scanty pasturage for our animals, which we were compelled, however, to eke out with the bark of young cottonwood trees.

Artemisia covered the ground over which we have travelled to-day, seriously inconveniencing the progress of our vehicles. This and the hills that we were compelled to cross, as mentioned above, were all, however, that marred the excellence of the road. We travelled 16¾ miles in all, or about 16 miles after crossing the river. Our course has been nearly magnetic south, or from 15° to 20° west of due south.

The promise of our Indian friends to overtake and accompany us has not yet been fulfilled, and our grief thereat is not wholly inconsolable.

Tuesday, September 6.—Our route to-day continued directly up the valley of the Big Horn, which at our last night's camp is not wide but cut into numerous islands by the river, the main portion of which here flows upon the eastern side, cutting the bluff and leaving the only practicable road upon the left bank, where we now are.

About three miles from camp we entered a wide, open valley, perfectly level, but travelling being still embarrassed by the artemisia. The hills upon each side sink and become less broken, and ahead seem to disappear entirely. The Big Horn mountains begin to be visible in the distance like faint blue clouds, and our prospects for rapid marching seem much more hopeful than for weeks past.

About 11 o'clock a herd of buffalo was discovered, and Bridger's skill with the rifle soon added two cows to our larder, in which fresh meat had for some days been a rarity.

About noon the mouth of the "Little Big Horn" came in sight. Here the river takes a wide sweep off to the east, coming back again beyond, and as our route would thus naturally lead some distance from the stream, a halt was ordered, as we were in possession of the three great requisites for camping—wood, water and grass. Though we had been in the saddle but six hours, and in that time had stopped to butcher buffalo, the distance travelled to-day was 13.86 miles.

Our camp is two or three miles below the mouth of the Little Big Horn. The Indian name of the Big Horn is *Ets-pot-agie*, or Mountain Sheep river, and of the Little Big Horn, *Ets-pot-agie-caté*, or Little Mountain Sheep river—the trappers' names for most of the streams in this country being translations of the Indian titles.

Wednesday, September 7.—Our route to-day continued up the Big Horn in the same broad valley travelled yesterday. Upon setting out in the morning we aimed directly for the distant bluffs, thus leaving the stream nearly two miles to the left. About two miles from camp we passed the mouth of the Little Big Horn, which flows through an apparently level valley of the same character as that of the main stream and of about half the width. About six miles from camp we crossed the bed of a stream, now dry, coming from the west, requiring some little labor with the shovel before it was passable.

Ten miles from camp the river cut the bluff on the west side, but just at this point we came upon a good ford and crossed without difficulty.

On the east bank we found fine grass, the best seen this season, but it does not extend over one-fourth of a mile from the river, the balance of the valley being clay covered with the interminable artemisia. Old corrals and the remains of lodges show that this is a favorite resort of the Indians. We encamped about three miles above the ford, having travelled 13¾ miles.

The Big Horn mountains are now in plain sight, apparently about 20 miles distant. After dark this evening a sudden gust of wind from the westward blew down a part of our tents, and set the whole party at work lengthening the cords and strengthening the stakes of our frail habitations. The gale was accompanied by a few drops of rain, but at 11 p. m. the sky was clear, giving promise of a pleasant day to-morrow.

Thursday, September 8.—We continued up the valley of the Big Horn, and for the first nine miles over as fine a road as could be desired, being almost level and with very little sage to obstruct our progress. Nine miles from camp we crossed a small stream coming in from the east, which Bridger, who seems to know every square mile of this region, calls Grass creek. Above this the road was a little rougher, but still good. About 15 miles from camp we crossed a small stream that Bridger calls "Soap creek," and two miles above this we pitched our tents for the night upon the banks of the river, where we had a plentiful supply of grass, though but little wood.

The Big Horn mountains, which in the clear morning air did not seem more than 10 miles distant, now appear but little nearer, notwithstanding our day's march of 17 miles.

The more immediate topographical features of these mountains are very peculiar. From our camp we can distinctly trace the Big Horn up its valley to this immense wall, rising over 3,000 feet in height, and crossing the course of the stream at right angles. The river here is large, deep, and nearly 300 feet in width, and yet at this distance there are no evidences of its cutting its way through this rocky barrier, and nothing in the conformation of the hills and spurs in the remoter ranges indicates the course of its channel. Its remarkable cañon is famous throughout the west, and as from this point our route would bear off southwestward towards the Platte, it was decided to visit this great natural curiosity this afternoon. I was accompanied by Dr. Hayden, Mr. Schonborn, and Mr. Wilson, and we rode up the banks of the Big Horn until a bend compelled its abandonment.

It was only after an hour's ride that the apparently smooth face of the lofty mountain wall afforded the slightest evidence of being broken, and two hours elapsed before we reached the foot of the cañon. During the latter portion of the ride we passed over luxuriant meadow land, whose rank and rich vegetation rose to our stirrups, while the soil was manifestly of extraordinary fertility, making this the garden spot of this entire region. This unusual productiveness is undoubtedly explained by the circumstance that in the vicinity of the mountains rain is more abundant, and this hypothesis is further strengthened by the fact already noted, that the valley of the Big Horn continually improves in agricultural characteristics as it is ascended.

This spot at the mouth of the cañon, however, is unsurpassed in this region, and I venture the prediction that not many decades will elapse before it shall become a thriving and important point on a road connecting the Platte with the three forks of the Missouri, and skirting in its course the Big Horn mountains.

The cañon is one of the most remarkable sights upon the continent. The river here narrows to a width of less than 150 feet, and bursts out through reddish tinted walls of perpendicular rock over 300 feet in height. Its current at this point is slow, but undoubtedly its course among the mountains is marked by successions of rapids and cascades.

We pushed up its banks until we reached the impassable wall of perpendicular rock, and after affording time for sketching and geological observations returned to camp. Bridger claims to have descended the lower cañon of the Big Horn some years since upon a raft during his service as a trapper with the American Fur Company, and his descriptions of the grandeur of the scenery along its banks are glowing and remarkable.

He portrays a series of rugged cañons, the river forming among jagged rocks between lofty overhanging precipices, whose threatening arches shut out all sunlight, interspersed with narrow valleys, teeming with luxuriant verdure, through whose pleasant banks the stream flows as placidly as in its broad valleys below. The conformation of the country—my measurements showing the mountains to be over 3,000 feet in height—render all these marvels natural, and if it were possible I should be glad to attempt the exploration of the cañon myself.

Friday, September 9.—We this morning left the valley of the Big Horn and struck off to the southward, passing up "Soap creek," and hugging the foot of the mountains. The rain of last night had fallen in snow upon their summits, suggesting the approach of winter, and demonstrating their unusual altitude.

The morning was cloudy and disagreeable, but the party seemed to regard this as a turning point in the expedition, and as we were now facing towards civilization jubilancy of spirits universally prevailed. The road, however, soon lost the excellence that characterized it yesterday, and became abominable. Short and deep ravines crossed it every half mile, not so abrupt as to require working, but, nevertheless, causing much delay.

For the greater portion of the distance we kept between the creek and the mountain, in order to avoid the bad travelling in the narrow valley. About eight and a half miles from camp a deep ravine gave serious trouble, retarding us an amount nearly equal to a half day's march, as we were compelled to double our teams, and even then a portion of the loads were necessarily carried across by hand. We travelled only a single mile after this delay, and encamped upon the stream up which we had been advancing.

Extensive fires have burned over much of this country, seriously injuring the grass, and as this seems to have been of recent occurrence, I imagine that it is the act of the Indians, who are thus seeking to impede our progress.

This evening I read the angle of elevation to one of the prominent points of the mountain range under which we are travelling, using the sextant and artificial horizon. The height, as thus determined, of the mountain above our camp is 4,818 feet, or 8,318 feet above the ocean, the barometer showing our camp to be 3,500 feet above the ocean.

Saturday, September 10.—We had this morning indubitable evidence of the immediate presence of Indians. Three of the picket ropes, with which our animals had been fastened, were found cut, and one of our mules was missing. An examination of the scene of the theft resulted in the discovery of the place of concealment of the culprit and of the tracks of the missing animal. The Indian had stolen into camp under cover of some thick low bushes growing upon the banks of a dry ravine, and had succeeded in driving off the mule without the knowledge of our sentinels. There was no hopes of recovering the missing animal without the loss of more time than we could spare at this season of the year, and it was, therefore abandoned to our Indian friends, (?) and we resolved to profit by the lesson taught by their amity. This occurrence prevented an early start, and the dry bed of a stream near camp gave further trouble by causing one of our teams to staul, making further delay.

After this, however, we ascended a ridge between the dry gully and Soap creek, and continued along it for three or four miles, when we crossed the main stream, which here is a clear mountain brook some five or six feet wide, flowing over a gravel bottom, and then passed, with much difficulty, over a steep hill dividing us from Grass creek, causing an additional delay of an hour or more. It was thus 2 o'clock before we reached the latter stream, though we had travelled only nine miles.

We found that it was entitled to the name Bridger gave it, for the grass was excellent upon its banks, and the temptation to halt was difficult to resist. The necessity of advancing was, however, more potent than the luxury of a good camping ground, and we, therefore, continued over the next ridge hoping to find a suitable spot in the valley beyond, but upon reaching it no water could be discovered, and all the grass had been recently burned.

A second valley, which proved to be in the drainage of the Little Horn, was at length reached, but with the same result. A third ridge having more gentle slopes was then crossed when we entered the valley of Grass Lodge creek, a branch of the Little Horn.

I preceded the party over the hill and was sadly disappointed as I looked down into the valley to see the black marks of fire along the west side, but on reaching the opposite bluff we ultimately found an excellent camping ground, which we were glad to occupy at 4½ o'clock, having traveled 14¾ miles.

In my explorations in search of a camp, in advance of the party, I discovered in a thicket on the banks of the stream the finest elk I had ever seen, and after encamping informed Bridger of the fact. He started in search of the game, and just before dark returned and reported that he had shot the animal about a mile from camp, and declared it to be one of the largest he had ever met. The head and horns were cut off to enable them to put his body in the cart, and as it lay stretched on the grass it seemed longer than that of any mule in our herd. We had not the facilities for weighing the carcass whole, but after it had been dressed according to the requirements of the commissary department, with the necks and shanks off, the four quarters aggregated 640 pounds. The head, horns, and hide were also weighed, and the total showed that the live weight of the animal was over 1,000 pounds. This supply of fresh meat was very acceptable, as we have had less than usual of late.

The evening was bright and unusually beautiful, filled with all the charming effects of a full moon and grand mountain scenery.

Sunday, September 11.—The rest of the Sabbath was doubly acceptable after one of the hardest week's work we have had during the summer, the last two days having been especially trying on our animals.

Dr. Hayden and Mr. Snowden wished to visit a bluff at the pass of the Little Horn this morning, but as Bridger was very decided as to the danger of parties going abroad alone while there were such evidences of the vicinity of the Indians, and as I could not encourage unnecessary work upon the Sabbath, the project was abandoned. Simply as a question of physical advantage, the propriety of the observance of the Sabbath as a day of rest has been demonstrated to my satisfaction by the experience of the expedition thus far.

The day is bright and beautiful and rather uncomfortably warm in a close tent, the thermometer standing at 70° in the open air.

Monday, September 12.—The first two and a half miles of our route to-day was a continual ascent, tasking our teams severely, but after climbing about 500 feet above the stream we entered upon an almost perfectly flat open plain some two miles in extent. This terminated in an abrupt slope into the valley of the Little Horn, which occasioned us considerable difficulty, the vertical descent being full 700 feet. Upon reaching the valley we found a beautifully clear stream of about 20 yards in width, and, at the point at which we crossed it, 15 inches in depth. The valley is quite wide, and the immediate banks of the stream are bordered by a thick growth of bushes and briers.

Leaving the valley of the Little Horn we ascended the hill on the eastern side where a deep gully intercepting our route caused considerable delay. A fine supply of wild plum was found upon its banks, and while the men were engaged in regaling themselves with the fruit, one of the party, James Stephenson, was suddenly attacked by a large she grizzly and knocked down. The wagon master hastened to his assistance and the brute retreated to a neighboring thicket.

A grand hunt was at once commenced by almost every member of the party, but soon assumed a ludicrous phase. The sportsmen attempted to obtain a shot at the bear, but the moment they came in sight through the bushes she would make a vigorous charge and scatter the crowd, beating immediately a hasty retreat to her lair. After this alternate hunt of the bear by the hunters and the hunters by the bear had been repeated several times she failed to respond to another approach, and some of the more daring of the party crept into the edge of the bushes to reconnoiter. They failed to find her, and at this juncture she was discovered crossing the crest of a neighboring hill with three cubs, just out of rifle range. Inasmuch as she had justly earned her right of escape, her exit was heartily cheered.

After finally reaching the top of this ridge we descended by an easy grade to the valley of Pass creek, where we encamped, having travelled 13 miles.

The country passed through is the best seen on our whole route. The hills are high and rugged; but the soil is good, and both hills and valleys are covered with a luxuriant growth of bunch grass. All that the country needs to make it a desirable residence is a better climate and a larger supply of timber. The latter is, however, more abundant than in most localities in this region, the valleys affording a present supply of fuel, and the neighboring mountains an indifferent species of pine.

A large portion of the grass has just been burned over, and the surface of the country is therefore black and forbidding; but it is evident that, in the spring, the prospect is most beautiful from the exuberance of verdure and foliage. The close proximity of the mountains not only adds beauty to the landscape, but they are the sources of numerous brooks of clear running water that fertilize the soil and teem with mountain trout.

Bears are very numerous, more than a dozen having been seen in the course of the day's march, and one, a yearling cub, was brought down by Bridger's rifle. Elk, deer, and antelope have also been seen in abundance, and we can now understand why the Indians cling with such tenacity to their country. No buffalo have been seen to-day, but the number of skeletons visible upon all sides show that at times they are to be found here in large numbers.

Tuesday, September 13.—We started this morning up the valley of the stream upon which we had encamped, and after crossing it found a good road to its source. We then crossed a low divide, reached a second branch of the same creek, and after ascending it to its head passed over a rather steeper hill, and arrived at the drainage of Tongue river, striking a branch which heads in a large hill to our left. In passing down this stream we encountered one or two difficult hills before reaching the river itself, upon the banks of which we encamped after a march of 14½ miles. Several of the carts were upset in the course of the march, causing vexatious delays; but, as a general rule, the travelling was fine. The general aspect of the country remains unchanged, but a thick smoky atmosphere has prevented our enjoying the full benefit of the scenery through which we have passed to-day. As we gradually approach the mountains they are increasing in grandeur. While Bridger was in advance of the train to-day he discovered five or six Indians in the distance apparently watching our march. They are doubtless the fellows who stole the mule on Friday night, and are now seeking opportunities to commit other depredations. Our camp has, therefore, been selected with special reference to safety, the river protecting it in front, while, upon the other sides, we have an open prairie, which they will not probably be bold enough to cross with hostile intent.

Wednesday, September 14.—Our precautions against Indian robberies prove not to have been thorough enough, and this morning we miss a number of minor portable articles (cups, axes, &c.,) which were left too near the river bank. The Indians appear to have crept along in the shadows on its edge, and thus reached them. The boldness of the theft is noteworthy, especially after we consider the fact that two sentinels were upon duty last night—one of the escort and one of the citizen employés detailed specially to guard against possible dangers. I question, however, their vigilance, as I have found it very difficult to impress upon the party the necessity of incessant watchfulness. The labors of the day they discharge uncomplainingly, but the guard duty at night they seem inclined to neglect, even at the risk of personal safety.

Our route to-day bore directly across Tongue river, (a beautiful mountain torrent about 40 feet wide and a foot or more in depth,) and thence over the hills in a southeast course, keeping nearly parallel to the mountains, but approaching them gradually. We crossed the heads of several small tributaries to Tongue river, the undulations of the surface being slight. A flat plateau separated the streams, the valleys of which were broad and beautiful. One narrow brook, flowing in a cut some eight or ten feet deep, was the only one that we experienced any difficulty in crossing.

The last descent into the valley in which we encamped was long and steep, but level, and accomplished without special difficulty. Our camp is on the right bank of Goose creek, the most eastern fork of Tongue river, and the stream at this point is 25 or 30 feet wide and 8 or 10 inches in depth. Our camp is about six miles in a straight line from the summit of the mountains which tower sublimely above us at a height which I find by angular measurement to be over 4,000 feet. The distance travelled to-day was 12¼ miles. Heavy clouds and a slight rain prevented observations at night.

Thursday, September 15.—Our route to-day still bore to the southeast, gradually approaching the mountains, and crossing the heads of several small tributaries of Tongue river. Our proximity to the mountains soon rendered the road somewhat broken, all the small water-courses becoming deep ravines. The hills seemed rounded, and were covered with grass; but the travelling became so bad that we determined to leave the mountain edge, and in about six miles turned down a small stream, running nearly east, that seemed convenient for our purpose. The road was good, and I drove in advance, as was my custom, to ascertain the nature of the country. Observing that the train did not follow as I had expected, however, I waited until Lieutenant Smith, commanding the escort, came up and reported that one of his wagons had broken down, and that a halt was necessary to repair damages. Returning, I found the party in camp after a march of only about seven miles. While returning to the train my first view of the camp struck me as one of most singular beauty. The dark and varied outlines of the mountains formed the background to a landscape of wide extent and attractive features. In the centre the circle of white tents and wagon covers reflected the bright rays of the sun, and the smoke of camp fires, the groups of men, and the grazing animals, added the charm of busy life to the scene; while, upon either hand, the striking contrasts were mellowed down by gently-sloping hills clad with verdure of all the picturesque tints of autumn. The canvass of the painter has perpetuated few finer scenes real or ideal. Upon parting with Lieutenant Maynadier it was mutually agreed that should either meet with misfortunes that demanded the assistance of the other we shall communicate by signals of smoke. I was, therefore, much troubled this evening at a large smoke visible to the north. Our compasses were brought into requisition, its position with reference to our route determined as accurately as possible, and, after careful consideration, it was concluded that it was so near to the route we have ourselves followed that it could not be the other party. Dr. Hayden came into camp this evening from a ride in the mountains, and reported that a snow-clad peak is in sight from the top of the mountain ridge, along the base of which we have been for several days travelling. I at once planned a little side excursion for to-morrow to enable me to see, and, if possible, locate it. The country traversed to-day is good, but not as fine as that we have found during the last few days. A few miles to our left (apparently not over 10 or 15) the hills stand out in all the naked deformity of "washed lands," showing that the belt of good land close under the foot of the mountains, and through which our route lies, is not more than 20 or 25 miles in width. A clear night enabled me to obtain good observations.

Friday, September 16.—Soon after the train was in motion this morning I left it, and in company with Dr. Hayden, Mr. Schonborn, and Mr. Wilson, started for the mountains. We rode for over an hour before we reached their base, climbing rising ground the entire time. Selecting the most favorable point we dismounted, and leading our horses, as we were afraid to leave them, we commenced a long and tedious ascent which lasted until about noon. We were repaid for our labors upon reaching the summit of the ridge, which, however, we found was very far from constituting the summit of the mountain. Far in the distance the rugged rocks were piled above us, several of the highest peaks being covered with snow. Looking to the left through a deep gorge the Clear fork of Powder river was seen sparkling in the sunlight, while in the distance Pumpkin butte appeared putting up from the level prairie.

The desire to visit the distant peaks was very great, and gladly would I have gratified it had it been practicable, but a single glance was enough to shrow that the attempt would require more time than I deemed it proper to spend at this season for this purpose. The journey would be a long and wearisom one; deep valleys and high ridges would have to be crossed and thick woods penetrated, all of which would not only consume time, but horse-flesh, neither of which can be spared just now. We were therefore compelled to content ourselves with visiting two well defined points that we knew had been fixed by intersecting lines from our route, and by compass bearings from them established the position of the highest point, with a considerable degree of accuracy.

While descending the mountain we discovered the train still on the march, though it was later than our usual hour for halting. When we reached the party at 5 p. m., they were hard at work ascending a hill which proved to be the dividing ridge between the waters of Tongue and Powder rivers. This hill was quite steep and about 200 feet high, with no level space at the top. The descent was also abrupt, but only about 40 or 50 feet, verticle measurement, before reaching the bank of the Clear fork of Powder river, the stream running literally upon the top of the hill, in such a manner that a cut of 200 or 300 yards would give a fall of about 150 feet and turn the water into Tongue river.

This peculiarity in the topography was so striking that it was observed by every one in the party the moment the summit was reached, and the remark was generally made "what an excellent location for a water-power."

The road to-day has severely tasked our animals, as it crossed a succession of steep ridges, rendering our progress very slow. One creek especially, caused delay, as nearly every wagon stalled in it. The elevation is getting to be so great that the mules fail to perform the labor they would be equal to in a less rarified atmosphere, and the barometer this evening reads only 24.8 inches, indicating a height of over 5,000 feet. We are to-night, for the first time, encamped among pines. All seem exhausted by the labors of the day, and as it was nearly dark before the wagons were all up, we were compelled to encamp at this point, though it was far from being secure from the visits of the Indians, whom we know to have been on our track for several days past.

The result was that at about 11 o'clock we were startled by the report of a gun and the cries of one of our sentinels. I rushed from my tent but only to see the form of an Indian dodging into a neighboring clump of trees, and meet the alarmed guard, whom I found had been shot with two balls through the muscles of the upper portion of his arm. He stated that he had seen a man near him, whom he supposed to be one of the party walking about camp in his drawers, and instead of hailing the individual as he should have done in obedience to his orders, he walked towards him.

The Indian did not perceive the sentinel's presence until he was but 10 paces distant, and then finding himself discovered, fired and ran. The wound received by the man proved to be slight, but the balls had passed on and struck one of our horses, which died from bleeding in a few minutes. The camp was of course greatly excited at this rencontre, and scouts were sent out in all directions but without finding any traces of the intruder or his comrades.

It is not probable that the savages intended anything more than a plundering visit to camp, and this hypothesis is confirmed by the fact that several portable articles are missing from the cook's fire, their number being so large also as to induce the belief that the Indian who fired was simply one of a band. After the excitement had subsided, and additional guards had been stationed, we returned to sleep, thankful that the adventure was without more serious results. The party have now a forcible conviction of the imperative necessity of continual vigilance.

Saturday, September 17.—A severe storm prevailing this morning would have prevented a change of camp to-day, had not the experience of last evening demonstrated the importance of such a step. About noon a temporary lull was therefore improved, and the train started.

The Clear fork impinged upon the bluff just below our camp, making it necessary to cross at once. The stream at this point is quite wide and cut up into several channels.

The bed is also filled with large boulders, many of which we were compelled to remove to make a passable road, and as a result of the consequent delay, we did not reach the opposite bank until 2 o'clock. Here we found a narrow bottom affording an excellent road, down which we moved rapidly for about four miles, to a point at which the valley widened sufficiently to furnish a camping ground away from any cover convenient for our Indian visitors.

Rain commenced falling again as we halted, and has continued till this time, (10 p. m.) The wind is also blowing a gale from the north, and as we are upon an open plain, exposed to its fury, both men and animals must suffer severely. The moon does not rise until late and a better opportunity for a night attack could hardly be imagined. Our camp is, however, excellently placed and no necessary precautions have been neglected.

Sunday, September 18.—The night passed quietly, aside from the storm, and the morning is bright and beautiful, though the mountain tops are glistening with snow. The day has been spent as usual in camp.

About noon a party of Indians were discovered approaching, headed by a Spaniard whom we had seen with them at Fort Sarpy, and they marched directly into camp. I was not disposed to give them a very cordial reception, as I deemed it probable that they are the fellows who have been tracking us for the past two weeks, and have been guilty of the thieving that has so annoyed us. They pretended, however, to be entirely ignorant of all these matters, but said that they had seen a Blackfoot trail, it being the custom of the Crows to place all rascality to the credit of the Blackfeet.

Upon more close questioning, however, they admitted that a party of five young men had left the Crow camp the day after we did, and doubtless these are the ones who have paid us so many unwelcome visits. I have little doubt also that our guests of to-day were fully conversant with all that had happened, if not themselves the guilty parties, and that they have adopted this bold method of ascertaining the results of the shot of night before last, which was apparently fired, rather to secure escape than with any murderous intention. As, however,

I had no proof of this I made a virtue of necessity, and ordered coffee to be given them. One of the party carried a shovel that had been missed by my escort and reported stolen, but he claimed to have found it and made no objections to its return.

The Indians located themselves on the bank of the river, and during the afternoon I had an opportunity of witnessing a curious spectacle, namely, an aboriginal sweat-bath taken by four of the savages. The modus operandi was as follows: They first erected a frame work some eight feet in diameter and five feet high, of long willows planted in the ground, bent in proper form and wattled together with great care and regularity, resembling a large open basket inverted, and having an entrance sufficiently large to admit one person. A hole 12 or 14 inches in diameter, and eight inches deep, was then excavated in the centre and all the dirt carefully removed. Around this a shallow trench was dug, as also four small trenches entering it at right angles from the circumference. Willow boughs were also carefully laid around the hole, and the whole of the structure was thickly covered with buffalo robes and blankets. A fire was then kindled and a large number of stones heated. These preparations having been completed, four men entered the bath, the attendants passed in the stones and vessels of water, and then carefully closed the entrance. Steam was generated in this close apartment, by throwing water upon the stones, so effectually that its inmates were compelled to call three times for fresh air, which was supplied by the attendants making a small opening at the door. The men remained in this bath some 15 or 20 minutes, when they emerged dripping with steam and perspiration. Three went at once to the cold mountain stream and washed off, while the fourth contented himself with laying on the ground until he was cooled. A more effective method of taking a vapor bath could hardly be desired, and I learn it is a favorite remedy with the Crows for almost all the ills to which savage flesh is heir.

In the afternoon an elk was seen some distance below camp, and two of the Indians at once mounted their horses, and giving chase soon succeeded in bringing it down.

As night approached the savages moved back of our location, and after dark burned torches for some time on each side of their own camp-fires. These were undoubtedly intended as signals to others in the distance, and consequently excited considerable suspicion, but they insisted that it was only for amusement, and we of course were destitute of all power of proving the contrary.

The Spaniard's explanation of his presence with the band is that he was sent by Richard at Platte bridge to bring the Crows there to trade, and that these 14 are all that he was able to induce to accompany him. His appearance is not especially in his favor, but I have entrusted him with a letter to be mailed at Platte bridge.

The night is bright and clear, and we obtained observations for time and latitude. The thermometer this evening stood at 42°.

Monday, September 19.—We left camp at 7½ o'clock, our course continuing to the southeast and nearly parallel with the mountains. On climbing the hill from the valley of Clear fork, the highest peak of the Big Horn range came in sight. From our point of view it is a regularly shaped and rather flat cone, surrounded by several other peaks of nearly equal height, all crowned with snow which has apparently not yielded to the heat of summer.

Passing over the ridge from the Clear fork of Powder river, we entered the valley of Lake De Smit, so called from a catholic priest, who has spent many years among the Indian tribes of this country. It is a small pond, some three or four miles long, lying between the branches of Clear fork. One or two small streams empty into it, but no outlet was discovered, and Bridger and Meldrum agree in saying that it has none. The barometer indicated that the pond was some feet lower than the streams upon either side, but this is not sufficiently marked to attract the attention of the casual observer, and I therefore attribute the frequency of its mention as something remarkable to the fact that it is the only sheet of water of the kind that we have met during our summer's wandering.

We passed upon its southwestern side, leaving quite a ridge between it and our route.

We soon reached the valley of a small creek flowing into the southeastern branch of the Clear fork of Powder river, down which we travelled for a mile or two, and then crossing the point of land near the junction, reached the stream itself upon the banks of which we encamped.

The country through which we have been passing to-day is less attractive than that about the head-waters of Tongue river, the soil being poorer, and sage in large quantities replacing the grass. The reddish broken hills immediately upon our left also show that we are now upon the borders of a different, and more sterile geological formation. Our camp is located upon a small patch of fine grass, but it is all there is in sight in the valley, which is here a mile wide. The creek has little or no timber upon it, and the cheerless prospect is before us of again encountering our old enemy—the "washed lands."

The Indians who encamped with us last night, left early in the morning, which was the occasion of our late start. We overtook them, however, at our camping ground this evening, but just as they were preparing to go on, which (much to our satisfaction) they did without their customary resort to promiscuous and importunate begging.

Several of the highest peaks of the Big Horn range are visible from this camp and loom up grandly and boldly against the clear western sky. I cannot help constantly regretting my inability to visit them, but it is clearly impossible to spare the requisite time at this juncture. I have, however, located them by intersections from our line of route, and, reading the angles of elevation with the sextant and artificial horizon, I find the highest visible point to be over 7,000 feet above our camp, or about 11,500 feet above the sea level. The night is cloudy, and consequently observations were impossible. The distance travelled to-day is 14.7 miles.

Tuesday, September 20.—Our route to-day has still continued parallel with the mountains, but a change in the direction of the range has made our course almost exactly south. The road has been good though rather hilly, but the elevation, averaging over 5,000 feet, has told upon our animals by reason of the rarity of the atmosphere, and decidedly impaired their capacity for labor.

We crossed one or two small streams, but the country is by no means as well watered, nor is the soil as good as that found before leaving the Big Horn. Sage covers much of the surface of the earth, and grass is becoming scarce. The mountain range on our right is also of less height, and the lofty peaks visible for some days past have disappeared. The country to our left and in front of us seems also much more level, and the hills on the other side of Powder river can now be seen in the distance.

Far out on the plain "Pumpkin butte" is also visible—a long hill with a level summit, standing between Powder river and the headwaters of the Shayenne, and forming a marked feature in the landscape.

The larger portion of our route to-day lay through valleys parrallel with the mountains, the hills to our right rising to considerable heights, and a distinguishing characteristic of the topography being the fact that all the dividing ridges between the streams were lower at the foot of the mountains than at a distance of some miles. We crossed a small tributary of Powder river that Bridger calls Sandy creek, and continuing down it some three miles, encamped upon one of its lesser branches, having advanced nearly 16 miles.

The day has been quite comfortable, the thermometer standing this afternoon at 79°. One of our mules broke down and was necessarily abandoned, and all the animals reached camp with difficulty. The grass is here, to my regret, no better than at our last camp, and I can see but little opportunity for their recruiting. The only fuel here also is drift-wood from the mountains, and buffalo chips which are not very plenty. The early part of the evening was quite clear, but it soon clouded up.

Wednesday, September 21.—We continued to-day nearly due south, still skirting the mountains and crossing several small streams flowing into Powder river.

The country travelled over has differed in no essential respects from that through which we have passed in the last few days, consisting in the main of gentle undulations that were traversed without difficulty, but occasionally varied with sharp, rocky hills. About five miles from camp we crossed a small brook only a foot or two wide, but very mirey, giving on this account much trouble. In crossing it a member of the party, Mr. Wilson, refused to aid me in lifting one of the carts from the slough, upon the ground that he had not been assigned to this special class of duty by the Secretary of War. I promptly released him from duty of any kind by discharging him upon the spot, only permitting him to remain with us until we should reach the Platte road. This disagreeable occurrence was the legitimate result of the presence of men who simply owe their connection with the party to the order of high authority and not to the needs of the expedition, and are therefore more guided by motives of selfishness than a sense of duty.

While en route to-day we were joined by three Indians who came with us to camp, and were there re-inforced by three others. They proved to be Arapahoes, and among them were "Little Owl," one of their head chiefs, and "Friday," also a chief, who speaks English quite well, having spent some time while a boy in St. Louis. They told us that their whole village of 180 lodges was within six or seven miles; and they also brought some fresh meat, for which we exchanged bacon. This, with a cup of coffee and a few buiscuit, seemed to make them well satisfied with their visit.

Friday informs me that Major Swiss, the Indian agent on the Upper Platte, has letters for us, and this assurance is the nearest approach to news from our homes that we have enjoyed since leaving the Missouri. It is at least a gratification to know that there are letters for us somewhere, although weeks may elapse before they shall reach us.

A warm south wind has prevailed all day, threatening rain, but about 8 p. m. the wind shifted to the northeast, and it has become uncomfortably cold. This would be a bad place to encounter a storm of any duration, as there is no fuel excepting a little driftwood, and the grass is miserable. The distance travelled to-day is 10.7 miles. The Indians left at 8 p. m. to return to their village.

Thursday, September 22.—The morning was dark and rainy, but our camp was so unsuitable, being almost destitute of grass or wood, that I determined to move, and accordingly we commenced our march in the middle of a heavy shower, though with fair prospects of the early return of clear weather.

We crossed the first stream about two miles from camp, and would have stopped had there been an adequate supply of fuel and grass; but as these essentials were still lacking, and the day was not as yet very disagreeable, we pushed on in search of better quarters.

The storm, however, did not abate, but settled down into a steady rain with a driving northeast wind. A thick fog also closed around us, shutting out all view of the country, and greatly embarrassing our selection of a route, even the mountains fading from our sight in the thick mist. Our guide, however, did not falter, but pointed out our course with every mark of complete self-confidence, and as coolly as if on a broad turnpike in clear weather, and amid familiar landmarks.

The first part of our course was over high rolling ground, and the dividing ridge between Sandy and Willow creeks, being an elevated level plateau, gave us four or five miles of excellent travelling. The descent to the valley of Willow creek was quite abrupt, however, and here we again found ourselves surrounded with the "washed lands," which had before occasioned us so much trouble, and now compelled a long detour to the left before we could enter the valley, along which we passed to the bank of the creek, upon which we encamped, having travelled 14.7 miles.

The march has been very trying to our animals, the cold rain and driving wind, with the bad roads, causing several to give out, and another mule had to be abandoned. We are to-night partially protected from the wind by a high bluff, which is a decided improvement upon encamping in the open plain. It is raining steadily now, and the darkness is intense.

Friday, September 23.—The cold northeastern storm of yesterday has continued almost without intermission, and consequently we have not moved camp. The day has been spent in efforts at work, but it has been so exceedingly disagreeable that little has been accomplished. The rain has stopped this evening and a few stars are visible, giving "token of a goodly day to-morrow."

Saturday, September 24.—The storm being over and the morning bright and clear, we struck our tents at an early hour and resumed our march. After following down the valley of Willow creek for some to or three miles, we crossed it and ascended the ridge between it and Powder river. The road was very heavy, the ground being saturated with rain, giving an idea of the difficulties that would attend travelling in this country in the wet season. At many points it was with the utmost labor that our animals could move, and our course had to be selected with great care. Wherever the surface of the ground was exposed by the absence of grass, it was about impossible to even ride upon horseback, but by following the ridges we made tolerable progress, and reached Powder river about 1 o'clock, having travelled 11 miles.

Powder river at this point possesses the same characteristics as nearer its mouth. The stream is, however, very muddy from the recent rain, and its bed is filled with mire and quicksands, rendering the selection of a crossing a matter of much care. The banks present that "washed" appearance with which we have become so familiar, although it is not quite as forbidding here as further down. There can be no doubt of the truth of Bridger's statement, that the same general features prevail throughout the whole extent of the stream, and in this case the non-arrival of Lieutenant Maynadier and party is fully explained. I shall await them at this point, as per agreement, and hope that a rest will much improve the condition of our jaded animals. The night is clear, and we observed for time and latitude.

Sunday, September 25.—The day has been spent in camp, with the customary services.

The weather has been bright and beautiful, to the intense pleasure of every member of the party.

Monday, September 26.—Mr. Snowden, Dr. Hayden, and Mr. Schonborn applied this morning for permission to visit a pass over the mountains that is visible from camp, each wishing to advance the interests of his own department. I gave my consent gladly, and with a single attendant they left camp to be absent until to-morrow night.

Bridger and myself turned our faces down stream to try and obtain some information in regard to Lieutenant Maynadier. After a ride of about 15 miles we came to the ruins of some old trading posts, known as the "Portuguese houses," from the fact that many years ago they were erected by a Portuguese trader named Antonio Matéo.

They are now badly dilapidated, and only one side of the pickets remains standing. These, however, are of hewn logs, and from their character it is evident that the structures were originally very strongly built. Bridger recounted a tradition that at one time this post was besieged by the Sioux for forty days, resisting successfully to the last alike the strength and the ingenuity of their assaults, and the appearance of the ruins renders the story not only credible but probable. I shaved off the pickets at two or three places, and wrote on the bright surface information as to our whereabouts for the benefit of Lieutenant Maynadier, if he should chance to pass in this direction, and then, after an unsuccessful reconnoissance of the surrounding country from the summit of a convenient hill, returned to camp.

During my absence Lieutenant Smith, in accordance with consent previously obtained, had moved camp about a mile further down stream for the purpose of securing better pasturage, and I found the party just settling themselves in their new quarters.

Tuesday, September 27.—The day was spent in camp, still awaiting the arrival of Lieutenant Maynadier, concerning whom I am commencing to feel somewhat anxious.

Bridger made a short excursion to-day towards the Platte to select a route, but returned with a rather unfavorable report. The course recommended I judge to be anything but direct, but as he strenuously insists upon its superior feasibility I shall follow his advice.

The party returned from the mountains in good season and fine spirits, each having abundantly gratified his special tastes and pursuits. Mr. Snowden claims to have decidedly improved his acquaintance with the mountain ranges. Dr. Hayden found several new plants and many fossils, and Mr. Schonborn obtained a number of admirable sketches.

They described a singular topographical feature of the country they visited. A small stream pierces through a low hill in its course, forming one of the cañons so common in this country, where the water-courses pay so little respect to the ridges crossing their paths. After emerging, however, it makes a sharp turn, and at a distance of but a few yards again flows through the hill, making thus a strange double cañon. A sketch of Mr. Schonborn's has well preserved this curious freak of nature.

Bridger and Doctor Hayden will to-morrow make a second reconnoissance down stream in search of Lieutenant Maynadier, and if they are unsuccessful I have decided to push on with my detachment without further delay, sending a guide back to find and bring up the others, if it shall be possible.

Wednesday, September 28.—A dark and lowering sky did not prevent the departure of the down-river party, consisting of Lieutenant Smith, Doctor Hayden, Bridger, and Stephenson. They left camp with the expectation of being absent three days.

About noon the wind shifted to the northeast and rain set in, but about 4 p. m. it changed to snow, and for a time the flakes fell as thickly as I have ever seen them. It melted as rapidly, however, the thermometer not sinking below 36°. About dark the fall of snow ceased, and there were indications of clearing up, the thermometer rising to 40°.

Thursday, September 29.—The morning was bright and clear, the thermometer standing at 7 a. m. at 28°. Thick ice formed in camp last night, but the bright sun rapidly warmed the air, and at noon the thermometer had risen to 60°, with a south wind prevailing.

The day was spent in camp, computing, making copies of notes, &c., &c.

At 5 p. m. we were visited by a war party of 11 Indians on foot, who proved to be Arapahoes on their way to join another band of their own tribe, or a body of Sioux, in a horse-stealing expedition among the Utes, with whom they are now at war. I may remark *en passant* that horse-stealing appears to be one of the grand objective points of Indian campaigning. They were each armed with a rifle, and all carried *lariats* for the purpose of securing their plunder. As usual I furnished them with supper to avoid arousing any unnecessary ill will, and at its close they repaid us by one of their native concerts, the music of which may be soothing to the savage breast, but is decidedly irritating to the civilized ear.

They formed a circle about the fire, standing shoulder to shoulder, and then sang in a species of aggravatingly-monotonous strain, marking time by a swaying motion of their bodies, at intervals enlivening the proceedings by ferocious yells, preceded by short, sharp barks like those of an angry dog. This entertainment having been closed, the Indians proceeded to comfortably locate themselves about our camp fires, where they now lie, to all external appearance, in a state of supreme content.

Friday, September 30.—Our Indian guests left us this morning immediately after their breakfast, but not without characteristically begging a supply of provisions to take with them.

The day was spent in camp awaiting the return of the reconnoitring party, who arrived about 5 p. m., without any tidings of Lieutenant Maynadier. They report that they reached a point not far from fifty miles from camp, and state that a train would be compelled to travel much further to pass over the same ground. This proves that if Lieutenant Maynadier is coming by Powder river, as he expected, he is so far behind that he cannot join us for several days, possibly for a week.

I have, therefore, decided to push on myself to the Platte, and, if he is not heard from before, send after him from that point. My party is too small for another division, and my animals are too much exhausted for such a journey, even if I felt justified in sparing the men.

Saturday, October 1.—We left camp at 7½ o'clock a. m., for the Platte, our route lying west of direct, the guide claiming that he knows the country perfectly, and that this course is indispensable to securing a good road. Following up the valley of Powder river we found our progress impeded by high sage and deep ravines, which compelled us to cross the stream repeatedly, the hills on either side being so high and steep as to forbid our venturing among them.

About nine miles from camp we crossed the mouth of Red Cañon creek, a stream very appropriately named, as it flows between high rocky banks of the brightest red, the water itself, also, taking on the same brilliant hue. After the crossing a bold point gave us some trouble, but we ultimately reached the valley of the Powder, upon which is located our camp to-night, in the midst of a small bottom, covered with tall, coarse grass and rushes, upon which our animals are faring sumptuously.

The country we are now in is generally identical with that we have uniformly found about the course of Powder river, wherever we have met that stream. The geological formation of the opposite banks of the river is strikingly different. The right is of dark brown or slate color and of the setaceous formation, while the left is of the jurassic, and consists of rugged rocks, upheaved and outcropping in all directions. The soil in the narrow valley cannot be regarded as good, the luxuriant growth of sage proving too plainly its sterility.

The distance travelled to-day was 11 miles, to accomplish which we were compelled to be moving eight hours and to use the shovel and pick freely.

Sunday, October 2.—This is the only Sabbath of the season upon which I have moved camp, but I have deemed it in this instance to be a case of absolute necessity, as it is of the utmost importance that we should reach the Platte at the earliest possible moment, in order that we may send back for Lieutenant Maynadier's party, should not news from them reach us by that time. I was amused on the march at a discussion between two of the party in regard to the day of the week. One insisted that it was Sunday, but the other replied: "I tell you it ain't. Don't you know the captain never moves on Sunday?" This was conclusive at first, and until I explained the fact and the reason of our deviation from an established rule.

Our route still bore up the valley of Powder river, or at least of one branch of it, and the stream we are on seems to be the main fork. As to the road it is only necessary to say that our progress was but about a mile an hour. A succession of deep gullies were crossed in the first part of the march, and after about four miles advance, we passed through the thickest undergrowth I have seen in this country. Willows, vines, and briers had to be cut out of the path, but at length we struck a wide Indian trail that brought us through with comparatively little further trouble.

During our march the stream was also crossed and re-crossed several times. Our camp for to-night is at the "Red Buttes of Powder river," which constitute a very marked geological feature. One large butte, standing in the middle of the valley and seen from a distance, greatly resembles a crumbling castle. The towers and bastions are all complete, and the likeness to an old ruin is indeed extraordinary. Similar buttes extend up the right bank of the stream for miles above our camp, all preserving the ruin-like appearance, innumerable birds' nests clinging to their sides completing the picture. The rock is a hard, indurated clay, and the red tinge it gives to the water proves it to be easily soluble and therefore of no great economical value.

The day has been bright and beautiful, and the evening is clear, but chilly.

Monday, October 3.—Our route to-day still continued up the valley of Powder river, having on our left the remarkable red bluffs encountered yesterday, which are a constant source of admiration and amazement. A striking feature is their steep sides, which render them almost impassable. Dr. Hayden succeeded in reaching the summit some distance below camp, and after following the crest for some miles, all the time in sight of the train, he was obliged to retrace his steps before he could again descend into the valley. If these rocks were in an accessible region they undoubtedly would attract more attention from wonder-seeking tourists than the famous Palisades of the Hudson.

Our road lay on the left bank of the stream for some distance, but deep gullies compelled us to make several crossings and necessitated the free use of the pick and shovel. Four miles from camp the valley becomes very narrow and our only feasible route led through the cañon, with high, rocky banks upon either side. About six miles from camp we entered the cañon of a small branch coming in from the left, up which we passed for half a mile before we could emerge, when we crossed the point and again reached the stream, which we have since followed. The cañon above us is impassable, however, and we will be obliged to again abandon the stream at this point. As Bridger says we will not find water for nearly ten miles, I ordered the train to halt, although we had advanced only seven and a quarter miles.

Tuesday, October 4.—Our route this morning was directly over the hills, and thence parallel to the stream. The first mile or two was a gradual ascent over hard ground and with good travelling then for five miles. The road ran along a level plateau, whence it at last descended by an abrupt hill into the valley. Here we encountered one of the few evidences of the existence of industry among the Indians. We were following a trail which was plainly of much importance.

The steep descent which it here met had been originally rendered nearly impassable by an immense number of boulders, but these had been carefully and systematically piled up in low pyramids on the side, leaving a road of comparative excellence. Bridger claims, however, that this was never finished as a single undertaking, as no Indians would have been guilty of such a sensible work, and his theory is that separate parties have consumed a long series of years in accomplishing this result.

The valley reached over this highway is from one to two miles wide, and ten to twelve long, and, although it is 6,000 feet above the ocean, is closed on all sides by mountains. On the left are the Red Buttes before spoken of, while to the right lay the dark, frowning heights of the Big Horn mountains, cut by numerous cañons. The valley is so nearly level that, but for the stream flowing gently through it, the slope would scarcely be perceptible. It is a bright gem in a rough mountain setting, and apparently fulfils all the conditions of the "happy valley" of Rasselas, save the inhabitants. A single Indian grave, the body deposited on an elevated platform, was the only evidence of even the presence of Indians at any time within its rocky walls.

We continued some eight miles further up this valley and encamped under a bluff on the right side, after a march of 15½ miles. The day has been dark and dreary, and a cold northeast wind has prevailed, making us fear a storm at any moment, and rendering the shelter of the rocks very desirable.

Wednesday, October 5.—Our "happy valley," through which we yesterday travelled so pleasantly, proved, like a bad habit, exceedingly difficult to forsake. Our egress was barred by a succession of rugged spurs of the mountains, with deep ravines interlying, and their steep sides blocked up by large and jagged boulders; the road being thus as bad as it could possibly be and yet be passable. The high red bluffs on our left still continue, and have compelled us to travel far to the westward of a direct route in order that we might avoid them.

After severe labor until 3 o'clock in the afternoon, we found a small spring near the summit of the ridge bounding the valley on the southwest, and near this we encamped after a march of 11¾ miles.

The country traversed has been exceedingly barren and destitute. No timber exists save stunted pines on the mountains, and a very thin growth of bunch grass upon some of the ridges, and the neverfailing sage (artemisia) completes the vegetation. Our camp is immediately under a bluff, and a scattered growth of stunted cedars upon it, with driftwood in the gullies, constitutes our entire stock of fuel.

Thursday, October 6.—A gradual ascent of about a mile and a half brought us easily this morning to the summit of a pass, leading into what we at first supposed to be the valley of the Platte. After travelling down a small stream for a few miles, however, it became evident that we were in the eastern drainage of the Big Horn. Leaving the stream we skirted the eastern edge of the Wind River basin, passing over an almost level country without a stick of timber visible, and but little sage and still less grass. The excellence of the road was an advantage, as the nature of the country compelled us to make an unusually long march.

About 12 miles from camp we found a small spring, which would have given us a scanty supply of water, but as there was no pasturage nor fuel it was thought advisable not to halt. Four miles further we entered the valley of the Platte. Flanking parties were thrown out to look for water, but we were compelled to travel until after sundown before any was found. The supply of grass was then most miserable, and not a stick of wood was visible. Sage and buffalo chips answered, however, for fuel, and we were glad to break a fast of over 13 hours.

The country passed over to-day has been a barren desert, its soil being a light clay, which is baked by the sun and produces absolutely nothing of value. To the right the level plain is as monotonously cheerless as can be imagined. A slight deviation from our route enabled us to look down the valley of Powder river, and the prospect in that direction was equally desolate, with the addition of the fact that the ground was much more broken, presenting all the disagreeable features that appear to uniformly mark the course of this river. Our animals are to-night crowded into the narrow bed of the stream, the only spot where grass is to be found.

Friday, October 7.—Our mules and horses were too much exhausted by yesterday's labors for either an early start or a long march. We moved off about half past 8 o'clock, and after travelling over a barren, sandy plain for six miles, found some rain-water standing in pools in the old bed of a dried-up stream

There being no prospect of a better camping ground, and the condition of the animals being exceedingly reduced, I determined to halt and encamp.

This country is the most barren yet seen, and except in the very narrow valleys the only vegetation is a sparse growth of grass, varied with clumps of very small sage. From a cursory inspection of the land adjacent to our line of march, I have roughly estimated that the vegetation of all kinds (sage, grass, &c.) only covers about one-fifth or one-sixth of its surface.

The small valleys are our sole reliance for subsistence for our animals and for our supply of fuel. The soil when wet becomes a thick and clayey mud, clinging to the feet in large masses, and rendering locomotion almost impossible.

Saturday, October 8.—On gaining the summit of the first hill encountered this morning, the mountains on the south side of the Platte came in view, and by their proximity encouraged us with the expectation of soon reaching the much-talked-of Platte road. Our route led southeast, leaving the stream upon which we had encamped, and crossing several valleys draining into it.

The road was tolerably good, and our progress fair; but our animals are too much worn out for long marches, and we therefore encamped by a small pond of rain-water on the prairie, with no fuel but sage, after a journey of 11 miles. The hardships of the past week have been enormous, and a similar experience in the next seven days would compel the abandonment of our wagons.

Sunday, October 9.—The day was spent in camp as usual, as notwithstanding my anxiety in regard to Lieutenant Maynadier's party, the exhaustion of both men and beasts renders rest indispensable.

Monday, October 10.—From camp this morning our route bore across the hills, leaving the stream upon our left. After advancing three or four miles we reached the valley of another branch, down which we followed. It soon became wider, and contained far better grass than has been found for some time, though in several places the soil was covered to the depth of several inches with a white salt, or, as Bridger calls it, "alkali." This is an impure soda, although in some places it is found of sufficient purity to be used for culinary purposes.

The stream where we first struck it was a running brook of palatable water, but five or six miles below it became very salt, and the water was found only in holes. After we had travelled 15 miles we halted for the night at a point far less eligible for a camp than many localities we had passed.

After encamping I rode in advance to ascertain our exact whereabouts, and soon came in sight of the valley of the Platte, the Red Buttes, and the Laramie hills. It was evident that another day's march would bring us to the Platte road.

Tuesday, October 11.—As the train was leaving camp this morning, I started with Dr. Hayden and Wilson for the Platte bridge. We followed down the stream upon which we had been encamped some distance, finally turning to the right, and after riding for about six miles reached the Platte road, near the Red Buttes. Before starting I had in my ignorance asked Bridger if there was any danger of crossing the road without knowing it. I now understand fully his surprise, as it is as marked as any turnpike at the east. It is hard, dry, and dusty, and gave evidence of the immense amount of travel that passes over it. Indeed we had not followed it a mile before we came upon an ambulance with ladies in it, bound for the "States," and we were very seldom out of sight of some vehicle upon this great highway.

The fact of again reaching a regular road appeared to impart new life even to our jaded horses, and we rode on at a rapid rate until we reached Richards's trading post at the Platte bridge, having travelled about 18 miles. Here I received the pleasing news that Lieutenant Maynadier was close at our heels, on our trail, some Indians having just arrived at the bridge who had seen his party near the head of Powder river. I was also so fortunate as to receive a single letter, which constituted our latest news from home, though it was four months old. I learned also that a mail was waiting for us at the Indian agency at Deer creek, and engaged Richard to send for it. I also made arrangements to get up our winter supplies from Fort Laramie; and after taking dinner under a roof, off from a table, and on a stool—luxuries we had not known since leaving Fort Pierre—returned to the Red Buttes, where my party was in camp, having reached that point about 1 o'clock.

I found some evidences of our return to "civilization" that were not so agreeable. Two neighboring houses were devoted to the sale of liquor, and a large number of the party were consequently in a state of uproariousness that had converted the camp into a bedlam, which it required great efforts upon my part to subdue. The commander of the escort was invisible, and had certainly made no efforts to maintain order or enforce discipline.

My object was now to select a suitable place for winter quarters and detail a portion of the party for their preparation, while the others should be engaged in procuring provisions and making a reconnoissance in the direction of the head-waters of the Shayenne and Pumpkin Butte, to develop a district of country that had not been reached by either Lieutenant Warren or myself. I determined first to examine the valley of Carson's creek, which empties into the south side of the Platte above Red Buttes, and if that should not prove suitable for a winter residence, then go east until I found an eligible location, knowing that at the worst we could obtain a resting place at Fort Laramie.

Wednesday, October 12.—I left the party in camp to-day, while I accompanied Bridger to look at the valley of Carson's creek, as previously determined. As I was about departing I observed that the escort were also making preparations for moving. I inquired of the officer in command what his purpose was, and learned that he intended taking his command to Carson's creek. I replied it was my wish that they should remain in camp, and accordingly gave him orders to that effect. He replied with an oath that he should do as he pleased, as I had no power to give him orders. Knowing that I certainly had not the means of enforcing my commands, I rode on to make the proposed examination, and was satisfied that the place was not such as was required, the grass being poor and the timber unsuitable for building huts. Upon my return I found my escort gone and Lieutenant Maynadier in camp, having come on in advance of his party.

I wish here to state the result of the disobedience of orders upon the part of the commanding officer of the escort. He was tried by court-martial for the offence, and *acquitted;* not for want of proof, but because the court held that I, as an engineer officer, could not *command* troops, basing their finding on the 63d article of war, which provides that engineer officers shall not be put upon or *assume* duties out of the line of their profession, and paragraph 14 of the Army Regulations, which provides that engineers shall not *assume* the command of troops.

If the finding in this case is correct, then an engineer officer, in discharge of his legitimate duty, requiring the co-operation of troops, is at the mercy of the line officer, who is not obliged to co-operate with him further than his own inclinations may prompt. It seems to me that such a conclusion is far from warranted by either the Articles of War or the regulations. An officer of engineers is regularly assigned to duty, *in the line of his profession*, by a common superior having the right to issue the order. If such duty cannot be performed without troops, I submit that he does not *assume* command of troops by exercising the authority due to his rank.

The right to order on duty carries with it the right to order in command of the troops required to perform that duty, it being distinctly understood that the duty is such as legitimately pertains to the functions of the engineer officer. Any other construction involves the military absurdity of supposing a junior has the right to thwart the purposes of the officer giving the original order.

I have stated my views in this case because I deem it a matter of vital importance to the engineer corps. In the discharge of their duties they are held fully responsible; and yet whenever these duties require co-operation of troops, they are placed at the mercy of the officer in charge of such troops without the slightest regard to relative rank.

The arrival of Lieutenant Maynadier's party, followed by that of the mail towards evening, caused excitement enough, however, to divert our thoughts from other matters, and the close of the day was spent in acquainting ourselves with the first news from home and friends obtained since leaving St. Joseph. Lieutenant Maynadier, it was found, had travelled some 90 miles further than had we, and this fact accounts for the delay. He met with no accidents, however, and struck our trail near the selected point of meeting on Powder river. Lieutenant Maynadier's report of his expedition will be found in full herewith, marked Appendix A.

The period from October 13 to October 17 was consumed in search along the Platte road for a suitable location for winter quarters, and it is not necessary to describe our march over a route so well known. We finally settled upon some unfinished houses near the Indian agency of the Upper Platte, which the agent, Major Swiss, kindly invited me to occupy. The buildings had been commenced by the Mormons some years ago as a way station on the route to Salt Lake, and part of them had been finished and were now occupied by Major Swiss. The others were in a half-completed state, and by taking these we were saved considerable labor, and obtained far better quarters than otherwise would have been possible.

On the 16th snow fell all day, but did not last long, the temperature being about 32°.

On October 18 I gave Mr. Snowden instructions to make a reconnoissance to the northward of our present location and determine the sources of both branches of the Shayenne. His report will be found herewith, marked Appendix B.

On the 18th, also, we commenced work on the corrals and shed for our animals, but found the day too windy for effective labor.

From October 19 to November 3 I was engaged in a trip to and from Fort Laramie, and in procuring supplies and provisions for the winter. I was kindly received by all the officers in the fort, and my thanks are due to all, especially to Major H. Day, 2d infantry, commanding, for his efforts to aid me in all possible ways.

I started for Laramie with a supply of provisions, my tents, and a cook, taking it for granted that we should be obliged to camp out and rely upon our own commissariat for provisions, as on our journey since leaving Fort Pierre. I soon discovered my mistake, however. Houses were found every ten or fifteen miles, and I was much surprised to learn that if one would be satisfied with the accommodations they afforded, the journey could be made from the Missouri to the Pacific with reliance upon these frontier hotels, which are found about every fifteen miles along the whole route.

The Indians were perfectly peaceable, and it was not unusual to see men riding singly along the road, though for company more than for considerations of safety they generally travelled in parties of two or three. The Platte road is truly a national thoroughfare, and until the railroad is completed must remain our most important channel of communication with the Pacific States.

On my return to camp I found the quarters progressing, but not as rapidly as I had hoped. The want of proper tools, and the inexperience of the men in the use of such as we did possess, were difficulties that could only be overcome by patience and perseverance. At last some of the party got into quarters on the 11th of November, the thermometer that morning standing 6° below zero.

On the night of the 12th and 13th a number of the men were still in tents, the thermometer indicating — 17°. On the following morning all found shelter in our yet unfinished houses.

CHAPTER III.

WINTER QUARTERS.

It is not necessary to submit a detailed report of our life during the six tedious months spent in winter quarters. After we reached our creek, several parties passed down the road on their way to "the States," and we could have done the same, thus saving the expenses of the party for about four months, and still returning in time for the resumption of our explorations, but my instructions were explicit in directing me to winter in the mountains, and therefore the course named was impossible.

The words "winter in the mountains" apparently embody the idea of discomfort and privation, but in our case they possess no such significance. We were thoroughly comfortable in all our surroundings. Our log houses, although they had no floors, and only decidedly primitive roofs, were still dry and warm. These roofs consisted of logs, with brush filling in the interstices, and covered with a coating of clay mortar, and above all a foot or more of earth well packed. This is the common roof of the plains. A slope of about one foot vertical to five horizontal serves to shed the rain perfectly, and the amount that falls is not sufficient to wash off the dirt within one winter, as we fully proved. The winds are in fact much more destructive.

With such a device repairs are very simple, consisting of only a few moments' labor with a shovel. The fact of the general use of this style of roof among the settlers on the plains, decidedly sustains the theory of the great want of rain in these regions.

Two or three times during the winter we had "snaps" of very cold weather, the thermometer in one instance falling to minus 25°. The cold of December 4th, 5th, and 6th was intense, the thermometer ranging from 15 to 25 degrees below zero. On the 6th the wind was terrific, and the air was filled with minute particles of snow and ice, which penetrated every crack and crevice in our buildings.

In my own quarters I had a bank of snow two feet deep that sifted through a crevice of whose existence I was previously unaware. A snow bank also formed on the exterior of our quarters as high as the roof, completely blocking up the doors. It was strange that we did not lose all our animals, but only one was killed, though they had but little or no shelter from the fury of the storm.

Excepting these cold "spells," the weather during the winter was delightful. The meteorological records, which were carefully kept and given elsewhere in detail, show the mean temperature for the different months, and the amount of rain or melted snow that fell, to have been as follows:

November 25th to 30th	30° 25′	370 inches rain.
December	20°	660 inches rain.
January	29° 4′	512 inches rain.
February	34° 2′	575 inches rain.
March	42° 4′	310 inches rain.
April 1st to 15th	48° 8′	140 inches rain.
		2, 567 total rain.

Our general occupation was picking up the loose ends of the summer's work, reducing and copying notes, making charts, computing, &c., employment that was both agreeable and profitable. With a view to determining the longitude of our camp I had proposed observing noon culmination during the winter, and for this purpose had ordered a transit instrument to be forwarded to me at Fort Laramie. On the occasion of my visit to that post, however, it had not arrived, and I then ordered it forwarded by the Overland Mail Company's wagons, paying express charges upon it at the rate of a fraction over letter postage, and receiving it with promptness and safety on December 9th.

It was mounted on the 12th, the moon being considerably past the full. The meridian passage was observed that night, and on the 13th and 15th, which ended observations for that lunation. The instrument remained mounted until the 6th of May, when it was taken down preparatory to the summer's journey.

During this period, of the 69 meridian passages of the moon, which occurred when the sun was belew the horizon, 56 were observed, and only 13 lost by cloudy weather—that is, four nights out of every five were clear enough for observations.

From the 29th of February to the 14th of March, inclusive, the passage of the moon over the meridian was observed each night, excepting March 6th. From March 26th to April 9th, inclusive, six nights were cloudy. This was the least favorable of any lunation. These facts, taken from the records, are enough to show that, unless the winter of 1859–'60 was a very unusal one, which I have no reason to think was the case, the snow that falls in the mountains is not sufficient to prevent the running of railroad trains at all seasons.

If our animals had not been broken down by the arduous labors of the summer, there would have been little difficulty in our continuing our explorations by parties sent out from our fixed camp during a large portion of the winter. The necessity of so doing was not great, however, as we were in a country comparatively well known, while it was of supreme importance that we should recruit our horses and mules as fully as possible. Therefore, the only explorations made after reaching winter quarters were by a party sent to the headwaters of the Shayenne, another detailed to find the nearest possible approach to a direct route from Deer creek to Powder river, and a third sent out for geological researches to the southward, along the western slope of the Rocky mountains to Long's peak. The first of these expeditions was in charge of J. Hudson Snowden, and started three days after we reached Deer creek, being absent about ten days.

The second expedition was made in April, under the charge of Mr. James D. Hutton, the object being, as stated above, to find a more direct road to Powder river than that we followed, thus obtaining, in connection with the route already explored along the base of the Big Horn mountains, the map of the entire route to the Big Horn river. The report of Mr. Hutton will be found herewith.

The other expedition was made under the direction of Dr. F. V. Hayden, the geologist of the expedition, and as the country visited was comparatively well known, no topographer accompanied it. The results of the geological investigations will be found embodied in Dr. Hayden's geological report, submitted herewith.

Throughout the whole of the season's march the subsistence of our animals had been obtained by grazing after we had reached camp in the afternoon, and for an hour or two between the dawn of day and our time of starting. Often the grass was very scanty and of poor quality, requiring them to feed over a large extent of ground, thus giving them no opportunity for rest. The water, also, was in many cases so impregnated with salt as to act as a purgative, thus lessening their strength.

The consequence was that when we reached our winter quarters there were but few animals in the train that were in a condition to have continued the march without a generous grain diet. Poorer or more broken-down creatures it would be difficult to find. They were at once driven up the valley of Deer creek and herded during the day, and brought to camp and kept in a corral through the night. The distance grazed over covered perhaps 50 square miles, and in the spring all were in as fine condition for commencing another season's work as could be desired. A greater change in their appearance could not have been produced, even if they had been grain-fed and stable-housed all winter. Only one was lost, the furious storm of December coming before it had gained sufficient strength to encounter it.

This fact that seventy exhausted animals turned out to winter on the plains the first of November, came out in the spring in the best condition and with the loss of but one of the number, is the most forcible commentary I can make upon the quality of the grass and the character of the winter. The extent of territory ranged over by the herd also shows that the quantity of grass is very small per acre; and in this connection I wish to mention an incident that further illustrates this fact. On the 4th of March almost half the herd disappeared very mysteriously, and were not found for over a week, when a general and thorough search in all directions resulted in their discovery some fifteen or twenty miles from camp at a point whither they had strayed for better pasturage.

Among the most noticeable incidents of our sojourn in winter quarters was a visit from One Horn, a chief of the Minneconjoux tribe of the Sioux or Dakota Indians. He said that a large band of the Sioux were wintering about two hundred miles north of us, and that he had been sent to notify me that I must not pass through their country. I informed him that I had been sent by the President and must obey my orders, and reminded him that I had brought them a large present promised them by General Harney when he made a treaty with them, and that one of the conditions of that treaty was that persons sent by the President should not be molested. He answered, "We cannot restrain our young men; they will kill you." "Then," I replied, "your tribe will be held responsible." "Where are you going the coming summer?" he asked. I responded by sketching a rough map of the country, laying down the different rivers, all of which he seemed fully to comprehend, and told him I proposed to pass westward by the heads of the Yellowstone and Missouri. He at once exclaimed, "You are not going into the Sioux country!" "I know that," I replied, "until, on my return, I reach the mouth of the Yellowstone, where I intend crossing the Missouri and going directly south."

The following dialogue ensued:

CHIEF. "Keep on the east side of the river." Answer. "I cannot; you know that that route is the longest. It will be nearly winter; my horses will be broken down. I will be in danger of being unable to get out of the country. I must take the shortest route."

CHIEF. "Are any more parties coming?" Answer. "Not that I know of, unless my party does not get home at the right time. You know there are soldiers at Fort Randall; they know when to look for us. If we do not get there at the right time they will go for us, and if you want soldiers in your country that is the way to get them. Kill my party and then you will have enough."

This last seemed to stagger him, and after a few moments he replied, "It may be that they will not hurt you; we will try to restrain our young men. If any of them come into your camp don't let them shake hands with you?" He meant by this, do not permit too many around you at once, so that they may be able to surprise and overpower you. I was satisfied that this was good advice, and probably it was intended as such. I told him I would look out for this, but that he must remember that we were all armed and should defend ourselves to the last, and if we were attacked some of them would be killed before they could exterminate us. After giving him some food and a present of a few Indian goods, he left apparently well satisfied that the best course for them to pursue was to allow us to proceed quietly on our journey.

When we arrived at Deer creek we found at the Indian agency the Rev. Mr. Bryninger and three companions, on their way to establish a mission among the Crows. They were German Lutherans, and had been sent out by the German Evangical Synod of Iowa. God-fearing and devoted men, but ignorant of the world as well as of our language, and in consequence poorly fitted for the labors they had undertaken. They had started so late in the season that winter had overtaken them at this point. Their means were exhausted and they were awaiting funds from their friends in Iowa to enable them to prosecute their labors.

I have the satisfaction of believing that I was instrumental in enabling them to pass a more comfortable winter than would otherwise have been their lot, and also of enabling them to continue the prosecution of their undertaking in the spring, though they were never permitted to reach their destination.

Mr. Bryninger and his companions left Deer creek a few days before we left our winter quarters, proposing to establish their headquarters near the lower cañon of the Big Horn river, a point I had recommended to them and which I have mentioned as possessing more natural advantages than any I met with. I did not hear from them until the close of the season's operations, when I learned that after getting as far as Powder river, Mr. Bryninger got separated from his companions and was killed by the Sioux. His companions being thus left without a head became discouraged and returned to Iowa, and the attempt to establish a mission was abandoned. After my return to civilization the authorities of the synod under which they were acting refunded to me in full the small advance that I had made to the party.

Early in March preparations were commenced for our summer campaign. I had made requisition for a mounted escort, and knew that it would be necessary to take all our supplies in packs, as it would be impossible for our wagons to accompany us. This involved the purchase of a large number of additional animals and the procuring, either by purchase or manufacture, of pack saddles. A few of these were obtained from the quartermaster at Fort Laramie, but the balance we were compelled to make. Without suitable tools or material this was considerable of an undertaking, but we at last succeeded in producing an article that answered a very good purpose. Indian horses and mules were purchased of the traders, supplies were procured from the commissary at Fort Laramie, and by the first of May we were ready to resume operations.

The fitting out of the pack train with inexperienced packers, extemporized pack saddles, and unbroken Indian horses and mules, was, however, a tedious, and at times an amusing, operation. The animals were first loaded with packs of sand to get them used to their burthens, and for a time confined to the limits of the corral. As a general rule they only submitted to the incumbrance after they had been wholly exhausted by the most frantic efforts to free themselves, and I made up my mind that the Indians had sold us only such animals as they could not use, or were too lazy to themselves break for service.

Deer creek had been selected for our winter residence upon the recommendation of Major Swiss, the Indian agent for the Upper Platte, who is familiar with the whole country, and who had made this point the headquarters of the Indian agency. The fact that the Mormons had at one time commenced a settlement in the valley and commenced to build the houses which we had finished and used, also proved it to be one of the best locations in this section of the country, but notwithstanding these facts I was most agreeably disappointed in the excellence of our mail facilities. We were but three and a half miles south of the Platte road, along which the overland mail was carried, and shortly after we were settled the department complied with a request previously made by Major Swiss, and established a postoffice at the mouth of the creek, appointing an Indian trader postmaster. We were at once brought within about fifteen days of our friends, the mail coming once a week with such regularity that we could time it within a few hours. The walk to the postoffice soon became an established event to break the monotony of our life, and after our friends at home learned that we were within accessible distance of their letters, our weekly mail was as large as would be received at a respectable country village.

The pony express was also established while we were in winter quarters, and by it we several times received interesting items of news but three days old. To this enterprise I cannot forbear paying a slight tribute in passing. The sight of a solitary horseman galloping along the road was of itself nothing remarkable, but when we remember that he was one of a series stretching across the continent, and forming a continuous chain for 2,000 miles through an almost absolute wilderness, the undertaking was justly ranked among *the* events of the age, and the most striking triumphs of American energy.

Notwithstanding our mail facilities, our astronomical duties, our map-making, and other official duties, there were many weary hours in winter quarters, when we longed for the social enjoyments of home and civilized life. At times these were relieved by recounting incidents of adventure in life on the plains which had come to our ears, most of which were heard from the former trappers in this region, some of whom are yet to be found. From all that I hear I conclude that in the palmy days of the fur trade, before the silk hat was invented, and when the beaver was the great object of attraction, the bands of trappers in the west were little more than bands of white Indians, having their Indian wives, and all the paraphernalia of Indian life, moving from place to place, as the beaver became scarce, and subsisting like the Indians upon the products of the country.

Bridger says that one time he did not taste bread for 17 years.

Is it surprising that men leading such a life, not hearing from civilization oftener than once a year, and then only through the fur companies who send to them to get their furs, and supply them with ammunition and Indian trinkets, but who yet retained a recollection of the outer world they had left, should beguile the monotony of camp life by "spinning yarns" in which each tried to excel all others, and which were repeated so often and insisted upon so strenuously that the narrators came to believe them most religiously.

Some of these Munchausen tales struck me as altogether too good to be lost, One was to this effect: In many parts of the country petrefactions and fossils are very numerous; and, as a consequence, it was claimed that in some locality (I was not able to fix it definitely) a large tract of sage is perfectly petrified, with all the leaves and branches in perfect condition, the general appearance of the plain being unlike that of the rest of the country, but *all is stone*, while the rabbits, sage hens, and other animals usually found in such localities are still there, perfectly petrified, and as natural as when they were living; and more wonderful still, these petrified bushes bear the most wonderful fruit—diamonds, rubies, sapphires, emeralds, &c., &c., as large as black walnuts, are found in abundance. "I tell you, sir," said one narrator, "it is true, for I gathered a quart myself, and sent them down the country."

Another story runs in this wise: A party of whites were once pursued by Indians so closely that they were forced to hide during the day, and could only travel at night. In this they were greatly aided by the brilliancy of a large diamond in the face of a neighboring mountain, by the light of which they travelled for three consecutive nights.

I will end these specimen tales by one from Bridger, which partakes so decidedly of a scientific nature that it should not be omitted. He contends that near the headwaters of the Columbian river, in the fastnesses of the mountains, there is a spring gushing forth from the rocks near the top of the mountain. The water when it issues forth is cold as ice, but it runs down over the smooth rock so far and so fast that it is *hot at the bottom.*

I cannot pass over our winter in the mountains without mentioning the prevalent and entire disregard of the laws and regulations in regard to the traffic in ardent spirits in the Indian country. The evening after my party reached Platte Road, at the Red Buttes, liquor was obtained, and many of its members rendered almost uncontrollable. After we were established in winter quarters this continued to be a source of constant trouble, notwithstanding we were immediately under the eye of the Indian agent, and it was only by reminding the traders that I knew the law and should enforce it that I was able to preserve anything like discipline in my command. The sale of liquor in this country is an evil that demands the most effective and persistent remedies.

CHAPTER IV.

My escort, a detachment of 30 men, 2d United States dragoons, under First Lieutenant John Mullins, reported to me at noon of May 8. The next day was spent in making the final arrangements for starting, and on

Thursday, May 10, after nearly seven months in winter quarters, we again turned our faces to the westward, and resumed our march. After the usual annoying and unexpected delays at the last, we completed the packing by about 10½ a. m., and left the valley of Deer creek by the same route by which it was entered last fall.

The natural difficulties resulting from unbroken animals, and badly-adjusted packs had to be overcome, but still our progress was better than we had reason to expect, and we reached the Platte, beyond the Little Muddy, by 2½ o'clock p. m., having travelled 11⅜ miles. The parties living at the Little Muddy claimed to own the insignificant bridge across it, and charged me $10 toll for the transit of the party, a sum which I paid with the reflection that this was indubitable proof of the gratifying fact that we were still within the limits of civilization.

A few drops of rain fell during the afternoon, and a high wind has been blowing all day.

Friday, May 11.—Our route to-day led up the Platte road to the bridge, which we crossed, paying $50 toll for the whole train. The march was performed much more smoothly than yesterday, there being far less trouble with animals and packs, but it will still require several days to bring everything to perfect working order.

After leaving the bridge we passed over the Sand Hills—a continuation of the same range that is crossed on the route from Deer creek to Powder river—and, descending these, we made our camp on the Platte, having advanced a little over 16 miles, and accomplishing this distance in five and a half hours. The grass is as yet very scarce, and we have begun our summer's march quite as early as was practicable.

The mail overtook us while *en route*, and the postmaster at Deer Creek had kindly forwarded our letters by the carrier, thus giving us the last news we shall have from home until we reach Fort Randall.

Saturday, May 12.—We continued up the Platte road to the Red Buttes, where we encamped after a march of 13 miles. This road has been so often described that repetition is unnecessary, but I may say that it would be considerably improved if it should continue further up the south side, and cross some five miles above the Mormon crossing, as some of the hills now passed over are abrupt and difficult, and they could thus be avoided.

The wind was very high from the southwest all day, making travelling disagreeable, and towards night the weather became very chilly, threatening a storm.

After getting into camp the escort horses, from some unknown cause, became "stampeded," and tore off over the hills at full speed. Men started at once in pursuit, and returned about 11 o'clock p. m., bringing nineteen with them, twelve being yet missing.

Sunday, May 13.—Awaking this morning I found the ground white, and a snow storm still in progress. The fall continued till about 11 o'clock, and though it thawed constantly, yet at that hour the ground was covered to the depth of four or five inches. The sun came out in the afternoon, however, and at dark there was but little snow left in the valley.

According to custom, we passed the day in camp. This course, however, was not only dictated by inclination, but also by necessity, as the remainder of the stampeded horses were not captured till noon. They had gone about fifteen miles before they were overtaken, and returned decidedly the worse for the trip. It was a great misfortune to have them so completely exhausted at this early stage of the journey, and the horse belonging to the officer commanding the escort, Lieutenant John Mullins, was hardly able to get back to camp. Lieutenant Mullins at once bought two Indian ponies to meet the emergency.

Our camp is about half a mile up a small stream that flows into the Platte below Red Buttes. The water is brackish, and wood and grass are very scarce.

Monday, May 14.—A cold, disagreeable morning prevented an early start, and when we were ready to pack up three horses were missing. Whether they had been stolen or had strayed off after better pasturage we were unable to determine, but they could not be found. Upon leaving camp, my division and that of Lieutenant Maynadier separated. The latter will follow the Platte road to above Independence Rock; thence pass northward to the Popo-Agie and down that stream to its junction with Wind Row, while I shall diverge to the north of the road and join him on Wind river.

My division left camp in advance about half an hour, and we abandoned the Platte road at the point at which it forks to pass on either side of the Red Buttes. By turning to the west of a large butte that stands on the north side of the road, we passed once more out into the plains. Our route led over level ground in the main, but we met occasionally our old tormentors, the gullies, though in these cases so small as not to cause any serious delay. We passed over barren plains with here and there small quantities of grass, but no water, until we reached the stream down which we traveled in October last, and upon this we encamped after a march of 13¼ miles. Our hunter was out all day, but returned without finding any game.

Tuesday, May 15.—We left camp this morning at 8 o'clock. The day has been cloudy, but with very little wind, and has therefore been far more pleasant for travelling than yesterday.

We followed up our trail of last fall for about fourteen miles, or to near our camp of Sunday, October 9. The stream we are on is not as full now as then, and in many places its bed is perfectly dry. We pushed on in a nearly direct line, diverging to the southward of our last year's route, and, crossing a rolling divide, encamped upon another branch of the same creek. No fuel whatever could be found excepting sage, which answers very well for cooking. Grass still continues scarce.

During the march some Indians were noticed a mile or two to the left of our route, and after getting into camp three of them visited us, and proved to be Arapahoes, who report buffalo not far in advance. Numerous tracks and "signs" show that they have been here recently.

The Indians stated that they had plenty of meat, and were now going to a good place to eat it—a fair specimen of the providence of the whole race. If the wants of the day are supplied they have no further care.

We also learned from them that a small "war party" of Shoshones had left camp on Wind river and started for the Platte to steal horses from the whites. Stealing horses means making war in the Indian phraseology, the killing of men being considered as only an incidental occurrence.

The country traversed to-day is the same barren desert that we have been in since leaving the Platte—very little grass, no wood, and scarcely any water. I cannot conceive how it will ever be made inhabitable for the white man, and the whole country from the Big Horn mountains to the Platte is of this same character. We observed successfully at night. Our hunter brought in some game this evening in the shape of the carcass of an antelope.

Wednesday, May 16.—We left camp at 7½ o'clock a. m., the day being clear but chilly. Last night was the coldest experienced since leaving winter quarters, and at 6 a. m. the thermometer stood at 26° Fahrenheit. The weather moderated rapidly, however.

Our course was nearly magnetic west, passing over a succession of spurs from the Rattlesnake hills, which rendered the road very difficult. In the first six miles we crossed three deep gullies, which necessitated considerable work, while a fourth forced us to make a wide detour to the right before we could reach its opposite bank. Then resuming our westerly course over a gently rolling country, we encamped upon another branch of the stream that empties into the Platte at Red Buttes, having travelled 13.6 miles, requiring seven and a half hours of hard labor.

The country is becoming rather uneven, but not more inviting. Most of the hills crossed to-day are washed as bare as clay banks. We are now near the western edge of the valley of Poison Spring creek, and we know that the drainage of this stream covers an area of about 800 square miles, and yet it is dry at its mouth in the middle of May.

Dr. Hayden, who was south of our route near the Rattlesnake hills to-day, reports seeing a herd of Buffalo and some Indians watching them and waiting for the arrival of their village.

The wind is from the northeast this evening, and the weather is chilly, but the sky has kept clear and I have observed for time and latitude.

Thursday, May 17.—About three miles from camp this morning we passed the divide between the Platte and Wind rivers, which is an undulating prairie, rendering it difficult to exactly locate the summit. Our course thence bore rather more to the northward to avoid a washed land district, which would have retarded our progress. The country passed over was a gently rolling plateau, with no obstructions save the sage, which embarrassed the heavy wagons of the escort.

After travelling 20½ miles we encamped upon the banks of a clear running brook, into which men and animals rushed in haste to quench their thirst. The water proved so bitter and salt, however, that they turned away in disgust; but as there was no other resource we pitched our tents near a small patch of grass that had escaped the fires that have recently swept through this region. The surface of the ground in many places near our camp is covered with a white saline deposit, causing the standing water to be entirely unfit for use, and rendering even that in the stream exceedingly disagreeable.

Some of the hills crossed to-day were covered with a tolerable fair growth of bunch grass, but the greater part were barren in the extreme. Our last night's camp was near pools of water occasioned by the rain or melting snow, and which could not be depended on for a permanent supply, and in our day's march of over twenty miles not a drop was found, nor was a stick of wood visible large enough to make a picket pin. Our fuel has been grease wood (a species of sage) and buffalo chips.

Friday, May 18.—Our route this morning led down the valley of Bad Water creek for some five miles. This road was an easy, gentle slope, though the soil was sticky, and in places wet. After leaving the immediate valley we passed four miles further over a gently rolling prairie, hoping to reach camp at an early hour, but hills of loose sand were encountered, which extended to the bank of the creek on the south, while on the north deep gullies crossed the valley at short intervals. Choosing the least of two evils, we plodded wearily through the sand, the labor tasking severely all the animals, the wagon teams making progress with the greatest difficulty. Fortunately, the creek was close at hand, and we could thus encamp at any moment, and this we did at 2 o'clock, after a march of 13½ miles.

In the sand hills numerous bands of antelope were feeding, and our hunter killed five, while other members of the party brought down three, thus providing us with a bountiful supply of fresh meat. The water in the creek is less salt at our present camp than at last night's, though it is still far from palatable. The old bunch grass on the sand hills is tolerably good, and our animals prefer it to the new that is springing up in the valleys. A better supply of grass will soon be indispensable, for our animals are already showing the effects of short rations, though we have been out but a week. The fine American horses of the escort are suffering most, and it is evident that for hard service they are far surpassed by the tough Indian ponies.

Saturday, May 19.—Our route to-day still continued down the valley of Bad Water creek, which we were obliged to follow closely, as the hills upon each side were either of loose sand or cut up in deep ravines. The water in the creek diminished in quantity as we approached the mouth, and some eight or ten miles from camp disappeared entirely, the bed consisting of hard dry sand, which we crossed repeatedly. The travelling was poor all day, the road leading alternately through almost impassable sand and then high sage, but no hills intervened and our progress was moderately rapid.

After advancing some ten miles I ascended a bluff on the south side of the creek to look for the Big Horn river. I found the hill cut into deep ravines, and it was with the greatest difficulty that I picked my way to the summit. From that point I could see the timber along the river banks which we would be obliged to reach to find water.

About fifteen miles from our last night's camp Bad Water creek circled off to the southward, and crossing the bend by a gradual slope, the valley of Wind river came in full view only five or six miles distant. Turning to the southward we found some difficulty in again passing through the valley of Bad Water creek, as it was here a mere marsh; but once over we went on rapidly to the river, descending to the stream over a barren clay slope, the bluffs consisting of washed lands, with ragged rock projecting at or near the summit. Some of the slopes were covered with a scanty growth of grass.

The upper range of the Big Horn mountains has been on our right for the past two days, and when we left the valley of Bad Water creek the upper cañon of Big Horn river was plainly in sight, some twelve or fifteen miles distant.

Wind river, or more properly the Big Horn, for the junction of Wind river with the Popo-Agie should be considered as forming the Big Horn, is here a bold, rapid stream, somewhat swollen, doubtless, by the melting snow at this time. It is cut up by islands into numerous channels, but just below our camp, where it is united in a single stream, its width is eighty yards. Its depth is four or five feet, and it has a current of three and a half or four miles per hour. The water is now muddy, and the river presents all the characteristics of the Missouri upon a small scale. Our camp is in a fine grove of youg cottonwoods, the first trees seen, except on the remote hills, since leaving the Platte, now distant one hundred miles.

The altitude of our present camp above the sea level is ascertained by barometric measurements to be 4,991 feet. When leaving the Big Horn below the lower cañon on September 9 of last year the altitude of the river was recorded as 3,471, and it is thus shown that during its passage through the mountains the river falls 1,520 feet. The distance between the location of the measurements thus compared is a little less than 200 miles.

Sunday, May 20.—We spent the day in camp as usual. Our animals show evident symptoms of breaking down, and rest has become absolutely indispensable to them. The weather has been chilly and disagreeable, making a fire necessary, and proving that much snow still remains in the mountains.

Monday, May 21.—We started up the river this morning for the mouth of the Popo-Agie, the point of meeting agreed upon with Lieutenant Maynadier. Our route lay along the river bottom, the soil of which is barren sand deposited by the river, while sage is about the only vegetation.

Five or six miles from camp we passed the dry bed of a stream which seems to head in the ridge crossed three days since. Several low swales were also crossed, and one of them, consisting of many acres, was covered with a white, saline deposit, so light and dry that the passing train raised a cloud of most disagreeable dust.

A succession of low spurs marred the latter part of our route, being but a slight improvement upon the "washed lands." Just below the mouth of the Popo-Agie we encountered one that necessitated a wide detour, and from it we descended to the banks of this river just above the forks, and crossing, pitched our tents in a fine grove of cottonwoods amid tolerable pasturage.

The Popo-Agie at this point is about 60 yards wide, three feet deep, and has a current of about four miles per hour. Both it and Wind river, which here is about the same size, are doubtless now considerably swollen.

I rode up the Popo-Agie some five miles towards evening, hoping to meet Lieutenant Maynadier, at whose non-arrival here before me I am greatly disappointed, but I could see no indications of his presence in the vicinity.

Tuesday, May 22.—We passed the day in camp, awaiting the arrival of Lieutenant Maynadier, and spent the time in readjusting packs and pack saddles and making preparations to abandon all wheels as soon as it may become necessary.

I sent a small topographical party up the stream to gain information, hoping also that they might meet the other detachment, but they returned without tidings from them. Our hunter was entirely unsuccessful in his search for game to-day.

Here I desire to state a fact of some importance with reference to the nomenclature of the Big Horn and its branches. The river which last summer we descended under the name of the Big Horn is formed by the junction of the Popo-Agie and the Wind river at this point, and should properly be called the Big Horn below the site of our present camp. By the trappers, however, it is always spoken of as the Wind river until it enters the cañon some 30 miles below here. There is no good reason for this arbitrary distinction, whereby the same stream passes into the mountains under one name and emerges with another, and it is necessary that these facts should be known to avoid confusion.

Wednesday, May 23.—We spent the day in camp, still waiting for Lieutenant Maynadier and party, who came up about 5 p. m., having travelled about 25 miles further than ourselves, a fact which accounts for their late arrival.

One of the party caught to-day in Wind river a mountain trout weighing about two and a half pounds and of the variety so common in the Rocky mountains, the spots being darker than those on trout found in the eastern portion of the continent.

I spent the evening with Lieutenant Maynadier, making arrangements for our future explorations. We are to separate again at this camp. My own division will ascend Wind river, and from its head cross to the Three Forks of the Missouri. Lieutenant Maynadier is to descend the Big Horn to the point at which we left it in September, and thence proceed westward along the base of the mountains, crossing the Yellowstone and reaching the Three Forks by Clark's route—the understanding being that we shall meet at the Three Forks on the last day of June.

I deem it important that we should effect a junction by this date at the furthest for the following reasons: On the 18th of July will occur the total eclipse of the sun, which is attracting such attention in all scientific circles. My orders from the department require that, if possible, I should visit the line of the total eclipse in British America, (permission having been obtained for this purpose from the authorities of those provinces,) and take such observations as may be possible. I propose, therefore, on reaching the Three Forks and meeting Lieutenant Maynadier, to leave the expedition, and with three or four attendants to push on ahead myself to the north, obtaining new horses at Fort Benton, and advancing into the wilderness beyond the international boundary, reaching the eastern base of the mountains north of latitude 52°, just within the line of total eclipse.

The distance from the Three Forks I shall be compelled to traverse will be about 500 miles, and if the two parties shall meet on June 30th, as agreed, I shall have 17 days in which to reach the desired point. As this will require only an average day's march of about 29 miles, I hope to be successful. It will be indispensable, however, that there shall be no delay at the Three Forks.

Thursday, May 24.—After a halt of a day or two it is always difficult to leave camp promptly, on account of the number of loose ends to pick up, and accordingly we did not this morning get started before 9 o'clock. Our route lay up the valley of the Wind river, keeping upon the south side of the stream, and for the first three or four miles we passed through fine grass. The valley is a mile or more in width, and the immediate banks of the stream for 300 or 400 yards are covered with a thick growth of cottonwood. Between this grove and the bluffs the valley contains little besides sage, which is the largest yet seen, many of the bushes being seven feet high, and four or five inches in diameter at the ground.

The valley becomes narrower as we ascend, and the bluffs are so high as to shut out the view of the distant mountains. About ten miles from camp the stream impinges upon the bluffs on the south side, compelling us either to cross or climb the hills. The latter was preferred, and we found a succession of gullies that made the road quite difficult, and after journeying about five miles among the hills we descended again to the river and encamped upon a small plat, accessible only by the route by which we entered it or by crossing the river. The distance travelled to-day was 15¼ miles, and over a road that would have been very difficult for wagons.

Friday, May 25.—Ice formed in our buckets last night, showing that the season in this valley does not keep pace with the almanac. Some of our party spent most of the night around the camp fires, being unable to sleep on account of the cold. These chilly nights and warm days are not proving healthful, and three or four are affected with severe colds, attended with ague and fever. Nothing serious has yet manifested itself, however.

A warm sun was shining when we left camp, and crossing the river at once we continued on our course towards the mountains.

The valley still possesses the same general features as in yesterday's march. A bluff on our right promised such an excellent prospect from its summit that it was ascended to obtain an idea of the neighboring topography. The barometer showed the elevation to be about 500 feet above the river level.

As we ascend the river we find the mountains upon either hand closing in upon our course. Upon our right are visible the dark peaks of the Big Horn range, relieved by here and there a snow-capped summit, but occasionally sinking to a very low altitude. One of these latter points Bridger calls "Gray Bull pass," and asserts that through it there is an excellent road into the Big Horn valley.

To the left lies the snowy ridge of the Wind River mountains, sharp granite crags projecting along its summit. The valley in which we are travelling between these chains of lofty hills naturally contains scenery of much grandeur. The soil, however, is very barren, the surface being parched and dry, and the progress of our train raises clouds of the most disagreeable dust. The geological features of the country are becoming more and more marked, the tertiary formation prevailing here and extending to the base of the mountains.

In its general appearance the plain is not unlike the sand beach of New Jersey, save that it lacks the freshness and greenness of verdure. The vegetation is very poor, and we were greatly troubled to find a spot for a camp that would afford sufficient pasturage for our animals. On the location ultimately chosen the old grass (there being little or no new visible) was as hard and dry as in midsummer. The day has been very cool, a strong wind blowing from the snow-capped mountains surrounding us, and most of the party have worn their overcoats during the march.

Some elk have been seen in the valley, and half a dozen antelope also crossed the plain to-day, but our hunter is on the sick list, and we are without fresh meat in camp.

Saturday, May 26.—We continued our route up the river, keeping on the north bank for some three miles, and then crossing to the south. Soon after leaving camp a bear was discovered on the opposite side of the stream, which Bridger's accuracy with the rifle promptly killed, and some of the men brought the carcass into camp. The guide had been previously complaining of illness, and was reluctant to leave camp in the morning, but the sight of game produced a sudden and remarkable convalescence. Our hunter was also fortunate enough to bring down an elk early in the morning, and thus our day's march was made with the pleasant prospect before us of fresh meat for dinner.

The river at the point at which we crossed it was divided by islands into three channels, but one of which (the last) was sufficiently deep to render care necessary in fording.

About nine miles from camp we crossed the Lake fork, a bold, dashing mountain torrent, which I estimate to contribute from one-fourth to one-third the water of the whole stream. Just above our point of crossing it fell from 15 to 20 feet in a few rods, forming beautiful rapids. My topographer and artist visited the lakes some three or four miles up the stream, and describe them as beautiful mountain ponds, distant from each other about one-fourth of a mile.

Before reaching Lake fork, a bold spur jutted out to the river bank, over which we were compelled to pass. It was covered with large granite boulders, and had only a narrow path leading to the summit. It was the first serious difficulty that the single pair of wheels we use for the odometer encountered, and the aid of the men was found necessary in taking them over the spur to keep them upright. Above this point we came upon a well-beaten trail extending a mile or two, and enabling us to make rapid progess for that distance.

I had estimated the Lake fork as nearly one-third as large as the main stream, but we found the crossing above its junction far more difficult than before, as the river was about three feet deep and so rapid as to make firm footing almost impossible. I felt decidedly relieved when all had safely reached the north bank.

Our route lay now on a wide open bottom, of which the vegetation was "salt" grass, while the surface of the ground was covered with "alkali." We again passed some very large sage bushes before reaching a fine spring, near which we encamped amid a tolerable supply of grass. The river is only a few rods distant, and this evening some of the men have caught quite a number of mountain trout, and as our hunter shot a deer just before reaching camp, we are now living upon the fat of the land, our bill of fare comprising elk, bear, venison, and brook trout.

Sunday, May 27.—We passed the day quietly in camp. The morning was cloudy and threatened rain, and about 2 p. m. it commenced falling and has not slackened up to this time. The escort have no tents, and, should the weather become cold, they will suffer severely.

Monday, May 28.—The rain of last night continued until after daylight this morning, but by the time breakfast was over there appeared some prospects of a clear day and the order to move was given. As the clouds lifted, the mountains were revealed covered with snow nearly to the valley, presenting an appearance æsthetically magnificent, but practically foreboding, as but little time will elapse before we shall be compelled to cross them.

Everything in camp was wet, increasing the weight of our loads and requiring more time than usual for the preparations for the start, but at 8 o'clock we were in motion After travelling some two miles we crossed the river to the south side, and for ten or twelve miles the road presented no difficulties, the valley being quite wide, with a branch meandering through it for several miles before uniting with the river. Another stream about 11 miles from camp proved to be a bold mountain torrent flowing over large boulders, which rendered crossing very difficult. A short distance beyond this the trail we have been pursuing crossed the river, but on attempting to follow it we found the fording so difficult that we concluded in preference to pick our way among the hills on the south side.

The large boulders on the hillside made the travelling so bad that I ultimately gave orders to leave our odometer wheels behind, and after a march of over 18 miles our tents were again pitched for the night. As I was very anxious not to give up our odometer measurements, I sent back for the wheels after getting into camp, and they were brought in just before dark.

We are now fairly among the mountains, and the bluffs that come out to the river are almost impassable. On the south side the formation is drift, and the large boulders that lie scattered in all directions constitute the greatest obstacle to travelling. On the north side the country is cut into deep ravines and the "washed" or "bad land" formation is predominant. Red rocks, similar to the "red buttes" of the Platte, occur just above our present camp, and all the bluffs on the north side present the peculiar coloring in belts seen on Powder river, except that the black (lignite) is wanting.

We have ascended rapidly to-day and our camp is about 400 feet higher than that of last night. Cedars were first found in our course to-day and the barometer indicates an elevation of 6,100 feet above the sea level.

After reaching camp rain again commenced and is now falling quite rapidly. If, as I fear, this is snow on the mountains, it will undoubtedly seriously embarrass our journey among them.

Tuesday, May 29.—We left camp at 7½ a. m. and crossed the river after travelling about a mile. The current was very rapid and we found the water about four feet deep. The recent rains have swollen the stream, so that it is now far more difficult to ford than it was nearer its mouth. It was only by stationing men in the water to keep the animals headed up stream that we led them across in safety.

After travelling between one and two miles further the train was again taken to the south side of the stream, these two crossings being made to avoid a bold red bluff on the south bank, the foot of which is washed by the river. Between four and five miles from camp we passed the forks of Wind river, the north branch at this time being much the smaller of the two. Our route bore up the south fork, which had to be crossed twice before reaching what Bridger called Otter creek, where we encamped after a march of only 13 miles.

The last portion of our journey lay over a narrow foot slope of high drift ridges coming down from the mountains, the opposite or northern bank of the stream being bold, cut bluffs of "washed lands" with the usual horizontal strata of varied colors, in this special locality a pinkish red predominating.

The grass at our present camp is the best found since leaving winter quarters, and this fact induced me to make the day's march unusually short.

Wednesday, May 30.—Passing over the hills from our last night's camp, (on Otter creek,) we reached the valley of Wind river after travelling about a mile. We made four crossings during the day's march, this being necessary to follow the most feasible road.

Toward the close of the day we crossed a high spur, from the summit of which we obtained a fine view of the valley. To our front and upon the right the mountains towered above us to the height of from 3,000 to 5,000 feet in the shape of bold, craggy peaks of basaltic formation, their summits crowned with glistening snow. Upon our left smooth ridges clad with pine rose to nearly equal height, while behind us lay the various-hued bluffs, amid whose singular and picturesque vistas we had for days been journeying. Through the valley, in the centre, the stream could be seen placidly winding its way, a subduing element in the grandeur of a scene whose glories pen cannot adequately describe and only the brush of a Bierstadt or a Stanley could portray on canvass.

About the middle of our day's march we passed the last of the "washed lands." Above that point large boulders cover all the surface of the hills, those upon the north being balsaltic and on the south granite.

Our camp is on the south fork of the stream about two miles above the Upper forks, and at the base of the mountains. From this point we propose crossing the dividing line to the waters of the Pacific. It was my original desire to go from the head of Wind river to the head of the Yellowstone, keeping on the Atlantic slope, thence down the Yellowstone, passing the lake and across by the Gallatin to the Three Forks of the Missouri.

Bridger said at the outset that this would be impossible, and that it would be necessary to pass over to the head-waters of the Columbia, and back again to the Yellowstone. I had not previously believed that crossing the main crest twice would be more easily accomplished than the transit over what was in effect only a spur, but the view from our present camp settled the question adversely to my opinion at once. Directly across our route lies a basaltic ridge, rising not less than 5,000 feet above us, its walls apparently vertical with no visible pass nor even cañon.

On the opposite side of this are the head-waters of the Yellowstone. Bridger remarked triumphantly and forcibly to me upon reaching this spot, "I told you you could not go through. A bird can't fly over that without taking a supply of grub along." I had no reply to offer, and mentally conceded the accuracy of the information of "the old man of the mountains."

After dinner Dr. Hayden and myself rode out to the basaltic ridge, being anxious to examine it more minutely. Passing down the stream about a mile we effected a crossing, but not without getting both our horses mired and ourselves drenched, the results of over-confidence, as we had become so accustomed to hard bottom that we plunged into the stream without a thought of finding mud, and with difficulty avoided serious consequences from our mistake.

On reaching the North fork we found it impossible to effect a crossing, though the stream was only a few rods wide, until we had travelled up it for not less than six miles. Here we found the faint traces of an old lodge trail, which led us to a point at which the bottom was firm enough to enable our horses to obtain a passable footing. The North fork, for 10 or 12 miles above the upper forks, flows through a marsh about a mile in width, which at no very distant day has been a lake, and in this marsh and the hills immediately surrounding the stream seems to rise.

After the last crossing we rode rapidly over the hills, passing some of the finest grass yet seen, and finding snow upon all sides. Upon setting out we had selected a perpendicular crag that we determined to reach, and at length we arrived at a point from which we supposed we should be able to do so without further trouble. The cliff was not more than a mile off, but between us and it we found a deep ravine filled with a thick growth of scrubby pines, which was impenetrable at such a late hour in the day. We were, therefore, compelled to retrace our steps without effecting our object. I felt well paid, however, for the afternoon's work, as we obtained a fine view of the crest of the mountains entirely around the head of Wind river, forming a natural amphitheatre which cannot be excelled.

Throughout our entire ride we saw abundance of buffalo "signs," showing that they had been here recently, and tending to confirm a statement I have frequently heard that the Snake Indians keep the buffaloes penned up in the mountain valleys, and kill them as their necessities require. Our camping ground for the night is evidently one much used, as the remains of numerous lodges and hundreds of lodge poles cover the ground, and it is evident that a camp at this point would effectually "pen" anything not winged that should chance to be in the valley above it.

Game is certainly abundant in the valley, and during our return ride we came upon an immense animal feeding amid the long grass at a distance of but 250 or 300 yards. We supposed it to be a buffalo, but upon its seeing us and rising we discovered that it was an enormous bear, whose equal for size I have never seen. As we were armed only with revolvers we did not molest it, nor did it seem in the least disconcerted by our presence. Antelopes are also numerous, and we saw many bands of at least 40 or 50. From the marshes close by immense flocks of ducks and geese were constantly rising.

We reached camp at dark, and just before a drenching shower, after a brisk ride of over 20 miles. The regular day's march had been 14½ miles.

Thursday, May 31.—We started at 7 o'clock, elated at the prospect of making our next halt upon the Pacific slope of the mountains. Bridger said that our camping ground for the night would be upon the waters of the Columbia, and within five miles of Green river, which could be easily reached. I therefore filled my canteen from Wind river, with the design of carrying the water to the other side, then procuring some from Green river, and with that of the Columbia making tea from the mingled waters of the Gulf of Mexico, the Gulf of California, and the Pacific—a fancy that the sequel will show was not gratified.

Our route bore up the point of a spur that reached the valley at our camp, and in some localities the road was rather steep, but on the whole our progress was good, and we advanced nearly three miles and ascended about 1,000 feet in the first hour. Then following the ridge, we had a gradual ascent and a tolerably good road for three or four miles among stunted pines, reaching at last a large windfall, which it was necessary to pass directly through, a programme involving much labor and the liberal use of the axe.

We then commenced another rapid ascent and soon found ourselves in the snow. By making our horses take the lead by turns we forced our way through, and finally stood upon the last ridge on the Atlantic side of the dividing crest. A narrow but deep valley separated us from the summit, the snow in it being too deep for an attempt even at crossing.

Turning to the left to avoid this ravine, and picking our way through thick stunted pines, we soon found ourselves floundering in the snow. Bridger, for the first time, lost heart and declared that it would be impossible to go further. To return involved retracing our steps fully half way to the Popo-Agie, then turning north into the valley of the Big Horn, and perhaps following the route of Lieutenant Maynadier, to the Three Forks of the Missouri—a course plainly inadmissible until every other hope had failed.

I therefore determined to reconnoitre myself, and if possible find some escape from our dilemma. Dismounting, I pushed ahead through the snow, which was melting rapidly, and rendered travel both difficult and perilous. At times the crust would sustain my weight, while at others it would break and let me sink, generally up to the middle, and sometimes in deep drifts up to my shoulders. In some instances I was able to extricate myself only by rolling and stamping, and in many places I was compelled to crawl upon my face over the treacherous surface of the drifts. After great labor I found myself alone on the summit of the Rocky mountains with the train out of sight.

An investigation of the topography of the surrounding mountains convinced me that if the party could reach this point the main difficulties of the passage would have been surmounted, and I therefore started to return and pilot them through. Following my own tracks for nearly a mile I came upon them, and found that they had followed me slowly.

My attendant, who was leading my horse, stated that he should think they had advanced two or three miles since I left them, making the distance I had pushed forward alone some three or four miles. I found myself very much exhausted, and my clothes saturated with snow-water, but I succeeded in guiding the party through and at last reaching the summit of the crest. The descent upon the south side was gradual, but very difficult, the snow being deep, while at the few points at which it was gone the ground was a perfect quagmire, and it was not until we had advanced some six miles from the summit that we found a scanty supply of grass upon which we could encamp in the midst of pines and snow.

The day's march was by far the most laborious we have had since leaving Fort Pierre; and wet and exhausted as I was, all the romance of my continental tea-party had departed, and though the valley of Green river was in plain sight I had not the energy to either visit or send to it.

Our last night's camp was at an elevation of 7,400 feet above the sea. The summit of this pass is very nearly 10,000 feet, and our camp to-night is 9,250 feet, so that the whole day has been spent in an atmosphere so rarified that any exertion has been most exhausting.

The weather has been a mixture of smiles and tears. Two or three flurries of snow passed over us attended with thunder, while at times the sun shone out brightly, renewing our life and vigor.

To the left of our route and some 10 miles from it rises a bold conical peak, 3,000 or 4,000 feet above us. That peak I regard as the topographical centre of the continent, the waters from its sides flowing into the Gulf of Mexico, the Gulf of California, and the Pacific ocean. I named it Union peak, and the pass Union pass.

Friday, June 1.—I was anxious to give our poor animals all the opportunity to graze that was possible, and did not, therefore, leave camp until nearly nine o'clock. We are now on waters flowing to the westward and into a branch of Lewis fork, which Bridger says is known to the trappers as Gros Ventre fork, the Gros Ventre Indians having been commonly in the habit of passing by this valley in their annual trips across the mountains.

The ground was frozen when we started, just hard enough not to bear our horses, and the poor beasts breaking through the crust into the mud, had as difficult travelling as could be well imagined. About a mile from camp we crossed a little rivulet not more than 18 inches wide, flowing between perpendicular banks four or five feet high. We endeavored to make the animals jump across, but four of them got in and had to be lifted out.

The valley soon became quite narrow, and the stream commenced a rapid descent over a rocky bed. Winding our way down the hill-sides over the rocks or through the mud, some four miles, we reached a bold clay bank 75 or 100 feet high, the foot of which was washed by the stream. A narrow bridle-path led over it, along which our pack-animals passed in safety, but the odometer wheels could not be kept upright even with the aid of ropes, but rolled over, carrying the mules with them, bringing up, at last, at the water's edge, where we left them for the time.

At the end of only a six-miles' march, we encamped upon a small tributary of Gros Ventre fork, having descended about six hundred feet, carrying us below the greater part of the snow and into pasturage that was much better than at our previous camp, though by no means good, the new grass not having yet started. Two or three snow-storms passed over us during the day, although the sun was shining at the time.

After getting into camp, the odometer wheels were sent after, and brought in by making a long detour on the south side of the stream.

My guide seems more at a loss than I have ever seen him, and after reaching camp he rode in advance to reconnoitre, and returned saying, "it would be necessary to make a short march to-morrow," which I do not regret, as our animals are greatly broken down.

Saturday, June 2.—The ground was covered with snow this morning. The sun shone out brightly when the herd was brought up, but, by the time we were prepared to start, snow was again falling rapidly. Crossing the stream, which is here about forty feet wide and two and a half deep, we continued down Gros Ventre fork, our course being north of west. The road was better than any before found on this side of the mountains, but the rapidly falling and melting snow caused mud that retarded us somewhat.

After a march of but three miles, Bridger advised a halt, as he did not know of another good camping ground within accessible distance. The grass is improving in quality, and I hope the rest of the Sabbath will be of essential benefit to our broken-down animals. Our object now is to keep as near to the dividing crest as possible and recross, as soon as we shall be able, to the head-waters of the Yellowstone.

The animal life of this region differs essentially from that on the Atlantic slope. Even in Wind River valley many birds new to us were seen, and Dr. Hayden and his assistants have been very busy collecting specimens of all kinds. Three or four squirrels previously unknown to us, double that number of birds, and a large and new species of rabbit have been obtained. Yesterday, Bridger shot a "mule deer," and the day before our hunter killed one on the eastern side of the crest of the mountains, a locality out of their usual geographical limit.

Sunday, June 3.—We passed the day quietly in camp. The sky has been cloudy, and we have been visited by occasional showers.

Monday, June 4.—Our course to-day has borne nearly northwest, and we are no longer following the course of the stream, but crossing the ridges separating its different branches. The road was found to be almost impassable. The snow had scarcely gone, while the ground was perfectly saturated with water. The depth of the mud, and the exhausted condition of the animals, made marching almost impossible.

A spirit of insubordination and discontent was also manifest among the men, showing itself openly in their apparent determination to abandon all further efforts to bring along the odometer wheels, which they permitted to turn over five times in about half a mile. It was with the greatest difficulty that I succeeded in enforcing discipline and inducing the men to continue the faithful discharge of their duties. A long march was plainly out of the question, the spirit of the party, the condition of the beasts, the state of the roads, and the scarcity of grass, all forbidding it. We halted therefore for the night after advancing but eight miles.

Tuesday, June 5.—We left camp at 7½ a. m., starting off rapidly to the northwest across the spurs running down to Gros Ventre fork. The hill-slopes were not as steep as those passed over yesterday, and had it not been for the mud the road would have been good. As it was, the animals labored hard, sinking over the fetlock at every step. A month later in the season, however, there would probably be no especial difficulty encountered in travelling here, the late rains being chiefly responsible for our troubles. Crossing one or two inconsiderable streams, at about 10 miles from our morning's camp we reached the valley of what was supposed to be another branch of Lewis river, but which subsequently proved to be a northern fork of the Gros Ventre. Here the mud became far more impassable than before, while our labors were greatly augmented by occasional banks of snow through which we were compelled to force a way.

After travelling some two miles in this valley, further progress in it became impracticable, and an attempt was then made to push on along the side of the mountain. There, however, among the pines the snow was found in impassable banks, while the open ground between presented even more obstruction than the snow itself, the soil being loose, spongy and saturated with moisture, so that the animals were constantly and helplessly mired.

I counted at one time 25 mules plunged deep in the mud, and totally unable to extricate themselves. To go on was clearly impossible, and as we were now above grass, to remain here was equally out of the question. The only course left, therefore, was to return, and we retraced our steps for about two miles, and pitched our tents at a point where our animals could pick up a scanty subsistence.

After getting into camp Bridger ascended the summit of a high hill to obtain an idea of the country, and returned after dark with far from a favorable report Nothing but snow was visible, and although he seems familiar with the locality, it is evident that he is in doubt as to what it is best that we should next attempt. As I am exceedingly anxious to reach the upper valley of the Yellowstone, after a full discussion of the question in all its bearings with him to-night, it has been determined to make to-morrow a thorough examination of the mountains and pick out some path by which we may, if possible, find our way across them, and accomplish our purpose.

Wednesday, June 6.—Leaving the party in camp, I started with Bridger this morning, in accordance with our last night's arrangement, to ascertain if it was possible by some means to cross the mountain range before us. Following up the stream we soon reached the limits of our yesterday's labors, and seeing a westerly fork which apparently headed in a low "pass" that looked promising, we determined to explore it.

Before reaching this fork we experienced great trouble in picking our way around snow-drifts and through mud. After leaving the main stream the ground rose rapidly and the hillsides were covered with a dense growth of stunted pines, under which we found snow in abundance. Some of the banks were not so deep as to prevent our horses from plunging through them, but others had to be trodden down before we could effect a passage. The labor was of course excessive, but by perseverance the summit was at length reached.

Bridger immediately declared that we were on the wrong route and that our morning's labor had been wholly useless. This was evident by the course of the ravine upon the other side of the ridge, which tended so far to the southward as to show that the drainage was still towards the Pacific, and that we had expended our efforts in climbing a spur. We therefore returned to the valley and ascended the main stream, which carried us further to the eastward, and at first looked much less promising than the other.

After forcing our way through the snow-banks along the banks of the stream for about a mile, we reached a point where, for three-quarters of a mile above, the valley was comparatively wide, being bordered by steep cliffs, cut in deep gorges, filled with snow. The neighboring hillsides were clad with snow, and the level valley was covered to a uniform depth of from eighteen inches to two feet, without the slightest appearance of ever having been crossed by man or beast.

Bridger at once seemed to recognize the locality, saying, "This is the pass." Our own exhaustion, however, as well as that of our horses, was too great for any further attempts to-day, and we therefore returned to camp, determined to make another and final effort to reach the summit to-morrow.

Thursday, June 7.—I started this morning with a party of nine, all told, to make the last attempt to find a solution of the difficult problem imposed upon us. My companions were the guide, Bridger, Dr. Hayden, (naturalist,) Mr. Hutton, (topographer,) Mr. Schonborn, (artist,) and four men. One of the mules, however, fell into the stream soon after starting and was nearly lost, and we were compelled to send it back to camp, with its rider.

The rest of the party pushed on in our tracks of yesterday, without special trouble, till we reached the valley discovered at the close of our labors of the previous day. Here we encountered great obstacles. The deep snow in the numerous gorges rendered progress along the hillsides impossible, and compelled us to keep close to the stream in the valley, the descent into which was accomplished with much trouble. Our route here was crossed by side gullies from two to four feet in depth, entirely invisible beneath the uniform surface of the snow, and into which we tumbled, and out of which we floundered in a style at once rediculous and exhausting. We partially remedied this, at last, by probing the depth of the snow ahead by rods, and by this simple expedient saved ourselves much labor and annoyance. We ultimately reached the upper end of the valley, and by a steep climb over the snow scaled the last ascent and stood again upon the dividing crest of the Rocky mountains.

It did not require long to decide that further progress was impracticable. From the southward we had already passed over ten or fifteen miles of snow, but then we knew that there was a limit to it easily reached. To the north, or the direction in which our route from this point would lie, the view seemed almost boundless, and nothing was in sight but pines and snow. To bring the party to where we stood was next to impracticable, but this I had determined to attempt, if there were any hopes of getting through the snow on the Yellowstone side of the mountains. My fondly cherished schemes of this nature were all dissipated, however, by the prospect before us, as a venture into that country would result in the certain loss of our animals, if not of the whole party.

I therefore very reluctantly decided to abandon the plan to which I had so steadily clung, and to seek for a route to the Three Forks of the Missouri, by going further to the west and passing down the valley of the Madison. After taking in our fill of the disheartening view we returned to camp, to commence the execution of our new project on the morrow. The hunter to-day was sufficiently fortunate to kill two deer, which form a desirable addition to our rather empty larder. Occasional showers have fallen during the day, but the night is clear and cold.

Friday, June 8.—To-day the train resumed its march, this time in pursuit of a different route from that which had before imposed upon us such serious hardships. The herd was scattered far over the surrounding country, as a result of the scarcity of grass, and an early start was therefore impossible. We were compelled at first to retrace our steps for about three miles, passing down one of the branches of the Gros Ventre fork to its mouth, and finding the road so very muddy that our progress was necessarily slow.

On reaching the fork, we took to the hills bordering the valley of the stream, and notwithstanding the pines and the ravines, were enabled to greatly accelerate the speed of our march. After advancing several miles we crossed, with considerable labor, a steep spur and came down into the valley of a stream (which I deem to be the one whose sources we visited yesterday) near the Indian trail from Green river, and encamped close by its junction with the Gros Ventre, in fine pasturage. The crossing of the spur was of course useless, as it turned out, and resulted from a mistake of Bridger's. These little errors in matters of detail, upon his part, are not remarkable, as it is 15 years since he last visited this region, and they fade into insignificance compared with his accurate general knowledge of the country.

The length of our march was 12 miles, and it was accomplished amid weather of remarkable variableness. About noon we were visited by a storm of mingled rain, snow and hail, accompanied with vivid lightning and heavy peals of thunder, and coming from the mountains behind us, which were shrouded in the densest clouds, while ahead the sun continued to shine brightly and its rays were brilliantly reflected from the snow-clad peaks before us, unveiled by any apparent vapors.

The change in the appearance of the country traversed to-day has been marked. From the barrenness of the mountain summits we have passed into a region of fertility and richness. The evergreens have disappeared, and we are now among cottonwoods. The willows are far larger in size; grass has become abundant, while flowers surrounded us upon every side. The alteration in these characteristics has been perceptible in each step of our march to-day, and has afforded substantial gratification, as well as pleasure, to the eye of taste. The soil at this spot is unquestionably excellent, and its productive capacity is only impaired by the lack of warmth on account of its elevation.

Saturday, June 9.—An early start was effected this morning, with the view to a long day's march. On scaling the hill lying between our camp and the main stream, a prospect of much beauty was unfolded before us. The verdure-clad valley of the Gros Ventre was bounded upon either hand with mountains, whose sides were covered with dark evergreens and whose summits were capped with snow. Far off, a barrier apparently stretched across the valley in the form of a ragged cliff of brilliant red, above whose centre shone with even greater brilliancy the snow-covered peaks of the Great Tèton, dazzling in the clear atmosphere, with the reflected rays of the newly-risen sun. The magnificence of this view elicited universal admiration, and the accompanying sketch fails to do justice to the theme, the artist confessing his inability to represent the gorgeous coloring.

From the summit of the spur we entered the valley and journeyed rapidly down it for five miles, when it became necessary to either cross to the opposite bank or again resort to the hills. The rapidity of the current in the stream dictated the latter course, and we passed over two steep ridges, deriving material aid from several convenient ravines. At this point in our march, one of our dragoon horses slipped and was badly snagged, the wound bleeding profusely. By using cotton the blood was stanched and the gash then sewed up, but the animal was too much exhausted to proceed further, and we abandoned it temporarily.

We reached the river bank again at the foot of the high red bluff, over whose summit we had seen the peaks of the Tèton in the morning. We passed around it, along a narrow foot-path close to the water's edge and at the bottom of a lofty precipice. Here another accident occurred. Three of the pack-mules escaped from their drivers, and pushed up so high among the rocks that the men refused to follow them. Two returned in safety, of their own accord, but the third lost its footing and fell down a vertical descent of over 50 feet, rolling into the river and swimming to the opposite shore.

Part of the pack came off at the foot of the precipice and was picked up, but the remainder was carried across, containing two bundles of bedding. I immediately ordered the party to encamp, and one of the men succeeded in crossing the stream despite the rapid current. He found the mule dead, but the pack unharmed save by water. The rapidity of the current rendered some expedient necessary to bring the latter across, and a stone was thrown over with a twine attached, by which a rope was drawn to that bank and made fast to the pack. The latter was then turned adrift and swung around to our side of the stream. The man swam the current without apparent difficulty on his return.

We found also, on counting up at night, that one of our pack-horses was missing, thus adding another to the mishaps of the day. The distance travelled has been 15 miles, and our course has borne westward.

Our camp is well located, and the river here is thirty yards wide, four feet deep, and has a current of five or six miles an hour.

Sunday, June 10.—We passed the day in camp, the rest being most welcome to all. Both the injured dragoon-horse and the missing pack-horse were brought in at noon, and I am in hopes the former will be soon able to again do duty. The day has been changeable, sunshine, rain and snow, alternating, and at evening the sky was clear, but clouded up before I could complete the observations I had commenced.

Monday, June 11.—We continued down Gros Ventre fork to-day, and, as we are upon the regular Indian trail, found excellent travelling. For the first seven miles the road was rather hilly, crossing a succession of spurs running down to the river's edge, but as we climbed the last we saw before us a wide, level valley, known as Jackson's Hole. It extends up the river apparently to the main chain of mountains, and is bounded on the west by the Tèton range, along whose foot the Snake river flows, and on the east by the spurs just crossed by us. Its probable area is 100 square miles, and its surface was covered with luxuriant vegetation, the prevalent green being agreeably relieved by the bright yellow of a small variety of sun-flower that was singularly abundant. Through this valley we rode rapidly, crossing Gros Ventre fork in its midst, and pushed down Snake river in search of a ford, Bridger declaring that we could find none above.

At the junction of the fork and the main stream we were forced to cross a bold butte, and after this we encamped upon the river bank, our day's march having been 25½ miles, the extraordinary distance being explained by the excellence of the road and the weather.

While *en route*, Mr. Hutton reported that he had discovered a band of Indians watching us from the hills, and that when approached they fled rapidly. This fact led me to conclude that they were Blackfeet, to whom we are supposed to be indebted for previous hostile visits. I have no special fears from their neighborhood, as they will probably be greatly alarmed at the fact of their discovery, but as measures of precaution I ordered the train to close up, and have this evening doubled the guard.

After encamping, general search was made for a ford, but without success. The Snake is here divided into innumerable channels, and its current has the rapidity of a torrent. We discovered a band of Indians upon the opposite bank, and a party visited our camp, swimming their horses across the stream. They proved to be Snakes, and confirmed our suspicions that the others seen to-day upon this side of the river were Blackfeet. Our visitors were totally inoffensive in appearance and action, and after begging a few plugs of tobacco and gratifying their curiosity, returned.

Tuesday, June 12.—We moved camp this morning down the river for 2½ miles to the Indian crossing, hoping that it might prove available for our purposes. Lance Corporal Lovett started to inspect the ford, and I asked him to go as far as he could, and report to me. Lance Corporal Bradley followed him, and within twenty minutes Lovett came back with the startling news that Bradley was drowned. All hands started for the rescue, but the thickness of the underbrush and swiftness of the current rendered any serviceable effort impossible, and, as it was ascertained he had been swept away at the swiftest part of the current, all hope was abandoned. I sent men below to find the body, and also offered the Indians a reward for its recovery, but thus far all has been in vain. The calamity is deplorable, but it is one of those sad accidents for which blame attaches to no one.

All attempts to find a ford have proved futile, but we have picked out a point, at which it is hoped that we may succeed in making use of a raft. A party under charge of Mr. Hutton was, therefore, detailed to construct one, and completed it late in the afternoon. We shall try the experiment with it to-morrow.

I spent most of the day with a single attendant exploring the river above Gros Ventre fork in search of a feasible crossing. I drove up its bottom for some eight miles, finding it to be some forty feet lower than the plain we had traversed and composed of a black, vegetable mould, through which it would be impossible for the train to pass at this stage of the water, aside from the trouble they would subsequently encounter from the miry bottom of the stream. After a ride of thirty miles, I returned to camp without accomplishing anything. The river has now been examined for a distance of 25 miles along its bank without the discovery of any kind of a ford.

We have been again visited to-day with heavy showers.

Wednesday, June 13.—For the purpose of being near the spot at which the raft was to be tested, I this morning moved camp half a mile further down stream, halting the train in the edge of the timber. We launched the raft and attempted to guide it by a rope to the shore, the current being too rapid to turn it adrift, but it even then behaved so badly that it was promptly pronounced a complete failure.

Before this, however, I had resolved to try Bridger's ingenuity, and had ordered him, with such men as could be spared, to construct a boat. After the raft fiasco I found that he had made good progress, and I immediately put all hands at work upon this undertaking. The framework was of course easily constructed, but our great difficulty was to devise a covering, there being no skins in our possession, and our gutta-percha blankets, which were purchased in New York, being almost worthless. We were compelled to make use of them, however, protecting them by a lodge-skin of Bridger's, and to render them more completely impervious to water I had large quantities of resin gathered from the pine in the vicinity, and thickly coated them with this substance. By night a very respectable boat was completed, rude in appearance, but promising to be serviceable. Its length was 12½ and its beam 3½ feet, and it was remarkable for the fact that it was constructed entirely without nails or spikes, the framework being bound together with leather thongs and the covering fastened on by this common device of the traders of this section.

At the point at which we shall to-morrow attempt to cross there are three channels about 100 yards in width. Through two of these a loaded horse can swim without difficulty, but in the third the current is far too deep and swift. Between these channels we shall have to carry our packs by hand.

To-day, for the first time since coming among the mountains, we have not been visited by rain.

Thursday, June 14.—We launched our boat at 9 a. m. and were compelled to carry it for nearly a mile over sloughs and islands to a suitable point of starting. It was then manned by four of our best swimmers and laden with a few goods, and thus succeeded in safely crossing the first channel. A point was then selected at which the other two channels could be crossed simultaneously, but the crew of four were compelled to carry the boat and goods again for nearly half a mile. They succeeded at last in reaching the other bank, and then carried the boat to a point above at which they could avoid the three channels and thus make the return trip at one crossing. It was 5 o'clock, however, before they reached our side of the river again, and we were thus compelled to suspend further labor for the day, save preparations for an early start to-morrow. The boat requires a crew of three men to manage her, and it will thus be necessary to load her lightly and make many trips. I regret the delay, but it is unavoidable, and the fact that the river is apparently rising this evening is additionally discouraging.

Friday, June 15.—We this morning commenced systematic labor in crossing the river. One detachment carried the goods from camp nearly a mile through marshes and among small channels to the point at which they were loaded in the boat. In crossing, the frail craft would reach the opposite shore fully one quarter of a mile, by actual measurement, below. She would then be carried by another party 700 paces up the stream and again launched, reaching our shore 200 paces below the point of original departure, and being carried up that distance by another detachment and reloaded for the next trip.

After these arrangements had been perfected and placed in working order, the round trip consumed but three-quarters of an hour, and we made 17 during the day. As the current was so swift we were compelled to carry over everything in the boat, and the result is that many goods still remain upon the east shore this evening, as well as 15 of the party. I hope to-morrow to complete the work. We have made several ineffectual attempts to-day to swim the herd across, but the moment they reach the swift current they put back, and thus far our efforts have been in vain, no one daring to venture to lead them. This evening they are in charge of the sergeant of the guard.

Saturday, June 16.—We resumed operations this morning by getting the herd across the river. They were driven to the three channels, at which the boat first crossed, and Lance Corporal Lovett volunteered to lead them. They were divided into two bands, and after great trouble were finally induced to follow him. All at last reached the west bank in safety, although some swam or drifted fully a mile down stream. After this the boat resumed her trips, notwithstanding the fact that the crew were so sore and sunburnt from their yesterday's exposure and efforts as to be almost incapacitated for further labor.

Ten trips were made, and all persons and effects ferried across save the odometer wheels, which I have decided to abandon, as the attempt to bring them across would be manifestly attended by too great risk. Everything is greatly scattered and disordered and repacking will be a serious task, necessarily consuming much time. The river at the point at which we have crossed it is 100 yards in width. The boat has drifted in each trip one-quarter of a mile down stream, and yet, notwithstanding an eddy in the middle which has been improved by paddling up and across stream, the time consumed in each passage has been but two minutes. From these facts I estimate the rapidity of the current here to be at least 10 miles per hour.

Sunday, June 17.—After our arduous week's work the rest of to-day has been most grateful. The only work done was the gathering together of the packs and a few such preparations for the journey to-morrow. Mr. Alexander, my foreman, attempted to bring the odometer wheels across on a raft, but failed, and was compelled to abandon them in the middle of the stream.

We were visited by Indians to-day, among whom was Cut-Nose, whom Bridger declares to be the hereditary chief of the Snakes. I made him a small present, and from the others the men purchased some capital trout.

The day has been warm and mosquitoes very annoying. Last night, however, there was a heavy frost, and yesterday a slight snow-storm, and the weather is thus well spiced with variety.

Our camp is now on the right or west bank of Lewis or Snake river and about 10 miles southeast of the highest of the Tètons, the most noted landmarks in this region. They are basaltic peaks, rising not less than 5,000 feet above the level plain of Jackson's Hole, and are visible from a great distance in all directions. Our route out of this valley will be to the westward and across the mountain chain of which they form a part, and which forms the western boundary of the valley we are now in.

Monday, June 18.—The straying of some of the herd prevented an early start, but by 8 o'clock we were in motion, marching due westward towards the mountains and crossing a fine stream about one and one-half mile from camp. In ascending the Tèton range we took advantage of the valley of a mountain stream flowing down its side, following a narrow bridle-path, skirting the foot of a precipice upon one hand and the bank of the dashing brook upon the other. Towards the last the slope became quite steep, but the road was far from bad for a pack-train. We passed across the summit of the range without difficulty, but upon coming to the western slope found our descent seriously obstructed by immense snow-banks, completely blocking up the Indian trail which we were following.

We had previously seen a number of these, but had succeeded in avoiding them. It seemed to be indispensable that we should do so in this case, and we therefore climbed a spur some 200 feet higher, passed over it and picked out a path along the mountain side until we had descended below the snow region. At some points the difficulties encountered were very great, and at one time in the descent the safety of those ahead was seriously endangered by rolling stones loosened by those in the rear. This pass is probably a capital one when not obstructed by snow, but it was with the greatest difficulty that we found our way through. Its summit is seven miles distant from the river and 1,900 feet above it. On the west side we descended 1,000 feet, vertical measurement, in a distance of less than two miles. On the summit I noticed a pine tree bearing this inscription: "J. M., July 7th, 1832; and July II, 1833."

After passing over the steepest part of the descent we entered the valley of a small stream, much more gradual in its downward slope, and after a further advance of about eight miles encamped upon its banks on the edge of Pierre's Hole, the length of the day's march being by estimate 18 miles. Among the pine through which we passed to-day I noticed some splendid trees fully four feet in diameter. The larger part, however, are about of telegraph-pole size.

Tuesday, June 19.—Our course to-day has borne nearly due north, passing down through Pierre's Hole, which almost deserves the extravagant praise bestowed upon it by Bridger, who declares it to be the finest valley in the world. It is between 20 and 24 miles in length, and seven or eight in width; its gently undulating surface being covered with vegetation of the greatest luxuriance, and carpeted with innumerable flowers of brilliant hue and the richest variety. It is bounded upon all sides by snow-capped peaks, while through its centre flows a fine stream fed by many branches finding their sources in the neighboring mountains.

The latter, whose banks are uniformly muddy, have retarded our progress somewhat, but we have advanced very rapidly, and encamped at 10 o'clock, after a march of between 17 and 18 miles. The Tètons have shown off finely upon our right to-day, and in front and to the left of our course a lofty, snow-clad peak is visible, which Bridger declares to be at the head of the middle fork of the Jefferson. We are seeking the head of the Madison, and at present there are no obstacles in sight threatening to intercept our route. Notwithstanding the beauty and fertility of the valley we have seen no game, squirrels being the largest animals that have crossed our path, while of birds only a few curlew and others of the smaller varieties have been visible. These circumstances are to be regretted, as with our limited stock of provisions a constant supply of fresh meat is very desirable.

Wednesday, June 20.—This morning we left the charming valley of Pierre's Hole, and continued our march northward over an open, rolling country, the hills varying from 100 to 200 feet in altitude, and occasionally sloping steeply to the banks of small streams, now greatly swollen and difficult to cross for this reason. A marked peculiarity of these hills is the decaying trunks of aspens scattered about, showing that at no remote day they were covered with this tree.

The soil is uniformly good, and a fine growth of grass prevails everywhere. About 10 o'clock we passed a fine stream and an excellent camping ground, but as I was anxious to get ahead as rapidly as possible, I decided not to halt, but to push on for an hour or two longer. On ascending the next hill we found a thick growth of pines and aspens, with dead timber lying in all directions.

Bridger and myself pushed our way carefully in advance among these obstructions, passed over the ridge, and thence down by a steep descent into the valley of a large stream, which Bridger declared to be Henry's fork, confessing that he had entirely mistaken his locality, and that he was greatly surprised at finding this formidable river here.

As it constituted an insuperable barrier to our immediate progress, I ordered the train to return to the camping ground passed early in the afternoon and halt there for the night. With the guide I commenced a thorough examination of the stream; we found it apparently too deep to ford, flowing between high banks and with a swift current. We went down its valley and attempted to find fords at a number of points, but unsuccessfully. I at last left Bridger to continue explorations, and crossed over the hills to camp and ordered the men to immediately commence the construction of another boat.

By night its framework was finished and ready to be carried to the river bank early in the morning. Bridger returned and reported having found an excellent place for crossing the stream by boat, with a good camping ground upon both banks. The pack-master and one of the men whom I had sent up stream in search of a ford came back after an unsuccessful trip.

The day has been chilly, rendering overcoats not only comfortable but necessary, and this afternoon a hail-storm, accompanied by a squall that blew down our tents, visited us and left the atmosphere even colder than before.

Thursday, June 21.—We made a very early start this morning and reached the river bank at 7 a. m., after a march of three miles. We commenced putting the boat together and had half completed the work, when one of the men whom I had sent below returned with the announcement that he had found a ford that was practicable for our larger animals. We immediately availed ourselves of this discovery, and by making two trips with our more powerful beasts, carried everything across and encamped upon the opposite bank, the day being far advanced and Bridger desiring to reconnoitre the country ahead. After a long absence he returned and stated that some thick pines would constitute the only serious obstacle to our progress that need be immediately dreaded. As the herd is in excellent condition, and the roads promise well, I still hope to fulfil my engagement with Lieutenant Maynadier and reach the Three Forks of the Missouri by the last of the month.

Friday, June 22.—We left the bank of Henry's fork this morning, passing directly over the hills, our course being about north-northwest. The country traversed differs but little from that through which we passed day before yesterday, save that the aspens and pines have increased in thickness and threaten to become impenetrable. The fallen timber also forms a serious obstacle, and I greatly feared (though in this I was agreeably disappointed) that we should lose some of our animals by snagging. The services of a pioneer party, to both clear and "blaze" the way, were needed throughout the entire march.

Early in the day we passed a large stream which Bridger declared to be Spring fork. Some distance further on we reached a second, about 40 yards in width, which he hesitatingly pronounced to be Lake fork, and up the valley of the latter we determined to go, preferring this course to further continuing among the timber. After about three miles advance, however, we came to the "spring," showing that Bridger had been mistaken, and that this was Spring fork. The "spring" is the largest I have ever heard of, and furnishes two-thirds of the volume of water in the stream, bursting forth from the hillside and reaching the main channel by a beautiful waterfall of over 30 feet in height. This feature of the country is not easily to be forgotten, and is famous all through this region.

We continued up a small branch of this fork for two or three miles above the spring, when the valley becoming too narrow we left it and entered an open marshy spot among the pines, upon which we encamped, as it afforded sufficient grass (though of a poor quality) for our animals. The mosquitoes have been very troublesome during the day, but the night was so cold that not only did their persecutions cease, but ice formed in our buckets to the thickness of a quarter of an inch.

This afternoon our hunter killed a large bear, giving us thus our first taste of fresh meat for nearly a week. The camas plant also abounds in this vicinity, and it has been to-day gathered and cooked, adding the vegetable element to our bill of fare. The camas is a bulbous plant that bears a beautiful blue flower. Its bulbs, which alone are edible, are from a half to a single inch in diameter, resemble onions save in their peculiar flavor, and apparently contain a large proportion of glutinous matter.

A fine comet is this evening visible in the heavens.

Saturday, June 23.—We started this morning with the determination of pushing ahead until we should emerge from the woods that now surround us. We have been journeying between the Spring and Lake forks of Henry's river, and found our road obstructed by stunted pines, fallen and decaying trees, a series of low marshes, and occasionally by sharp basaltic rocks. Our progress was thus necessarily slow and laborious, save when we were enabled to assist ourselves by a deserted Indian trail which was occasionally available.

After much of this hard travelling we at length reached an open prairie of firm basaltic gravel, over which we marched rapidly for more than an hour, passing through one or two marshes caused by small tributaries of the river and populated by myriads of mosquitoes that annoyed us immeasurably. From this we were compelled to again enter the pines, but soon succeeded in finding the trail, and by following it ultimately reached the bank of Lake fork itself. We found this stream to be here 100 yards wide, three feet deep, and with a current of two miles per hour. We crossed it without difficulty and encamped in a clear space upon its right bank, some ten feet above the water.

Game has been abundant to-day, and we have seen two large herds of elk. The hunter has also killed two deer and an antelope. Bridger says that we are now through the timber, and that there is nothing to further delay our progress to the Three Forks. Our latitude to-night is 44° 30′, a distance of about 25 miles from the point at which the divide is placed on the maps.

Sunday, June 24.—We have passed the day quietly in camp, holding the usual service. The morning was warm and pleasant, but it has rained all the afternoon, and this evening the temperature is much cooler.

Monday, June 25.—We started this morning in a northeasterly direction for the Madison, our route running through a strip of woods of about a mile in width, and then emerging into an open and almost level prairie, in which is located Henry's lake. At first we found the travelling quite marshy, but soon reached firm ground and advanced with unusual rapidity. The prairie was beautiful with its luxuriant growth of young grass, and bands of antelope were scattered about us on all sides, three or four being killed in the course of the march.

About ten miles from camp we re-crossed Lake fork, which is here a rapid stream, 25 yards wide and three feet deep, flowing between muddy banks, and then passed to the east of Henry's lake, being obliged to keep some distance from its immediate banks on account of their swampy nature, and thus skirting the foot of the mountain sides. The lake is from three to four miles in length, and after leaving its head we commenced ascending the gradual slope of the neighboring pass over the Rocky mountains. As we approached its summit I put spurs to my horse and galloped ahead over the boundary line and into Nebraska.

The pass is only four miles from, and 200 feet above the lake, and so level that it is difficult to locate the exact point at which the waters divide. It is about a mile in width, with the sides sloping gently to the centre. The barometer stood at 23.65 inches, indicating a height of 6,350 feet above the sea level, or 1,500 feet lower than the summit of the South pass. The approaches upon either side are remarkable, being of about a uniform ascent of 50 feet to the mile, and thus affording unequalled facilities for either wagon road or railroad purposes. I named it Low pass, and deem it to be one of the most remakable and important features of the topography of the Rocky mountains.

After passing over the mountain we marched about ten miles and reached the banks of the Madison below the cañon. We found this river to be here about 80 yards in width, flowing very rapidly over a bed of huge boulders, and presenting insuperable obstacles to our crossing it at this point; we accordingly encamped after an unusually long march. During the day I find that by observations we have made a northing of 20′. We have seen one band of buffalo among the hills, and hope to soon be surrounded again by this species of game. Appearances now favor our reaching the Three Forks by the last of the week, and if Lieutenant Maynadier is prompt, I shall start for the Eclipse on Monday next.

After crossing Lake fork, Mr. Hutton, Dr. Hayden, and two attendants turned to the east and visited the pass over the mountains, leading into the Burnt Hole valley. They found the summit distant only about five miles from our route, and report the pass as in all respects equal to that through which the train had gone. From it they could see a second pass upon the other side of the valley, which Bridger states to lead to the Gallatin. He also says that between that point and the Yellowstone there are no mountains to be crossed; and if this is true, these passes unquestionably offer the best route for a continental railroad. From them to the westward, there is an easy road over Camas Prairie and thence down to Lewis fork.

We narrowly avoided a serious casualty to-day, the carbine of one of the escort being accidentally discharged while lying across his saddle; the contents fortunately missed any of the party, but seriously wounded one of the dragoon horses. I am in hopes, however, of being able to save the animal's life.

Tuesday, June 26.—One of the men this morning accidentally shot himself while wiping out a loaded gun; a part of the iron ramrod struck him near the left nipple, passed through the fleshy part of the breast, hit and glanced off from the shoulder-bone, and emerged a little below the point of the right shoulder. It was at first feared that the wound was mortal, and I ordered back the herd which was at the time being driven up for the start. A careful surgical examination, however, revealed the fact that it was only a flesh wound, and after it had been dressed I gave the order for the march. A litter was at first prepared for the injured man, but a *travais* being recommended, that was ultimately tried.

By 10 o'clock we were under motion passing down the valley of the Madison, which is at this point from one to two miles wide, and consisting of three distinctly defined terraces, nearly level but with precipitous sides. Occasionally these run together, rendering some steep climbing necessary, but aside from this the travelling was excellent. After a march of about six miles it was found that the wounded man was growing worse, and a halt was ordered for the day. I have had a horse litter prepared for him for to-morrow, and trust that this will prove a relief.

Wednesday, June 27.—We encamped last night at the junction of the Madison and Rosse's fork, and this morning were compelled to retrace our steps for a short distance to reach the Indian trail that led to a ford through the latter stream. We crossed it after descending steep banks, and then passed on down the Madison. For ten miles the terrace formation continued, necessitating the occasional passage up and down of steep slopes, but at this distance the trail we were following ran along the precipitous side of a hill some 300 feet in height; it thence passed down to a narrow bottom and around the base of a huge bluff, whose frowning crags overhung a narrow path along the edge of the river. After this it again ascended to the summit of the hill, where we found ourselves upon a broad and level plain, over which we travelled rapidly, being in one or two instances compelled to descend to the river bank and again scale the hillside. Towards the latter part of the day it was difficult to find a good camping ground, and it was only after a march of 25 miles that we were able to obtain a suitable location. Even here only driftwood and a few willows furnished us a scanty supply of fuel. Our injured man has fared finely to-day, and the horse litter has answered its purpose perfectly. Three antelopes have been shot during the march, and we are thus abundantly provided with fresh meat; our other supplies are giving out, however. Some small snow banks have been seen, affording evidence of the great depth of the fall in this region last winter.

The face of the country has changed greatly, and is rapidly assuming the appearance of the Missouri near Fort Pierre and below. The rugged mountains are receding, and their places are being taken by rounded and barren hills. The valley is also almost destitute of wood, and the grass is becoming brown and scarce. The banks of the numerous small streams emptying into the river are skirted with a narrow figure of willows, alders, and aspens, and the valley thus presents the appearance of a farm divided into lots by hedges. It is needless to add that the prospect is far less inviting.

Thursday, June 28.—We continued our course down the Madison, following the river bottom for the first six miles, and crossing in our route a large number of sloughs and miry streams. For most of the distance the river was fringed by a low and narrow growth of cotton, woods, and willows. At one point a couple of buffaloes were discovered on the opposite bank, which became alarmed at our appearance, dashed headlong down stream, crossed it ahead of the train, and climbed the hill just in time to meet our hunter, who killed one, thus providing us with the first buffalo meat of the season.

After leaving the bottom we followed the first plateau, finding the travelling somewhat improved. Our route diverged slightly from the course of the river which here bears off to the right, entering a cañon through a range of broken hills crossing the valley. We pushed on to this transverse range and encamped at the foot of its slopes on the banks of a stream taking its rise in the mountains and emptying into the Madison at a distance of about four miles. The ground in its immediate vicinity was marshy, but the location of our camp on the hill-side is perfectly dry. The distance of the day's march was 18 miles.

This range of hills makes the valley down which we have been travelling a "hole," resembling, but larger than, Pierré's or Jackson's holes already passed. It has steadily widened as we have descended the river, and at last night's camp its breadth was at least 15 miles. The surrounding mountains are rugged, and in many instances covered with snow. They slope steeply to the plateau upon which we have been advancing, and thence descend by irregular steps to the river bank. All the terraces of which the valley is constituted are now covered with a luxuriant growth of bunch grass, affording at this season pasturage of the finest quality and great extent. Antelopes have been visible in large numbers upon all sides.

Friday, June 29.—To-day we have climbed the hills that last night intercepted our path. The summit of the first ridge was reached by a long and easy slope of about five miles. We then descended into an interlying valley forming the bed of a small stream, and after a not very difficult march of 10 or 12 miles, scaled the summit of a second ridge from which we obtained our first view of the three forks of the Missouri. A march of five miles further brought us to the edge of the level plain in which the Jefferson, Madison, and Gallatin effect their junction, and as there was no available camping ground to be found we pushed on until, at 5 p. m., we reached the Madison again, having travelled the very unusual distance during the day of 35 miles. We then encamped, finding but little timber in our vicinity, although considerable is seen on the banks of the Jefferson, and some on those of the Madison, chiefly on the sides next the bluffs.

The valley at this point is wide and inclined to marshiness. The Madison flows in a winding channel, badly cut up by islands and sloughs, and as the barometer indicates a fall of 1,000 feet since we left it last night it must be a continuous rapid through the canon, or a succession of cascades. Bridger, however, denies the existence of any perpendicular fall, and I am inclined to regret not having explored it throughout its entire length, if it had been possible.

There are no signs of the arrival of Lieutenant Maynadier, and I fear that he will not reach here in time to enable me to undertake my northern trip to visit the line of the total eclipse on the 18th proximo. Rain and thick clouds prevented observations at night.

Saturday, June 30.—Our energies have been to-day devoted to preparations for crossing the rivers. Early in the morning a small party was sent up the Jefferson in search of a ford while, with Dr. Hayden, I rode over to the same stream and thence down to its point of union with the Madison in pursuit of a better camping ground, and a feasible point of crossing. Meanwhile the others of the expedition were employed in the manufacture of another boat, which it was evident we should need to communicate with Lieutenant Maynadier, if for no other purpose. I found an excellent camping ground 400 yards above the junction of the two rivers on a narrow neck, only 37 paces in width, while those exploring the Jefferson reported that they had discovered a ford practicable for the animals but not for the packs.

I therefore determined to move camp to the selected spot, complete there the boat of which I found the frame nearly constructed, by it convey the goods and supplies across, and send the animals around by the ford A severe rain storm delayed us somewhat, but after it was over we moved camp and consumed the rest of the day in finishing the boat.

Observations for latitude locate us at 45° 55′, some distance north of Lewis and Clark's calculations, but corresponding with the position of the Three Forks in Lieutenant Warren's map.

The valley of the Three Forks has been most accurately depicted by Lewis and Clark. I ascended to-day a hill in the vicinity of our morning's camp, and compared the details of their journal with the scene before me. Their description was verified in every respect, even to the point they specified as suitable for a fortification. With their judgment in this respect, however, I must differ, as the location is commanded by higher hills, and any work thereon could be easily carried by a suitably armed force. If, however, it should be only intended to defend the cañon, which the Missouri enters just below, it would perfectly meet that requirement.

Sunday, July 1.—The day has been passed quietly in camp. One of the men this morning swam the Jefferson and reported that we were encamped upon simply one channel of the river, a large island intervening, and two others equally formidable will have also to be crossed before we shall reach the opposite bank. This fact, together with the non-arrival of Lieutenant Maynadier, has decided me to cross the Madison and Gallatin, instead of the Jefferson, and go down to Fort Benton by the east bank of the Missouri. If the other detachment shall not arrive before we have completed our crossing we can advance towards the Yellowstone until we meet them, and thence push to Fort Benton. By this course we shall save them the trouble of crossing to the Three Forks, and will also explore a country less familiar than that to the west of the Missouri. We observed this evening lunar distances for longitude, but the moon was so low that they were not very valuable.

The day has been warm and the musquitoes exceedingly troublesome.

Monday, July 2.—In accordance with my new plan adopted yesterday, all hands were set at work upon the boat this morning, that it might be immediately completed for the crossing of the Madison and Gallatin. Both these rivers were crossed by swimming by the same man that crossed the Jefferson, and on his return he reported that we should probably be able to ford the Gallatin. At 2 p. m. the boat was launched, and worked admirably, so that by 7½ p. m all our goods and the entire party had been safely landed upon the eastern bank of the Madison. The animals swam the current without difficulty, following one of the horses led by the boat.

Tuesday, July 3.—The ford of the Gallatin being pronounced practicable upon further examination this morning, we started at 9½ a. m. and crossed it at a point at which it was separated into two channels. In the first of these the water was four feet deep and the current very rapid. The second was not even three feet in depth. The crossing was effected without much trouble, and we emerged about half a mile above the mouth of the Gallatin. We at once scaled the bluff and started up the river, heading almost due east.

After a march of about three miles we came upon the hunter of Lieutenant Maynadier's party, who reported the main body to be but five or six miles distant and coming towards us. We rode on and met them as they were commencing to cross the Gallatin to the bank which we had left. This was stopped immediately, and both parties encamped on the north bank upon a small plateau at the foot of a high bluff, at a distance of 6¼ miles from the Three Forks.

Lieutenant Maynadier reports that he experienced great difficulty in crossing some of the streams in his route; that he was compelled to abandon all his wagons and carts, and that at the Stinking Fork of the Big Horn he lost a large number of his instruments and many of his notes by the sweeping away by the current of the wagon in which they were carried.

I regret this exceedingly, as it will render it almost impossible for us to hereafter make such observations as will be necessary to fix our positions. The report of Lieutenant Maynadier accompanies this.

Observations for longitude by lunar distance were attempted again this evening, but also proved unsatisfactory for the reason that the moon was so low, though nearly on the meridian.

Wednesday, July 4.—The day was spent in camp by the entire expedition, the lack of means limiting our demonstrative ebullitions of patriotism to the burning of a little extra gunpowder. Our labors were confined to preparations for another division of the party, as from this point I shall go northward to Fort Benton, while Lieutenant Maynadier will push down the Yellowstone to Fort Union. The contemplated trip to the remote north into the line of the total eclipse, (north of latitude 52°,) on the 18th instant, I am reluctantly compelled to abandon.

There now remain but 13 days in which I could travel, while the distance is 500 miles. It would thus require average journeys of 38 miles per diem, which, considering the nature of the unexplored wilderness through which we should be compelled to pass, is manifestly impossible. Had Lieutenant Maynadier succeeded in rejoining me by the last of June, I should have attempted to comply with the request of the department, but unforeseen obstacles have delayed him four days beyond the appointed time, and as I did not feel justified in leaving the party until assured of his safety, this plan must be from necessity relinquished.

On leaving Deer creek (winter quarters) I had simply procured a three-months' supply of short rations; one pound of flour and six ounces of bacon, with coffee and sugar, per diem for each man. A considerable percentage of this had wasted by the sifting of the flour through the sacks and the trying of the bacon under the sun's rays during the marches. Game has therefore been indispensable to the subsistence of the expedition, and the question of supplies is thus attended with serious embarrassments.

During the day I have taken a careful account of the stock on hand, and after issuing to my own party a short allowance for fifteen days for the trip to Fort Benton, the balance has been turned over to Lieutenant Maynadier, who thinks that with the buffalo he will surely find on the Yellowstone, he is thus sufficiently provided for his journey to Fort Union. I hope to find further supplies for my party at Fort Benton, but if not we shall be compelled to rely upon game on the trip from that post to Fort Union.

Lieutenant Mullins will accompany me, and my present intention is, after leaving Fort Benton, to continue our explorations by both land and river parties, putting Lieutenant Mullins in command of the former, with instructions to follow the divide between the Missouri and the Yellowstone, while with the latter I shall descend the Missouri itself. The early evening was marked by a beautiful aurora borealis, followed by thick clouds, which prevented observations.

Thursday, July 5.—We left camp this morning before Lieutenant Maynadier, advancing a little distance up the Gallatin, but bearing off to the left over the hills in a northeasterly course. On reaching the summit of the first ridge the beautiful valley of the Three Forks was spread out before us. The Jefferson could be seen in the western distance, while the Madison was visible to the cañon, and we could trace the course of the Gallatin apparently almost to its sources. In the lofty mountains upon the east the marked depression of Clark's Pass was especially noticeable, and through its vista could be discerned the distant peaks of the ranges beyond the Yellowstone. The landscape was also rendered additionally charming by the serenity of the weather and the freshness of the vegetation.

Our route bore over a series of spurs, with the dry beds of streams tending towards the Gallatin interlying; and we continued to rapidly ascend, the hills being destitute of timber, and out-cropping lime rock constituting their main feature. After a march of 15 miles we reached the summit of the divide between the Little Green (which Bridger describes as emptying into the Missouri about 30 miles below the Three Forks) and the Gallatin. We descended into the valley of a tributary of the former, and five miles further on came to that stream itself, ascended it for some two miles, and then encamped after a march (estimated) of 22 miles.

The Little Green is a beautiful mountain brook, 20 feet in width and 18 inches in depth, flowing through a narrow valley bounded by high and steep bluffs, whose surface is covered with fresh grass, jagged rocks, and occasional pines. The course of the stream is nearly south, heading towards a lofty spur, through a cañon in which it passes, but after this it must turn to the northward if Bridger is correct in his location of the point at which it enters into the Missouri.

The day has been the first of the season that has been disagreeably warm and oppressive throughout.

Friday, July 6.—Our course continued up the Little Green river this morning, the forks of which we reached after a march of about a mile. Crossing a high table-land lying between the two streams that form the river, we continued up the more northerly one for some nine miles, the narrowness of the valley compelling us to reapeatedly cross the fork. After reaching this point we were compelled to climb the steep sides of a lofty spur through which the stream passed in a cañon. Its height was from 800 to 1,000 feet, and we found both its ascent and descent to be very difficult; in the latter case the travelling being obstructed by a succession of rugged ravines, the sides of the gorges covered with pine and large ledges of outcropping rock. We found, however, a narrow footpath that, with some trouble, we followed to the valley again, and up this we advanced for another mile. The stream then bore off to the right, whereupon we abandoned it, and crossing over a second spur came out upon the open prairie, with the head of Smith's river in sight, and the Belt mountains filling the northern horizon. We crossed two small tributaries of the Little Green river, and encamped upon the second amid a grove of willows and aspens, which have furnished our night's supply of fuel. The distance accomplished in the march has been 14 miles, but the travelling has been as bad as any this season except the descent of the Tetons and our march through the pines on Henry's river.

Clouds were gathering threateningly as we halted, and by the time our tents were up the rain was falling in torrents, continuing till after nightfall and followed by a slight drizzle. The weather has been raw and chilly, and thus in disagreeable contrast with yesterday's warmth.

Saturday, July 7.—The direction of our march this morning was still northward over a high rolling prairie, crossed by several small tributaries of the Little Green. No timber was seen upon the banks of any of these—a fact which proves the fortunate wisdom of our selection of a camp last evening.

Upon the open prairie our view was unusually extensive. Through a gap at our left the mountains west of the Missouri were plainly visible. In the southeast could be seen the snow-covered peaks of the broken range in which the Muscleshell and Twenty-five Yards rivers take their rise, while the course of the former could be traced for miles along the eastern horizon. Far in the south we could dimly see the mountains beyond the Yellowstone, while stretching directly from east to west ahead of us were the pine-covered ridges of the Belt mountains, a poorly defined gap marking the location of the cañon of Smith's river.

A march of about 10 miles over a series of prairie hills brought us to the summit of the divide, from which we looked down upon Smith's river. This stream was flowing through a wide, open valley, and its banks were wholly destitute of timber.

I determined to follow down its valley to the plains of the Missouri, and we therefore changed our course to the north-northwest, and headed towards the cañon in the Belt mountains. After a march of 10 miles we reached the banks of the river, and found it to be from 30 to 40 feet in width and 18 inches in depth, flowing over a gravelly bottom. The valley was, however, so marshy that we were frequently compelled to cross the stream, and generally keep at a considerable distance from its immediate banks.

After a march of five miles we crossed a small spur through which the river cañons, and finding there some half a dozen dry cottonwoods that would answer for fuel we encamped upon a level, gravelly plateau, 30 feet above the water. The grass along our route has been both excellent and abundant, and would at this season furnish grazing for enormous numbers of cattle. Antelope and deer are the only game found, however, save a bear which was this morning started by the train and shot by Lieutenant Mullins.

The surrounding hills are covered with scattered pines and cedars, and other evergreens grow down to the very edges of the valley. The summits of the more lofty of the adjacent mountains are still covered with snow. An Indian trail was crossed directly after entering the valley this afternoon, and it was plainly that of a large band with lodges, and also fresh. The probable destination of the savages was Fort Benton.

Observations at night were decidedly marred by obscuring clouds.

Sunday, July 8.—The day was passed in camp, with religious services at the usual hour. The weather has been delightfully cool, and we have also enjoyed a relief from the persecutions of the mosquitoes. Some fine trout were caught in the river by members of the party, aiding us in eking out our scanty stock of provisions. I now hope to reach Fort Benton by the last of the present week, and there obtain fresh supplies.

Monday, July 9.—We still continued down Smith's river, heading to the northwest. The stream soon turned off in a bend to the left, and we passed over an open prairie, reaching the valley again after a march of ten miles. A spur of the mountains was then crossed, and we came to a branch of the stream, beyond which the river itself bore off to the west towards a cañon in the hills. We selected a route more to the northward and passed over a series of high prairie hills, reaching another branch of the river upon which we encamped after a march of 20 miles. Throughout the day we followed the Indian trail that we found yesterday, and supposed that it would lead us directly to Fort Benton. Bridger reconnoitered ahead this afternoon for some miles, however, and reports that it shortly strikes off towards the Muscleshell or returns up Smith's river. From this point we shall therefore be compelled to pick our own way out of the Belt mountains, but fortunately they do not present any very serious obstacles, being little more than prairie hills, occasionally covered with pines and out-cropping rocks. The only obstructions that are to be dreaded are the cañons that we may possibly encounter.

The grass through which we have passed to-day has been unequalled in luxuriance and richness, surpassing the fertile meadows of eastern farms. Its stalks average fully 18 inches in height, and branch at the top after the fashion of oats. Our animals are thriving freely upon the glorious pasturage. Some changes in the features of the country are noticeable, the rocks being now metamorphic, while yellow pine has for the first time made its appearance. A cold rain annoyed us during the latter portion of our march, but the afternoon has been beautiful and clear.

Tuesday, July 10.—Our route led this morning nearly due west for the first five miles, passing over high grassy hills, and then turned sharply to the northwest to avoid some rugged, rocky mountains that threatened serious obstructions to travelling. A large number of deep gullies embarrassed our progress now, and to this difficulty was soon superadded thick pines and fallen timber. After the severest toil, greatly exhausting our animals, we reached a clear space upon the summit of a high ridge, and found the continuance of our journey in its present direction forbidden by a series of ravines that were plainly impracticable. We therefore turned again to the west, and descending into the valley of Smith's river, which was about 1,000 feet below us and distant about two miles. The slope was gradual, however, and travelling again unattended with such severe labor, and upon reaching the valley we found an old Indian trail, marked at one point by two large heaps of stones. This was of course a favorable indication of a good road before us, and following this road we pushed on the river's edge, crossed the stream, and entered a small and beautiful prairie. The left bank was at this point formed by a bold and perpendicular limestone bluff, 300 feet in height, colored in places the most brilliant red, and forming a romantic and striking contrast with the dark hues of the surrounding evergreens.

These features of the landscape and the fertility of the natural meadow through which we were passing, rendered the spot charmingly delightful in all respects. The trail served our purposes well, being old but easily followed, and we advanced rapidly down the river crossing its bed three times, and keeping mainly in the narrow prairie upon its west side, the bold formation of the opposite bank continuing. After a march of three miles in this fashion, we found that the river turned to the right and passed through a narrow cañon, and we followed the trail in a narrow ravine up a rugged and steep ascent to the summit of the high spur, which occasioned the cañon. We found that on reaching this point we had left the pine region, and before us lay only high prairie hills, over which we passed rapidly, and encamped six miles further on, upon a small tributary of Smith's river. The stream enters the hills a short distance from this location, and the pines in the gorge furnish the only fuel in the vicinity.

The timber passed through to-day has been chiefly yellow pine and spruce. The rock has been mainly limestone, although one specimen was picked up, which was supposed to be cinnabar, the first ore yet found. Strawberry vines, with ripe fruit, have abounded along the line of our march. The trail that has aided us so greatly merits brief mention. It is plainly old and abandoned, but must formerly have been a great thoroughfare. It was originally very skilfully located, and in some spots has been artificially improved at the cost of considerable labor. It still affords excellent travelling, save in a few spots in which it has been impaired by natural causes, operating through a considerable period of time.

Wednesday, July 11*th.*—On leaving camp this morning we climbed to the summit of the high grass-covered hill before us, the ascent being about 1,000 feet, and on reaching its ridge were rewarded with a prospect of great magnificence. The rugged range of the Belt mountains through which we had just passed filled the horizon behind us. In the remote distance upon our left could be dimly seen the glistening snow upon the loftier peaks of the Rocky mountains, while upon the right the view was limited by the ridges along Highwood creek. Before us lay the valley of the Missouri, its varied features enhanced by the clear atmosphere of a summers' morning. The absolute solitude of the scene added to the striking effect its unaided grandeur would have produced.

We effected a descent from the ridge by a convenient valley and drove rapidly towards Smith's river, which we reached after a march of nearly 10 miles, finding it to be here about 50 yards in width and 2½ feet in depth. After crossing we descended its valley for half a mile, but finding the ground marshy, we at length, after two more crossings, ascended the hills upon its left bank and pushed to the north. We passed over a number of streams that afforded abundance of water, but could nowhere find sufficient timber to meet the requirements of a camping ground. After a march in all of full 30 miles, the Missouri came in sight upon our left, and turning sharply we marched five miles further, encamping upon its right bank under a high bluff, about three miles above the upper terminus of Lewis and Clark's portage. The valley of Smith's river, of which such frequent mention has been made in my journal for the past few days, is one of the finest upon the continent. It is very narrow, being barely half a mile in width, but the bottom and the adjacent hill-sides are covered with a luxuriant growth of grass, while the immediate banks of the river are fringed with considerable timber. At night I was successful in obtaining observations.

Thursday, July 12.—As we were now but a short distance from the great falls of the Missouri, I determined to visit them, and, having ordered the train to push over the hills and encamp on Willow creek, I started down the river bank accompanied by Lieutenant Mullins, Dr. Hayden, Mr. Schonborn, and two attendants. The river above the falls flows placidly between grassy hills, rising gently as they recede, and its surface is occasionally broken by wooded islands of much romantic beauty. At the distance of three miles from camp we came to the mouth of Flattery run and White Bear island, the upper terminus of the Portage. Three miles further on, our route still continuing amid exquisite scenery, we reached a spot upon the bank opposite the mouth of Sun or Medicine river. This stream is about one-half the width of the Missouri at the point of junction, and flows through a wide and beautiful valley. By the aid of our glasses we endeavored to see the Indian agency or mission station upon its banks, but although 10 or 15 miles of country were visible, nothing that could be identified as the buildings in question could be seen. Just below this point the falls begin, and we commenced their descent. In 1804–'5–'6, Lewis and Clark, in their extraordinary journey across the continent, passed up by these falls, being the first whites by whom they were ever visited. Their description is remarkable for its vividness and accuracy, and as I passed down I compared it point by point with the scene before me, verifying it in every essential respect. I can do no better than to republish here extracts from their journal. Under date of Thursday, June 13, 1805, their diary thus describes the ascent of the river.

Finding that the river here bore considerably to the south, and fearful of passing the falls before reaching the Rocky mountains, they now changed their course to the south, and leaving those insulated hills to the right proceeded across the plain. In this direction Captain Lewis had gone about two miles when his ears were saluted with the agreeable sound of a fall of water, and as he advanced a spray which seemed driven by the high southwest wind arose above the plain like a column of smoke and vanished in an instant. Towards this point he directed his steps, and the noise increasing as he approached, soon became too tremendous to be mistaken for anything but the great falls of the Missouri. Having travelled seven miles after first hearing the sound, he reached the falls about 12 o'clock. The hills as he approached were difficult of access and 200 feet high. Down these he hurried with impatience, and seating himself on some rocks under the centre of the falls, enjoyed the sublime spectacle of this stupendous object, which since the creation had been lavishing its magnificence upon the desert, unknown to civilization. * * The river immediately at its cascade is 300 yards wide, and is pressed in by a perpendicular cliff on the left, which rises to about 100 feet and extends up the stream for a mile; on the right the bluff is also perpendicular for 300 yards above the falls. For 90 or a 100 yards from the left cliff, the water falls in one smooth even sheet, over a precipice of at least 80 feet. The remaining part of the river precipitates itself with a more rapid current, but being received as it falls by the irregular and somewhat projecting rocks below, forms a splended prospect of perfectly white foam 200 yards in length and 80 in perpendicular elevation.

This 'spray is dissipated into a thousand shapes, sometimes flying up in columns of 15 or 20 feet, which are then oppressed by larger masses of the white foam, on all which the sun impresses the brightest colors of the rainbow. As it rises from the fall it beats with fury against a ledge of rocks which extends across the river at 150 yards from the precipice. From the perpendicular cliff on the north to the distance of 120 yards the rocks rise only a few feet above the water, and when the river is high the stream finds a channel across them 40 yards wide, and near the higher parts of the ledge, which then rise about 20 feet and terminate abruptly within 80 or 90 yards of the southern side. Between them and the perpendicular cliff on the south the whole body of water runs with great swiftness. A few small cedars grow near this ridge of rocks, which serves as a barrier to defend a small plain of about three acres, shaded with cottonwood, at the lower extremity of which is a grove of the same tree, where are several Indian cabins of sticks ; below the point of them the river is divided by a large rock, several feet above the surface of the water, and extending down the stream for 20 yards. At the distance of 300 yards from the same ridge is a second abutment of solid perpendicular rock, about 60 feet high, projecting at right angles from the small plain on the north for 134 yards into the river. After leaving this, the Missouri again spreads itself to its usual distance of 300 yards, though with more than its ordinary rapidity. Captain Lewis directed his course southwest, up the river. After passing one continued rapid, and three small cascades each three or four feet high, he reached, at the distance of five miles, a second fall. The river is about 400 yards wide, and for the distance of 300 throws itself over to the depth of 19 feet, and so irregularly that he gave it the name of the Crooked falls. From the southern shore it extends obliquely upwards about 150 yards, and then forms an acute angle downwards nearly to the commencement of four small islands close to the northern side. From the perpendicular pitch to these islands, a distance of more than 100 yards, the water glides down a sloping rock with a velocity almost equal to that of its fall. Above this fall the river bends suddenly to the northward. While viewing this place Captain Lewis heard a loud roar above him, and crossing the point of a hill for a few hundred yards he saw one of the most beautiful objects in nature. The whole Missouri is suddenly stopped by one shelving rock, which, without a single niche, and with an edge as straight and regular as if formed by art, stretches itself from one side of the river to the other for at least a quarter of a mile. Over this it precipitates itself in an even uninterrupted sheet to the perpendicular depth of 50 feet, whence, dashing against the rocky bottom, it rushes rapidly down, leaving behind it a spray of the purest foam across the river. The scene which it presented was indeed singularly beautiful, since without any of the wild irregular sublimity of the lower falls it combined all the regular elegances which the fancy of a painter would select to form a beautiful waterfall. The eye had scarcely been regaled with this charming prospect, when, at a distance of half a mile, Captain Lewis observed another of a similar kind. To this he immediately hastened, and found a cascade stretching across the whole river for a quarter of a mile, with a descent of 14 feet, though the perpendicular pitch was only six feet. This, too, in any other neighborhood, would have been an object of great magnificence, but after what he had just seen it became of secondary interest. His curiosity being, however, awakened, he determined to go on, even should night overtake him, to the head of the falls. He therefore pursued the southwest course of the river, which was one constant succession of rapids and small cascades, at every one of which the bluffs grew lower or the bed of the river became more on a level with the plains. At the distance of two and a half miles he arrived at another cataract of 26 feet. The river is here 600 yards wide, but the descent is not immediately perpendicular, though the river falls generally with a regular and smooth sheet; for about one-third of the descent a rock protrudes to a small distance, receives the water in its passage, and gives it a curve. On the south side is a beautiful plain a few feet above the level of the falls. On the north the country is more broken, and there is a hill not far from the river. Just below the falls is a little island in the middle of the river well covered with timber. Here, on a cottonwood tree, an eagle had fixed its nest, and seemed the undisputed mistress of the spot, to contest whose dominion neither man nor beast would venture across the gulfs that surround it, and which is further secured by the mist rising from the falls. This solitary bird could not escape the observation of the Indians, who made the eagle's nest a part of their description of the falls, which now proves to be correct in almost every particular except that they did not do justice to their height. Just above this is a cascade of about five feet, beyond which, as far as could be discerned, the velocity of the water seemed to abate. Captain Lewis now ascended the hill which was behind him and saw from its top a delightful plain, extending from the river to the base of the Snow mountains to the south and southwest. Along this wide, level country the Missouri pursued its winding course, filled with water to its even and grassy banks, while about four miles above it was joined by a large river, flowing from the northwest through a valley three miles in width, and distinguished by the timber which adorns its shores. * * * * This river is no doubt that which the Indians call Medicine river, which they mentioned as emptying into the Missouri just above the falls.

After thus pushing up the river, Captain Clarke took the courses and distances of the several rapids and cascades, and the journal of the expedition repeats the description, commmencing above the falls and following the same route that I did, as follows :

From the draft and survey of Captain Clarke we had now a clear and collected view of the falls, cascades, and rapids of the Missouri.

This river is 300 yards wide at the point where it receives the waters of Medicine river, which is 137 yards in width. The united current continues 328 poles to a small rapid on the north side, from which it gradually widens to 1,400 yards. and at the distance of 548 poles reaches the head of the rapids, narrowing as it approaches them. Here the hills on the north, which had withdrawn from the bank, closely border the river, which, for the space 320 poles, makes its way over the rocks with a descent of 30 feet; in this course the current is contracted to 580 yards, and, after throwing itself over a small pitch of five feet, forms a beautiful cascade of 26 feet 5 inches; this does not, however, fall immediately perpendicular, being stopped by a part of the rock which projects at about one-third of the distance. After descending this fall, and passing the Cottonwood island, on which the eagle has fixed its nest, the river goes on for 532 poles over rapids and little falls, the estimated descent of which is 13 feet 6 inches, till it is joined by a large fountain boiling up underneath the rocks near the edge of the river, into which it falls with a cascade of eight. It is of the most perfect clearness, and rather of a bluish cast, and even after falling into the Missouri it preserves its color for half a mile. From this fountain the river descends with increased rapidity for the distance of 214 poles, during which the estimated descent is five feet; from this, for a distance of 135 poles, the river descends 14 feet 7 inches, including a perpendicular fall of six feet and seven inches. The river has nowbecome pressed into a space of 473 yards, and here forms a grand cataract by falling over a plain rock the whole distance across the river to the depth of 47 feet 8 inches. After recovering itself the Missouri then proceeds with an estimated descent of three feet, till at the distance of 102 poles it again is precipitated down the Crooked falls of 19 feet, perpendicular. Below this, at the mouth of a deep ravine, is a fall of five feet, after which, for the distance of 970 poles, the descent is much more gradual, not being more than 10 feet, and then succeeds a handsome level plain for the space of 178 poles, with a computed descent of three feet, making a bend towards the north. Thence it descends, during 480 poles, about 18½ feet, when it makes a perpendicular fall of two feet, which is 90 poles beyond the grand cataract; in approaching which it descends 13 feet within 200 yards, and gathering strength from its confined channel, which is only 280 yards wide, rushes over the fall to the depth of 87 feet and three-quarters of an inch. After raging among the rocks and losing itself in foam, it is compressed immediately into a bed of 93 yards in width ; it continues for 340 poles to the entrance of a run, or deep ravine, where there is a fall of three feet, which, joined to the decline of the river during that course, makes the descent six feet. As it goes on, the descent within the next 240 poles is only four feet; from this passing a run or deep ravine the descent for 400 poles is 13 feet; within 240 poles a second descent of 18 feet ; thence 160 poles a descent of six feet ; after which, to the mouth of Portage creek, a distance of 280 poles, the descent is 10 feet. From this survey and estimate it results that the river experiences a descent of 352 feet in the course of 12¾ miles from the commencement of the rapids to the mouth of Portage creek, exclusive of the almost impassable rapids, which extend for a mile below its entrance.

As I have before said these descriptions are generally accurate in the extreme. The first five-foot fall does not now reach entirely across the river, and is so near the larger descent of 26 feet, as to be a part of it. The two falls, of 19 and 47 feet respectively, and the Crooked fall (31 feet) are in such close proximity as to be simultaneously visible from a point below, forming the finest view of the series. The "beautiful fountain" spoken of is an immense spring, boiling up through the rocks at numerous points, covering a quarter of an acre of ground, and sending a stream 100 yards wide into the Missouri, its water being clear as crystal, while its temperature was 53° Fahr. that of the river just above being 70° Fahr. A remarkable fact is that the eagle's nest, described in 1805, as above quoted, still remains in the cottonwood, on the island, in the stream, and as we came within sight a bald eagle of unusual size was perched in the tree by its side. This affords a very striking illustration of the habits of this peculiarly American bird, and from its known longevity it may have been the identical eagle that Captain Lewis made historical more than half a century ago. The description of the great fall is very correct, save that in the lapse of time the vertical descent is not now more than one-fifth of the entire width. Below this we turned up Willow creek, and found the party in camp on the spot I had described to them from Lewis and Clarke's journal in the morning.

During the day we were visited by a heavy storm of rain and hail accompanied by a furious wind, which wet us to the skin and chilled us through. The result was that the Missouri was as muddy at the falls, as we were accustomed to see it below, and in every gully we found a raging torrent. The air was agreeably cooled, however, and mosquitoes temporarily ceased their annoyances.

The banks of the Missouri down to the triple fall are low, and the edge of the river easily accessible. Below, however, it flows between high, rocky bluffs upon each side. The rock forming the falls is chiefly laminated sandstone, and is so soft that it must yield easily to the action of the water. Dr. Hayden made careful geological examinations as we passed down, and sketches of the leading points of interest were also taken by Mr. Schonborn.

One of Lieutenant Mullins' horses strayed to-day, and that officer and a party of three men have gone in search of the beast. At this time (10½ p. m.) they have not yet returned.

Friday, July 13.—Before breaking camp this morning, Mr. Hutton returned to the Great falls to obtain a photograph of them, taking with him two men, and expecting to rejoin us to-night. Mr. Schonborn also started off on a second expedition to the mouth of Portage creek, for the purpose of obtaining barometical observations. The train left camp about 7 a. m , passed out of the valley of Willow creek, and started nearly due east over a level prairie. We soon found, however, that the various streams crossing our paths formed deep ravines, several of which were crossed with great difficulty, before we reached the banks of Portage creek, which were mainly perpendicular rocks, through which the fortunate finding of an old lodge trail alone enabled us to pass. This stream is about 30 feet in width, and nearly 18 inches in depth, flowing in a narrow but comparatively well-timbered valley. Beyond it we ascended by a gradual slope to a high prairie, over which we advanced for some six miles, descending then again to the banks of Fall Timber creek—a stream which takes its name from the circumstance that the Fort Benton traders cut their timber about its head. We encamped in its valley, which is here three-quarters of a mile in width, in rich grass, and amid the finest grove of cottonwoods found since leaving the Three Forks.

This is our last camp before reaching Fort Benton, and we were sufficiently fortunate to encounter some officers from that post out upon a fishing excursion. They gave us the latest news from the east, including a newspaper of May 3, and stated that troops were still at Fort Benton awaiting transportation. We also found in this vicinity a gang of charcoal burners at work for the American Fur Company.

Mr. Hutton returned at nightfall, having indifferently accomplished the object of his expedition.

The distance accomplished in the day's march was 16 miles.

Saturday, July 14.—We left camp at 7 a. m. to-day, and abandoning the valley of Highwood creek, advanced over a level prairie at a speed which the prospects of soon reaching Fort Benton decidedly accelerated. Our route bore a little east of north, the Bear's Paw mountains being in sight upon our right, while across the Missouri was visible the valley of the Teton. Our road was crossed by but a single gully containing a few pools of water, this being all that was seen until we reached the Missouri.

Fort Benton was not visible until we ascended the summit of the bluff opposite, when it burst upon us as the central point of an inspiring picture. It is located in a beautiful valley amid an amphitheatre of lofty hills. The substantial trading-houses, the shining tents of troops, and several hundred Indian lodges, filled the small plain before us, the signs of life and business contrasting forcibly with the vast solitudes through which we had for weeks been journeying. After enjoying the beauty of the prospect we descended from the bluff and encamped opposite the fort after a march of 16 miles.

I crossed the river and called upon Major Blake, commanding the detachment of troops, and learned that no boat had arrived here for me. I at once ordered one built, and, as this will consume nearly a week, I shall be compelled to reconcile myself to the delay. I hope, however, to start Lieutenant Mullins and party upon their land exploration before that time.

Clouds at night prevented observations.

CHAPTER V.

FROM FORT BENTON TO FORT UNION.

From July 15th to 22d inclusive, was spent at Fort Benton in preparations for the farther exploration of the Missouri, and the region between it and the Yellowstone. The land party consisting of about 20 men in all, under command of Lieutenant Mullins, left camp on the 20th. The boat for my detachment, who are to descend the river, was finished on the following day, and is a large flat-bottomed craft, 50 feet in length by 12 feet beam. All the preliminaries having been arranged after a pleasant sojourn at Fort Benton, whose officers treated me with great courtesy and kindness, we left that post on Monday, July 23, at 9 a. m., after finishing our packing, settling bills, and receiving the mail we were to carry below, the order was given to cast off. At first, by means of a small skiff, following the boat in which a high mast had been erected, I attempted to survey the course of the river upon the principle of the *stadia.* The rapidity of the current, however, rendered it impossible to stop the boats, and also swept away our buoys, and I was at last compelled to reluctantly abandon the project. The river surface was two feet above low water, and the channel well-defined. It flows in a narrow bed, impinging alternately upon bluffs upon each side, in almost every case the opposite bank consisting of a small plateau elevated some 10 or 15 feet above the water's level. These bottoms are usually covered with fine grass, with a few cottonwood trees, and it is in one of these that Fort Benton is located. Beyond the bluffs the country appears to be an elevated and dry plain. The Bear's Paw mountains came in sight about noon, and the general course of the river has been towards it, *i. e.,* northeast.

The tributaries of the Missouri passed to-day have not been numerous. A few miles below Fort Benton the Shonkin joins it from the south, but of all Maria's river is by far the most considerable and important. This is quite a pretentious stream, but not now sufficiently so to explain the doubt, which perplexed Lewis and Clark on reaching its mouth, as to whether it was not the Missouri itself. In fact the volume of water in the main river was not very materially increased after the junction of the Maria. Nevertheless there may have been great changes since the first decade of this century. Below this the Little Sandy, a small stream, empties in from the northwest, and we halted for the night just below its mouth, at the point at which the river bends off to southeast to pass around the base of Bear's Paw mountains. This may be regarded as the northwest bend of the Missouri. The river has lost its limpid blue color during the day, and below the Maria has assumed an appearance of ashy whiteness, although it is not yet muddy.

Our latitude to-night, as determined by north and south stars, is 48° 4′ 38″, and the distance travelled is estimated at 50 miles.

Tuesday, July 24.—We started at sunrise and made rapid progress throughout the day with the current, the course of the river being directly southeast. Towards night we passed the mouth of the Judith, a handsome stream flowing through a wide bottom, and with more timber about it than has been previously seen since leaving Fort Benton. We encamped two miles below, upon the north bank, at a point which I believe to be the spot upon which the Blackfeet treaty of 1852 was negotiated.

The general character of the country has not greatly changed from that of the region through which we passed yesterday. For the first 20 miles, however, the hills gradually increased in height and ruggedness, a yellowish-white sandstone showing itself, with strata of a darker and tougher rock running through or overlying it. The sandstone is of course very susceptible to the action of the water and the elements, and has been thus cut into all conceivable shapes, picturesque and grotesque. At a distance, with such aid as the fertile imagination can easily supply, these take on an endless variety of fanciful appearances, resembling in turn massive temples, vast colonnades, fortifications of Titanic origin, or any of the mightier *reliques* of remote antiquity. In most instances the overlying dark rock appears as the cornice of the ruins beneath, while over all reposes the thick bed of stratified earth that forms the surface of the plain above.

In some points the sandstone is broken by dikes of trap which, withstanding the exposure more effectively, is left in many places isolated like immense rocky walls piled up by human skill. One of these singular formations was full 100 feet in height and 400 feet in length, and another was seen forming a distinct and nearly perfect horseshoe. These extraordinary freaks of nature have surrounded us on both sides during our voyage to-day, and in point of scenery the journey has been exceedingly pleasant.

Wednesday, July 25.—Two miles below camp we came into the region of the "bad lands" of the Judith. These resemble those with which we became so disagreeably familiar along the Powder, and consist of high clay bluffs, washed into deep ravines and steep slopes, the strata of earth running horizontally and being easily distinguished by their different colors. Over all lies the dark rock that capped the sandstone as described yesterday, and still supports the upper soil. It would apparently be impossible to approach the river from the banks among these "bad lands," and equally impossible to construct a road over them that would withstand the action of the water. The bluffs generally slope sharply to the river's edge, and only occasionally is a level spot to be found at their foot, and even these are wholly destitute of timber and of all fuel save driftwood.

Below Cow island, however, a change took place in the nature of the country. The hills, whose sides and summits are covered with pine, recede, forming a well-defined bottom, in which cottonwood trees in small quantities again appear. There is thus abundant fuel at this point along the river banks, while many of the pines would furnish passable lumber. Navigation is, however, embarrassed by numerous rapids, and for a voyage up stream it would be indispensable to have vessels of light draft and strong motive power. Boats drawing two feet could now ascend without difficulty, two and a half feet being the least water yet found. At low water no vessel drawing over 18 inches could pass. Navigation would also be decidedly improved by the removal of a number of large boulders from the river's bed. We encamped at night upon the north bank after a day's voyage of about 50 miles.

Thursday, July 26.—To-day the nature of both the river and its banks have undergone a great change. The stream is commencing to assume the appearance of the Lower Missouri, and the water is fast taking on its proverbially muddy appearance. The hills continue to recede, and the pines upon their summit are being replaced by the familiar burned brown grass. The valley is wider and contains more timber, while the immediate river banks are sharply cut and perpendicular, the strata showing the deposits of successive overflows. Game has been abundant. Yesterday mountain sheep were seen among the "bad lands," and to-day deer and elk have been started at almost every turn of the river. A few buffalo bulls have also been visible, but no large bands, notwithstanding the fact that a few years since this was one of their great feeding grounds. We encamped at night upon the north bank near the point at which the river bends off to the south to receive the Muscleshell.

Friday, July 27.—At 10 a. m. to-day we reached the mouth of the Muscleshell, and I halted to obtain observations for time and circummeridian observations on the sun for latitude. The Musclsehell, at its mouth, gives no evidences of draining the immense region it does, as it is not more than 30 feet wide and one or two feet deep at this point, its banks being muddy and the bed of the stream, therefore, difficult to cross. Its valley is wide and well covered with young cottonwood trees. It is a favorite resort for the Indians, a large band of whom have but just left it.

After a two hours' halt, we continued our descent of the stream until we reached the point at which the river resumes its eastward course, and here we stopped for the night. Our observations at both extremes and the middle of the Muscleshell bend of the Missouri should locate it accurately in latitude.

The valley of the river continues to widen, the hills receding and becoming lower, while the cottonwoods are vastly more abundant. Just below the Muscleshell, however, some of the "bad land" bluffs again appeared.

Saturday, July 28.—Our progress to-day has been decidedly intermittent. Shortly after starting a furious wind compelled us to lay by for over an hour. This was shortly followed by a shower which prevented the topographer from attending to his duties, and we were, therefore, again compelled to halt. At 10½ a. m., however, we got under way and made an excellent run, reaching in the afternoon a point within sight of, and a few miles from, the Round Butte, which is considered half way between Forts Benton and Union. Here we halted to kill buffalo, of which a large herd was in sight.

We have passed no streams of special consequence to-day, Quarrel river being the most pretentious of any. The mouths of all the tributaries of the Missouri in this region are dry and closed with a sand bar from two to four feet above the present river level, and this is even true of the gullies, which do not now run down to the water's edge. The country in our immediate vicinity consists of wooded points and "bad land" bluffs, the latter being whiter and more washed, but of less height, than those seen above.

At sundry points in the perpendicular banks of the river, I noticed large cottonwoods with their bark and roots imbedded from four to six feet below the surface of the plain, proving that the soil which the river was now washing away had also been deposited there by it during the lifetime of the tree.

Sunday, July 29.—We passed the day as usual without moving.

Monday, July 30.—An early start was effected this morning, it being my wish to reach the mouth of the Yellowstone by next Saturday evening, and we made a successful run of over 50 miles. At one point passed we landed two men who had come with us from Fort Benton for this purpose, who propose to remain there through the winter hunting wolves. As the nearest post is Fort Union, which is fully 200 miles distant, they plainly have no especial dread of Indian hostilities.

The valley through which we have passed to-day is not greatly changed from that above, although it is wider, while the hills continue to lessen in height, and the timbered points are becoming bolder. Snags in the river are getting more numerous rapidly, and to avoid them and the frequent sandbars requires skill and steadiness of navigation. The water in the river continues to fall, but has not yet settled into its regular low-water channel.

Tuesday, July 31.—The country surrounding us to-day is the same as that through which we passed yesterday, and a description of its characteristics would thus be mere repetition. We halted at noon a mile above the mouth of Big Dry creek, which I visited. As its name indicates, it is the mere dry bed of a stream that plainly drains a large area of territory, and at certain seasons must be filled with a great volume of water. I have not been able to hear, however, of but one person that ever saw any water within its banks. The channel is 87 paces in width; between the growth of willows the distance is 330 paces, while the banks proper are full 600 paces apart. The stream, however, can have but little fall, as no hills are visible up its valley.

Our progress in the afternoon was retarded by a gale, which compelled us to tie up for two hours, but we finally reached and halted for the night at El Paso Point, the limit of steamboat navigation on the Missouri until 1859, when the Chippewa forced its way up to within 20 miles of Fort Benton.

Wednesday, August 1.—Our voyage to-day has been rendered slow and uncomfortable by high easterly winds, accompanied by rain storms, which have chilled the atmosphere and necessitated frequent halts. The valley of the river continues without special change, and we have stopped for the night, after descending but a short distance, a few miles above the mouth of Milk river. We passed in the afternoon a party of five men erecting cabins and preparing to spend the winter here trapping for wolves.

Thursday, August 2.—Westerly gales to-day compelled us to halt after another short run, although our progress was very rapid until we stopped. We passed the mouth of Milk river early in the day, but as the Missouri is here very wide and shallow, and its deepest channel is quite narrow, and runs to the north of a large island, we were unable to obtain a close view of its important tributary. The day has been cold and raw, and considerable rain fell last night.

Friday, August 3.—The night was very cold for the season, rendering blankets indispensable, but the day broke clear and beautiful, and has so continued. We effected a prompt start, and have made an excellent run, although we halted early with the hope of securing game. In this we were disappointed, however, and as the Crows are just south of us, and the Assiniboines to the north, it is probable that we shall obtain no more fresh meat, as these tribes scour the hunting grounds most thoroughly.

The country below Milk river has become much more level than we found it above, and consists as a general rule of undulating prairie, stretching off uninterruptedly to the horizon. The river is wide, shallow, and greatly obstructed by snags and sand-bars. Several times in the course of the day our boat, which draws only 10 inches of water, has grounded, and rendered it necessary that all should jump overboard to get her off. Our pilot is experienced and careful, and I do not believe that it would have been possible to avoid the bars. For this reason I question if a boat drawing 18 inches of water would find it possible to navigate the Missouri at this time. However, the water is now falling rapidly, and has not yet cut out the channel to the depth it will possess at its lower stage.

Saturday, August 4.—We managed to make fair progress to day, notwithstanding the wind compelled an hour's additional halt at noon, and we stopped for the night at the upper end of the long northeast stretch above the Big Muddy. In the afternoon navigation was rendered very uncomfortable work by a heavy rain, while the wind made it impossible to obtain a satisfactory meridian altitude of the sun.

The country continues unchanged, timber lining the banks of the river, and prairie hills reaching away into the distance. Early in the afternoon, however, a few "bad land" hills were observed to the south, distant some ten miles from the river.

Sunday, August 5.—We did not move to-day, a fierce gale, as well as my inclination, forbidding it.

Monday, August 6.—The night was cold and attended by a very heavy dew, but the day has been calm and beautiful. We started promptly and halted for noon between Fort Stuart and the mouth of the Big Muddy. The latter is now a very insignificant stream, containing but little water. Fort Stuart is an old trading post of Clark, Premo & Co., now abandoned, that firm having been merged into the American Fur Company. Our afternoon's progress was excellent, notwithstanding another gale, and we halted for the night just below the mouth of the Little Muddy.

On the south bank of the river above Fort Stuart, and on the north bank below the Big Muddy, "bad land" bluffs again are seen, their horizontal strata being yellow, red, and black, the latter indicating the reappearance of the lignite. The red strata is plainly of burnt material.

Tuesday, August 7.—After a run retarded by winds and rain, rendering one halt and considerable trouble necessary, we reached Fort Union at 3 p. m. We found that Lieutenant Maynadier had been there a week awaiting our arrival, and we shall be compelled to halt now until rejoined by Lieutenant Mullins.

Lieutenant Maynadier's report of his explorations along the Yellowstone will be found in the Appendix.

CHAPTER VI.

FROM FORT UNION TO OMAHA.

Our halt at Fort Union lasted from August 8 to 15, inclusive. Lieutenant Mullins arrived on the 11th with his animals, greatly broken down by the hardship they had undergone. He reports having experienced considerable trouble with the Crow Indians, who are exasperated at the fact that the location of the payment of their annuities has been transferred to the Platte. The report of his exploration is given in the Appendix.

From this point it was my wish that Lieutenant Maynadier should continue the exploration of the Missouri, and I therefore turned over to him the boat in which I had descended the river. A second was also obtained in the fort, this being rendered necessary by the increase in size of the parties, and also by the fact that all over baggage was to be sent down the river in them. The two were named by Lieutenant Maynadier the Jim Bridger and the Bob Meldrum, respectively, after the noted pioneers of this region. With my party, I proposed to push directly through the Sioux country southeast from Fort Union to Fort Pierre. I found it, however, absolutely impossible to obtain a guide who would venture to lead us through, on account of the disaffection of the savages, and at last I was reluctantly compelled to abandon the project. Instead, I determined to follow down, with a land party, the valley of the Missouri, but at as great a distance from that stream as would be possible with safety. Lieutenant Maynadier started at 1 p. m. on August 15, but the miserable condition of the dragoon horses prevented my party from resuming the march until the following day.

While at Fort Union I sold 40 broken-down horses to Mr. Meldrum, at $5 each, being certainly the full value of the animals in their condition. During the halt I also obtained from Major Schoonover a record of his council with the Sioux, in which I found the following language recorded as having been addressed by him to the Indians. "General Harney sent you plenty of powder and balls. If there is any dissatisfaction with the goods, it is Captain Raynolds's fault, not mine." Against the tone and spirit of this I protested to Major Schoonover, and he denied having used such language. In conclusion I stated my determination to him to investigate the matter, and satisfy myself that I was right upon the record.

Thursday, August 16.—At 8 a. m. to-day we resumed our homeward march down the north bank of the Missouri. The road was of the best character, running along the second table-land, near the foot of the bluffs, and after a march of 24.87 miles, we halted on the banks of the Muddy river, about five miles above its junction with the Missouri. We ascended this tributary of the main river thus far on account of the statement of our Indian guide that we should not be able to cross it nearer its mouth. We found excellent grass at our camp, but the water was impregnated with salt, and "buffalo chips" constituted our only fuel. The hills upon the left of our course to-day have risen from 200 to 300 feet above us, and are generally covered with tolerable a growth of grass. In some instances, however, they have been washed into "bad lands," presenting the usual horizontal strata. The country in the vicinity is a beautiful and fertile prairie of almost level surface. The river bottom upon our right has been covered with a heavy growth of cottonwood, entirely concealing the water.

Friday, August 17.—We have travelled to-day almost directly eastward over the hills, leaving the immediate vicinity of the Missouri, which makes at this point a large bend to the south. We are thus afforded an advantageous opportunity of judging of the character of the country somewhat more remote from the river banks. We found ourselves among the high rolling hills destitute of timber and covered with the greenish brown grass of autumn. Water was very scarce, and the sight stretching away to the remote horizon could detect no change in the nature of the country. Not a tree was anywhere visible, and the monotony was only broken by small and scattered bands of buffalo. The soil is clayey, with occasionally drift rock and gravel, while the boulders are of granite and limestone, and greatly water-worn. The grass would furnish excellent pasturage, and with abundance of rain the region would without doubt yield abundantly such crops as are suited to the latitude. The dryness of the climate must, however, constitute a very serious obstacle to successful agriculture, while the severity of the winters would prevent stock from running at large, as is possible further south and nearer the mountains, (as witness the experience of the expedition in winter quarters.) Travelling among these hills was decidedly obstructed by deep gullies or water courses, with steep sides, in which a few scattered and stunted trees and shrubs are growing, not visible at a distance and making no perceptible break in the general surface level. The gully sides in some instances assume the "bad lands" appearance, and perhaps from the number of these ravines I should style the region rather a broken than a rolling prairie. Our progress was of course retarded by these obstacles, but we accomplished a march of 22 miles, and halted for the night upon the banks of a small tributary of the Missouri, which the guide calls Beaver creek.

Saturday, August 18.—On leaving camp this morning we advanced along the first table-land above the river bottom over a beautiful prairie of great fertility, six miles in length by four in width. The river formed its southern limits, having no timber at this point upon its north bank, while upon the east it was bounded by the dry bed of a small stream. The plateau was covered with grass of unusual thickness and richness, while the marshy spots were indicated by a low growth of bushes. After a rapid march through this charming valley we were compelled to pass along near the foot of the bluffs, which at this point came down almost to the river banks. For ten miles further we followed a path of this character, the river bottom being constantly in sight, but the water invisible on account of the timber, and ultimately after passing a lofty "bad land" ridge, which was noteworthy for the abundance of petrified wood and stumps imbedded in its clay, we reached the river bank on the edge of a narrow plain. The water was inaccessible here, however, and we continued on for a few miles further, encamping after a march of 20½ miles upon the bank of White Earth river. This is now a sluggish and muddy stream, which can be easily stepped over at any point at which there is much of a current, but its water is fresh, and the grass abundant, and it is therefore a suitable spot for a halt over the Sabbath. Our dragoon horses, which have been stabled and corn-fed during the winter, are giving out rapidly, being totally unfit for such a tramp over the plains, and some of the escort have been mounted to-day upon mules and ponies. The night is cloudy, and observations are impossible for this reason.

Sunday, August 19.—The day has been passed quietly in camp. The weather has been quite warm, and the thermometer rising to 90°, but a pleasant breeze has moderated the heat.

Monday, August 20.—Our march to-day was short, as after advancing 12 miles we reached the upper limit of the "big bend" of the Missouri, and the day was then too far advanced to cross the intervening country, and I did not wish to encamp far from the river's bank. We therefore halted a mile beyond Upper Knife river, and encamped on a bluff some 50 feet above the Missouri. The line of march to-day ran either along the river bottom or over the first tableland, and the general characteristics of the country traversed remain unchanged. Little Knife river was crossed without difficulty, and is now a mere brook with a muddy bottom and brackish water of a red tinge. The evening has been rendered unpleasant by high winds attended by some rain.

Tuesday, August 21.—We to-day followed the chord of the arc formed by the Missouri in the upper Great Bend, and after a march of 19½ miles encamped upon the river at the lower extremity of its long curve to the southward. Our route lay still over the undulating prairie peculiar to this region, the general surface being more level than we had before found it, and no marked drainage existing. In fact we found at two or three points that ponds of water had collected from rain and melted snow, and apparently are permanent. The grass along our course was decidedly better than that generally found since leaving Fort Union. Near our camp this evening, in a boggy spot below the bank, a fine spring has been discovered, whose water is very cool, and possesses a marked chalybeate taste. We have found it necessary to drive our herd nearly a mile to enable them to reach the river for water.

Wednesday, August 22.—On resuming our march this morning we crossed, about two miles from camp, a fine running stream, called by the frontiersmen, *L'eau qui monte*, and by Lieutenant Warren, Tide river. The striking point about it (and hence its name is probably derived) is, that its course is opposite to that of the Missouri, its head laying southeast of its mouth. Beyond this we passed for 15 miles over a gently rolling prairie, leaving the Missouri far to our right; until after this distance had been traversed, we found its valley directly in front of us. We then crossed two or three small tributaries, one being quite boggy, and reaching the bluffs saw Fort Berthold before us, lying about five miles to our left. We encamped by a pond of standing water, in the edge of the timber of the river bottom, after a march of 15 miles. I immediately mounted a fast horse, and, with Dr. Hayden, rode over to the fort. I found Lieutenant Maynadier there, and also Lieutenant White, 3d artillery, with a boat, and a detachment of 60 men, who wished to accompany him in the descent of the river. This re-enforcement will swell the river party to nearly 100 men. I made arrangements for crossing my detachment to the other bank of the Missouri to-morrow morning by means of the boats, and also endeavored to obtain a guide from this point to Fort Pierre. In this, however, I was entirely unsuccessful, no one being willing to venture it. A party of Sioux were here this morning and behaved very insolently, and this has unquestionably added to the general fear. This tribe of Indians is at present in great need of sound castigation.

Thursday, August 23.—We this morning proceeded to the fort, loaded our baggage upon the boats, and crossed to the west bank of the Missouri. Some difficulty was experienced in inducing the herd to swim the river, but at last it did so in safety. After the transit had been accomplished we loaded up and pushed ahead three miles further, encamping on an excellent spot upon Dancing Bear creek. The distance travelled during the day, exclusive of the ferriage, was 7½ miles. The boats started down stream at 10 a. m., immediately after our crossing. Dr. Hayden and Lieutenant Mullins have this evening returned to Fort Berthold to make a second effort to procure a guide.

Friday, August 24.—The attempt to obtain a guide proved a failure, and although a man promised Lieutenant Mullins last evening that he would accompany us, this morning he could not be found. All the whites in this region are greatly alarmed at the hostile tone of the Sioux, and they have predicted that we will be attacked. I do not apprehend, however, any systematic attempt to waylay us, as this would be too perilous an undertaking; but it is probable that we shall be closely watched and annoyed by petty depredations. The chief embarrassment attending the lack of a guide is found in the fact that we shall not possess any reliable information as to the localities in which water can be found, and our marches may thus necessitate decided hardships. We left camp (after the return of Lieutenant Mullins and Dr. Hayden from the fort) at 7.30 a. m., and marched to the southeast over a rolling prairie covered with an excellent growth of grass, especially in the valleys and upon the hill-sides. The summits of the ridges, however, were comparatively barren from the scarcity of moisture, and the lack of rain alone prevents the country from becoming one of the finest grazing regions in the world. After a march of 16 miles we reached Knife river, and encamped upon its south bank amid good grass and a tolerable supply of wood. This stream flows in a narrow bed, 20 feet below the general level of its valley, which is here, at least, two miles in width. The banks are of stiff blue mud, which we were compelled to bridge with willows, while the stream has been repeatedly dammed by beavers, rendering crossing additionally difficult. The valley is remarkable for the scarcity of timber. High winds in the evening placed a veto upon all observations.

Saturday, August 25.—We succeeded in making an early start this morning, and continued our southeasterly course. After a march of 11 miles we came in sight of the Missouri, with Fort Clark and the Ree village distant only about five miles. We were soon visited by some 40 or 50 Indians from the village who urged us to encamp near them, but I failed to appreciate the advantage of their vicinity during our Sabbath halt, and therefore pushed on to the south-southeast, changing our course to avoid the "bad lands" near the river. We found the country more broken, and marching therefore more difficult, and we ultimately halted, after having travelled 28 miles, upon the banks of Square Butte creek. Two of our dragoon horses broke down to-day, and one of them was left upon the road, and we are compelled to mount others of the escort upon mules. The evening has been calm and beautiful, and some excellent observations place our latitude at 47° 2′.

Sunday, August 26.—We remained in camp to-day, and were visited by two white men from the Ree village, who brought with them the acceptable present of a quantity of corn. Our customary religious service was held in the morning. Towards dark it was reported that some Indians had been discovered upon the adjacent hills, and, although I doubted the fact, I urged upon the party the importance of being constantly vigilant and prepared for emergencies, and as a precaution ordered the herd to be closed up, and a strict watch kept during the night.

Monday, August 27.—We resumed our march this morning, still continuing toward the south-southeast, the country traversed consisting of a broken prairie, not differing from that through which we have been journeying for the past few days. No hills have been in sight; and, notwithstanding our extensive range of vision upon all sides, the monotony of the prospect has remained unvaried. No comparison could be more apt than that which has likened this country to an agitated ocean suddenly stilled into immobility, and travelling through it has become latterly as uninspiring, through lack of change, as a sea voyage. In crossing Square Butte creek, some ten miles from camp, we obtained our only view of the Missouri. A mile further on we struck the head of a small tributary of Heart river, and followed down it to the banks of that stream, encamping near their point of union. The latter river is now of insignificant size, being not over 10 yards in width, although its bed shows that at times it must be from 60 to 70 yards across, and contribute an immense volume of water to the Missouri. Its valley is from half a mile to a mile in width, and contains much more timber than usual. Grass has continued good along our route to-day, that upon the summit of the hill being dry and hard. We were visited last night by a heavy thunder storm, the first since leaving the mountains.

Tuesday, August 28.—Leaving Heart river we crossed the rolling prairie country again, reaching, after a march of ten miles, the banks of Mule creek, a minor tributary of the Missouri. The water in its bed was formed in pools, and, although fresh, was strongly tainted by decayed vegetation. It being still early I decided not to halt here, but push on to another camping ground. Leaving Mule creek we crossed over to a level plain, some four miles in diameter, covered with salt grass growing on a chalky white soil, and again reached the rolling hills. At one point among them we found a small grove of oaks growing upon marshy ground in a ravine, furnishing more evidence of the fact that the scarcity of timber in this region is solely due to the absence of moisture. After a total march of 27½ miles we came to the north fork of Cannon Ball river, and encamped upon its banks. We found it to be a fine running brook, with fresh, sweet water and good grass in its valley. Fuel is, however, very scarce, and we have been unable to even obtain tent-poles. Observations this evening place our present latitude at 46° 22′.

Wednesday, August 29.—On scaling the low divide south of our last night's camp, we came to a peculiar valley covered by a rank growth of grass and weeds, and with its surface cut up with numerous ditch-like water-courses filled with stagnant water. After a difficult march of about five miles we came to a chain of "bad lands," and for three miles passed over them, reaching Cannon Ball river. The bed of this stream is nearly fifty yards in width, but at present contains but little water. Its banks on each side below us are of the "bad land" formation. We crossed to the south and encamped, while I rode ahead to "prospect." By ascending a hill overtopping its neighbors I obtained an extended view of the adjacent country, but nothing save broken rolling prairie was in sight, and I am convinced that this is the nature of the whole country between the Missouri and the divide of the Little Missouri. Observations have established the fact that our present latitude is 46° 15′, and render it certain that the Cannon Ball river, that here flows to the northeast, is placed decidedly too far to the south upon the maps. A high gale prevailed all the afternoon, and toward evening we were visited by a rain-storm of brief duration.

Thursday, August 30.—From our camp on the Cannon Ball we headed directly south, and at a distance of eight miles passed the head of one of its lesser tributaries. Beyond this for five miles we crossed a succession of steep hills, emerging upon an open and level plain, over which progress was easy and rapid. From the summit of the last ridge we obtained a distant view of the divide between the Grand and the Moreau, which is apparently more elevated than any other part of the country, several hills near the Missouri being of marked height. On the plain crossed the grass was of inferior quality, while sharp angular boulders of silicious rock were scattered upon all sides in great profusion. After a march of 27½ miles we encamped upon a small tributary of the Grand river. The country to the west of us is on fire, showing the proximity of the Indians. Good observations obtained this evening place our present latitude at 45° 53′.

Friday, August 31.—Our march to the south has continued to-day. At first we turned slightly to the eastward to avoid poor travelling in the valley of the stream upon which we had been encamped, and, after nine miles' progress, we came to Ree or Grand river. As this was flowing nearly due south we followed its banks for five miles, and then as it bent to the eastward crossed and encamped in the prairie a quarter of a mile distant. The bed of the Ree river is 60 yards in width, but the water is now standing in pools. As a general rule the bed is dry and hard, though in some instances quicksands were found. The valley is fully a mile in diameter, and its soil is excellent, producing fine grass, while the timber is also more abundant than we have found it upon any of the streams yet crossed. The trees are generally cottonwoods; but some ash is found, and in the ravines small groves of an inferior oak flourished, while wild plum and cherry bushes were very abundant. The nature of the country traversed remains without noteworthy change. Game was quite plenty, especially deer and antelope. Elk tracks have been also seen, but the animal itself has not been visible. A fire broke out in camp this afternoon and threatened serious damage, as a high gale was prevailing, but it was ultimately subdued without any disastrous results. The distance accomplished in the day's march was 13¾ miles.

Saturday, September 1.—We resumed our southward march this morning, and crossing a spur of hills suddenly found ourselves, after a journey of five miles, again upon the banks of the Ree river, which makes a great bend at this point. We left its valley here, however, and entered upon a level prairie, relieved only with an occasional knoll, over whose floor-like surface we advanced for ten miles to the banks of a small stream which I originally supposed to be a tributary to the Missouri. Our animals being weary, and having no knowledge of the distance to the next "water," we halted here and encamped amid excellent pasturage. After dinner I rode to the summit of a neighboring hill and ascertained that the stream was in reality a branch of the Ree following to the northeast and joining that river at a distance of about six miles. The grass found to-day has been greener and of more nourishing quality, and in this valley the luxuriance of its growth is remarkable. The stream consists of clear cool water, but its bed is greatly obstructed by beaver-dams. The timber is chiefly confined to the scrubby black oak found in ravines. A furious wind has been blowing from the southward all day, and the evening has been marked by thick clouds and a slight rainfall.

Sunday, September 2.—The usual Sabbath quiet has been maintained. Observations this evening place our latitude at 45° 33′.

Monday, September 3.—A heavy shower delayed our start until 8 a. m., but after ascending from the valley we came upon a prairie of wide extent, distinguished by some rather unusual features. It was so level that the course of drainage could with the greatest difficulty be traced, and several ponds of water had formed upon its surface. It was, however, marked by a considerable number of buttes, rising to the height of 20 to 50 feet above the general surface, constituting very prominent land-marks. These appear to be of the same material as the plain, but a few were apparently composed of gravel and drift. Owing to the prevalent flatness of the country, they possess at a distance an appearance of much greater elevation than actually pertains to them. Across this prairie and a few "bad land" hills we advanced to the banks of a tributary of the Moreau, (which we have seen to our left and in advance, its course being northeasterly,) known as the Little Moreau, the distance of the day's march being 18¾ miles. The stream now consists of mere pools, and the grass about its banks is the poorest found since leaving Fort Benton. Its valley is but one-eighth of a mile in width, and contains the only timber seen in the day's march. The soil of the prairie crossed to-day was good and grass abundant. Just at the close of the march Lieutenant Mullins discovered two Indians watching us from a hill, but they immediately disappeared. These are the only savages seen since leaving Fort Clark, and probably belong to some scattered lodges below us on the Moreau. Observations place the latitude of our present camp at 45° 18′.

Tuesday, September 4.—Our march to-day has been exceedingly difficult. Our course has still borne southward, and we have been travelling constantly among "bad land" hills, characterized by the scantiest vegetation, and with a loose and spongy soil that has most severely tasked the powers of our animals. Eight miles from camp we reached the Moreau river, whose bed is forty yards in width, but is now almost dry. The valley is a quarter of a mile in diameter, and contains good grass and considerable timber. Seven miles beyond we encamped upon the head of a small tributary of the stream, after a day's march of 17⅛ miles. The latitude of our camp to-night is 45° 13′, and we should reach the Shayenne to-morrow. Deer, elk, and antelope have been seen in large numbers to-day.

Wednesday, September 5.—An early start this morning brought us, after a march of two miles, to the edge of a high, undulating prairie, about four miles in width, and draining into the Moreau. After crossing it we found ourselves upon the summit of the divide between that river and the Shayenne. We had travelled thus far up a gradual slope, over a good road, and amid fine grass. Before us the prospect, however, was most forbidding. The "bad lands" of the Moreau were reproduced along the Shayenne, and for 15 miles the valley of the latter was spread out before us in a series of broken, dark, and desolate hills. Near the crest of the divide we came upon a wagon track which led us, at the distance of half a mile, to an old road used by Indian traders, affording us tolerably good travelling for 15 miles, when we reached the Shayenne, crossed the river, and encamped upon its south bank. We found it to be here 50 yards in width, and flowing over a bed generally of quicksand. At the point at which we crossed it, however, a fine, gravel bottom was found, while its depth was 15 inches, the current being rapid and the water muddy. The valley is about a mile in width, and covered with long grass and a scattered growth of cottonwood. Our point of crossing is only distant seven miles from the junction of the Shayenne and Missouri.

Thursday, September 6.—A march of two or three miles this morning, amid broken hills, brought us to the level plain again, where we found the road followed yesterday, and by its aid made very rapid progress. Leaving the ravines of the Missouri upon our left we soon reached the ridge dividing that river from Chantier creek, (one of its tributaries,) and advanced along its crest to the point at which the road crossed the stream. We then turned to the valley of the Missouri, but found no suitable camping ground until we reached the banks of the river itself, where we halted after a march of 27 miles. The Chantier we found with but little water in its bed, and that too thoroughly impregnated with salt to be used. The banks of the Missouri at our camp are high and steep, and we have been compelled to dig them down to afford the herd access to the water. The night is warm, but cloudy.

Friday, September 7.—A cold northeast storm visited us last night, and this morning the river was still falling, and travelling with packs and baggage utterly out of the question, the surrounding hills being slippery with mud. Leaving the train in camp, therefore, I rode on to Fort Pierre, accompanied by Dr. Hayden and an attendant. The journey was a most uncomfortable one, but after scaling the hills with great difficulty, we found good travelling, the road running along the divide between the Missouri and Willow creek, whose drainage lies very close to that of the main stream.

We reached Fort Pierre at noon, having travelled over 2,500 miles since leaving it in May of last year. I found that Lieutenant Maynadier and party had been at the fort for five days awaiting our arrival.

Saturday, September 8.—I remained at Fort Pierre over last night, and at 1 o'clock to-day the party came up under charge of Lieutenant Mullins. They encamped about a quarter of a mile above the fort, and we at once commenced arrangements for continuing our homeward journey. Our poorest horses I ordered sold, and steps were also taken to have the others properly shod. I had the pleasure of meeting here my Sioux guide, who piloted us through the Shayenne country last year, and deserted us near Powder river, taking with him a valuable mule. He greeted me very cordially, and appeared to regard his knavery as highly amusing. The stolen mule, however, was nowhere visible, and retaliating measures were, of course, out of the question. It is also worth mentioning that this Indian described to me the entire route of the expedition as far as the Yellowstone, proving that we had been carefully watched.

Sunday, September 9.—We observed the Sabbath as usual.

Monday, September 10.—This morning the party started for Fort Randall, Lieutenant Maynadier continuing in the boats. While settling my bills at the fort with a few attendants, I received a notification that an Indian delegation desired a "talk." On meeting them I discovered that the subject of their diplomacy was a dinner from our stores, and I therefore cut short the conference by stating that my supplies had gone down stream in the boats, and furthermore improved the opportunity by adding that I was acquainted with the recent depredations of the Sioux, and if their outrages did not cease, troops would be sent to the country, and severe punishment inflicted. I then rode on and rejoined the party, which I found had taken the wrong road, necessitating the retracing of steps for some distance. As we passed old Fort Pierre I noticed that but little was left of the structure, the remains consisting of the shell of one row of houses, and the demolition of this was in progress, the material being used in the new fort. Four miles from camp the summit of the surrounding hills is reached, and at this point commences the descent into the valley of the Shicha river. We found the stream swollen by the recent rain, and it was now 20 yards in width and 2½ feet in depth. It was forded without much difficulty, and passing through its valley, which is a mile in diameter, and contains good grass and considerable timber, we climbed the neighboring bluffs and came to a high plateau. Over this we advanced until we reached the head-waters of Cabri creek, upon which we encamped after a total march of 23 miles, although the morning's error rendered our aggregate advance only 18 miles. The road followed to-day has been good, but it passes to the west of our present camp and entirely avoids the Cabri. The grass upon the hills along our route has been of fine quality. After encamping it was discovered that one of Lieutenant Mullins's mules was missing, and his packer, who had come into camp originally, also rode off in a rather suspicious manner. A sergeant and two men were despatched after the missing animal and packer.

A cold east wind is blowing this evening and rain is threatening.

Tuesday, September 11.—The sergeant and men did not arrive until 1 p. m., and we therefore did not move camp to-day. They had returned to the fort and thoroughly searched the valley of the Shicha, but without finding the mule. The packer they brought into camp, having found him while apparently in search of the animal. As all the circumstantial evidence was strongly against him, Lieutenant Mullins discharged him at once. The sergeant reports that the Shicha is swollen to a depth of four feet by recent rains, and that he found it necessary to swim its current.

Wednesday, September 12.—We resumed our march to-day, the country traversed being an elevated and rolling prairie. We did not regain the road which we had left upon our right on Monday, but travelling in this region at this season is not attended by any serious difficulties at any point. The earlier part of the march was rendered excessively disagreeable by a driving storm of rain and sleet, from which the open plain afforded no shelter, while constant motion formed our only refuge. The wind shifted in an hour or two from the east to the southward, however, and ultimately we were refreshed by warmth of atmosphere and pleasant skies. Seven miles from camp we reached Cedar creek, finding the water only in holes, while but a few trees were scattered through its valley. After a march of 21 miles we encamped upon one of the banks of Medicine creek amid capital pasturage, but with no fuel save a few dry willows. The water in this stream is also found only in pools, and is rather difficult of access from the fact that the river bed is boggy in its nature. Below us wood is more abundant, and the distant valley of Medicine creek is apparently well timbered. The grass on the surrounding hills to-day has been of capital quality, consisting of a thick growth of that short and rich variety known as "buffalo"

Thursday, September 13.—We varied our course this morning more to the east, and after a march of five miles reached Medicine creek. We found the stream was destitute of running water, but its bed was deep and muddy, and crossing was only effected with much care and trouble over an old beaver dam. Beyond this we came to a slightly undulating prairie of the same general character as that traversed yesterday, save that the swells in the surface were so slight that it was in many cases difficult to detect the course of the drainage. In some cases we passed by several marshy depressions that in the wet season are unquestionably ponds. This prairie is probably the source of American Crow creek, which lies at the east of our route. After a march of 13 miles we reached the drainage of White river, and four miles further we again struck the road from which we diverged on Monday. Following this we passed among broken hills to the valley of White river, and encamped upon its banks after a total march of 22.8 miles. We are located upon the south bank on a handsome plateau, having crossed by a capital ford, although quicksands are found both above and below. The stream is about 60 yards wide, and from one and a half to two and a half feet in depth, possessing a rapid current. It is well named as the water is chalky white in color, and possesses a strong clayey taste. Coffee made from it could be changed but little in either color or taste by the addition of milk. We found that the water was greatly improved by digging holes near the bank and permitting it to filter through, as by this means it was obtained comparatively clear. The river valley is narrow and much broken up, (by the sinuous course of the stream,) consisting of a series of small bottoms averaging over half a mile in width. Grass and trees are both abundant. Clouds and rain prevailed at night, and we have not been able to obtain observations since leaving Fort Pierre.

Friday, September 14.—We were delayed this morning by a heavy shower, but succeeded in getting in motion by 8 o'clock, following still the old road. By means of a ravine we reached the summit of the bluffs without any hard climbing, and thence marched in a nearly direct line for the southeast, over a rich soil and amid abundant grass. Some distance before us two large buttes were visible, between which we passed, finding a small stream flowing near the base of the more easterly one, which is known as Yo-ke-oke-lo-ke, or Water Holes creek. At this point the country became much more rugged, while the hills upon our right were quite broken. The road, however, avoided all the more important obstacles to travelling, and following it we crossed the creek without difficulty, although it was now filled with running water on account of the recent rains. We then passed over a spur of hills, and came again to the same creek which makes here a complete turn, and, re-crossing, encamped upon its west bank after a march of 19½ miles. The course of our day's march has been magnetic southeast.

Saturday, September 15.—Our line of march this morning was directly up the valley of the Yo-ke-oke-lo-ke, keeping in the vicinity of the stream that it might be available for camping purposes in case this should become necessary. For 15 miles we thus passed through a region agreeably varied in its features from the monotony of the plains, trees being continually in sight, consisting chiefly of post oaks and elms, too small, however, to be used for aught save fuel. After leaving the head of the stream a gradual and long ascent brought us to the summit of the divide beyond which lies the valley of the Ponka river. We here abandoned the road for sake of shortening distance, and turning to the right pushed directly for the Ponka, and encamped upon its banks after a march of 27 miles. We found this river to be now an insignificant stream, with the water mainly in pools, but running here and there. The valley is flat but not wide, and timber is quite abundant, small post oaks being the prevailing variety. The hills behind us are comparatively barren, the grass being thin, coarse and hard. Those beyond the Ponka are rolling, and there are no obstructions to travelling visible. Near the summit of the divide crossed to-day I noticed a ridge capped with limestone in place, the first rock found in place since we left the upper Missouri. The sky at sunset was clear, but soon clouded up and during the evening we were visited with rain. This has been followed by a cold wind, and the heavens are now clear and illumined with a brilliant aurora.

Sunday, September 16.—Camp was not moved to-day, and the Sabbath was observed as usual.

Monday, September 17.—We resumed our march to-day heading down the valley of the Ponka, but diverging from its source, which passed further to the south than suited our purposes. We travelled over a level country crossed by two or three valleys containing water, but no timber save three small trees upon one of the streams. The monotony of the landscape has been greater than ever to-day, and the horizon has presented the appearance peculiar to it at sea. To the right the Forked Hills are plainly visible, and they have formed the only landmarks. After a march of 25 miles we encamped upon a small tributary of the Ponka, notwithstanding the fact that a few willows constituted the only fuel upon its banks. Some few sticks were gathered together, and we were thus enabled to do our immediate cooking, and I despatched a party to the Ponka for wood for our meals to-morrow. The wind shifted from the south to the northeast during the day, and the weather has been cold and chilly with a slight fall of rain. The sky this evening has been bright and clear, and observations place our present latitude at 43°.

Tuesday, September 18.—The prospect of reaching Fort Randall and obtaining mails from home led to an early start and a brisk march to-day. To avoid a detour we at first abandoned the road and struck off across the hills, the travelling being practicable for our pack trains but not for wagons. Two miles from camp we passed across a narrow valley containing a small stream with wood upon its banks, and four miles brought us to the road which we followed to Fort Randall. It keeps upon the irregular divide between the Missouri and the Ponka, and leads down to Fort Randall along the ridge between two small tributaries of the former river. Two miles from the fort we reached the valley of one of those streams, and following it down encamped near the Missouri, 400 yards above the fort, after a march of 26 miles. I dined at Fort Randall with Colonel Monroe, and found Lieutenant Maynadier and party there awaiting us.

As we were approaching the fort, and while it was yet two or three miles distant, and not in sight, we met a couple of soldiers, who saluted us with the question, "Whose party is this ?" On my replying, "Captain Raynolds's," I noticed a look of surprise, which was explained when I met Colonel Monroe, the commanding officer, who expressed great satisfaction at my arrival, as they had had a report for some days that my whole party had been cut off by the Indians.

It seems that a small command from Fort Randall had been over to Fort Laramie, and had there learned that some professedly friendly Sioux had reported that my whole party had been cut off north of the Black Hills, and at last accounts only two were alive, who were running for dear life. This rumor had been carried from Fort Randall to Sioux City and there got into the papers, causing no little uneasiness to my friends. Colonel Monroe said the story came so well authenticated that he was expecting orders to look me up.

I was happy to inform him that we were yet in the land of the living, and had not even seen a hostile Sioux, though I have no doubt many of them saw us. My explanation of the story is, that the Sioux, having said so much about destroying my party, thought it necessary to keep up appearances for a time by reporting they had done so, but that they could not screw up their courage to the point of making an attack which they knew would be vigorously resisted and result in the death of some of their number. It was the opinion of all the traders that we would be attacked, and they attributed our safety to our not having shown any disposition to yield the right, under the Harney treaty, to go where we desired.

September 19 *and* 20.—We spent these two days at Fort Randall, being employed in preparations for the continuance of our journey to Omaha, in which my detachment should again descend the Missouri along its banks, and Lieutenant Maynadier still take charge of the boats. At this fort I obtained money upon my checks, and paid to every member of the expedition a sum sufficient to take them to their several destinations, in order that they might be saved the necessity of purchasing coin at a premium at Omaha. I was greatly interested in a visit paid to the fort gardens, which richly repay the careful attention they receive. I have never seen finer vegetables, the beets especially being of gigantic size. The potato crop, for some unexplained reason, had this year proved a total failure. The fertility of the soil is great, and notwithstanding the fact that the past season has been attended by unusual moisture, and the luxuriance of agriculture is thus partially explained, there is no doubt that this region is fully as productive as any in a similar latitude.

Friday, September 21.—We resumed our homeward march at 9 a. m. to-day, passing down the valley of the Missouri. Four miles from the fort the river runs up to the foot of the bluffs upon the west bank, and the road passed over a series of broken spurs with interlying ravines, and at a distance of four to six miles again entered the valley. Eleven miles from the fort we came to the first house that we had seen in two years, built and inhabited by one of the inevitable Smith family, who had secured his claim by cultivation of the land. Three miles further on we encamped upon the river bank opposite the Yancton Agency. I crossed the river and visited Colonel Redfield, the agent, and the buildings and grounds of the agency. Many and important improvements were in progress. A large stone house and stables were in process of construction, and two or three comfortable log-houses were finished and occupied. I also found a steam saw-mill in busy operation. Attached to the agency there are 170 acres of land, well fenced and under cultivation. Colonel Redfield reports that his crops are doing finely, and he is raising corn, wheat, oats, and buckwheat. This agricultural experiment is more interesting from the fact that the farm is located upon the first table land, not upon the river bottom, and there is no diminution in the productiveness of the soil. I have no doubt of the supereminent qualifications of this country as an agricultural region, provided it can be demonstrated that there is a sufficient annual fall of rain.

Saturday, September 22.—On commencing our march this morning we were compelled to retrace our steps for some distance to reach the ridge between the Missouri and the Ponka, the drainage of the latter stream coming quite close to the valley of the former. Following this crest to the southeast for some 15 miles, we had both rivers constantly in sight. Upon reaching the Ponka we found it too muddy to cross, but after a short search a wagon ford was discovered, and by it passed through without difficulty. This river is not more than six or eight yards in width, and six to ten inches in depth, but the muddiness of its banks, and the fact that its bottom is to a large extent quicksand, render great care necessary in selecting points for crossing. Its valley is three-quarters of a mile in width, and covered with a rank growth of grass and weeds. Beyond the Ponka our road again entered the hills, and finally after a march of 20½ miles we encamped upon the banks of a small stream of running water, whose valley was marked by the presence of considerable timber. During the latter part of our march we passed an embankment of earth about three feet in height, forming a circular enclosure nearly 250 feet in diameter. Within were scattered about the remains of Indian lodges, indicating that this was the site of an abandoned Ponka village. The tribe still continue, it is said, to construct their villages in this manner. Near our camp upon the hillside are several mounds freshly thrown up, and constituting a Ponka cemetery. The *modus operandi* of erecting these mounds is as follows: Two perpendicular stakes are planted in the ground and connected by a horizontal bar resting on their tops. Slanting poles are then laid upon each side resting upon the ridge, and forming a species of wooden tent, within which the dead bodies are laid, when the whole is covered with earth forming a high circular mound. The fact that these practices still continue among the Indians of this age may possess some bearing upon the efforts being made to calculate the supposed great antiquity of the Indian mounds of Ohio and the west and south.

Sunday, September 23.—We passed the day quietly in camp, with the usual services. Last night I sent a messenger to the neighboring settlements of Niobrara and obtined a few potatoes, a luxury unknown heretofore during the expedition.

Monday, September 24.—Early this morning I left camp in company with Dr. Hayden and drove over to the town of Niobrara for the purpose of purchasing supplies and procuring a guide and interpreter. We found the country becoming somewhat more broken as we approached the river, and in crossing that stream we were greatly embarrassed by quicksands, being finally compelled to dismount to allow our horses to extricate themselves, thus getting most thoroughly wet. The Niobrara is broad and shallow, and a ride of two and a half miles from it across a level bottom, on which fine-looking corn was standing, brought us to the town. Niobrara consists of a three-story hotel and about a dozen houses, but its inhabitants now comprise but nine families, the others having gone on to the mines. I received an Indian guide for the train, and he brought it safely across the river without the trouble experienced by Dr. Hayden and myself. After leaving the town we advanced down the Missouri for three miles to the mouth of Basil creek. We thence pushed up the latter stream for a mile, crossed it, advanced through the hills to the southeast, and encamped upon the banks of one its branches after a march of 18 miles. Our camp is amid excellent pasturage and with abundance of water. Fuel is also plenty, although the banks of the stream are not very thickly timbered. Basil creek is larger at present than many water-courses in this country that are dignified with the title of rivers. Its width is 10 yards, its depth 18 inches, and its current quite rapid. Its valley is not wide but the soil is very fertile, and at the point of crossing there is a farm-house surrounded by 50 acres of cultivated land, corn constituting the chief crop. The latitude of our camp this evening is 42° 40′.

Tuesday, September 25.—Our course to-day has borne to the southeast, and we encamped at night upon the head of Basil creek. The country traversed has been more broken, and the soil poorer on account of the large admixture of sand. The grass, although abundant, is of a much coarser and less nutritious quality. Its stalk is hard and dry, and usually long, (not unfrequently from three to four feet,) and the blade is broad and of a reddish tinge. Ten miles from last night's camp we crossed a stream of running water, flowing over a gravelly bottom, and with considerable timber upon its banks. At our camp this evening water is only found in holes, and is scarcely accessible on account of the mud. Our supply of fuel has been obtained from half a dozen large elms. Observations this evening place our present latitude at 42° 29′.

Wednesday, September 26.—We have travelled to-day over more level country than we have found lately, and the undulations in the prairie have been barely sufficient to disclose the course of the drainage. Four miles from camp we crossed the ridge dividing the waters of the Platte from those of the Missouri, and seven miles further on we crossed one of the branches of the Elk Horn, whose muddy bottom troubled us decidedly. The bed of this stream is 50 feet in width, and a few scattered trees grow upon its banks. After a march of 20½ miles we finally encamped upon the banks of this same stream, and have now reached the limits of the land survey, and connected our line of reconnoisance therewith. At this point the stream, which is named Echo creek by our Indian guide, is 10 yards in width and 18 inches in depth, and its bed is sand gravel, the banks, however, being very muddy. This afternoon we have been visited by a small party of Ponka Indians, from a village distant but a mile or two. They report that a fresh wagon track, which we had noticed during the march, was made by a vehicle from the town of Ponka, and that it passed by this point yesterday. The weather has been beautiful to-day and the air bracing. The night is also clear and pleasant, and observations place our latitude at 42° 14′.

Thursday, September 27.—We followed the general course of Echo creek this morning, diverging slightly from it to the left, and heading south by east, passing over a level country with an inferior and sandy soil, and striking the Elkhorn two miles from the junction of its tributary. The valley of the river, which is wide and level, is much more fertile than the surrounding plains, and the growth of minor vegetation and of shrubbery is luxuriant. The Elkhorn itself is about 50 yards in width and nearly two feet in depth, flowing over a sandy bed with a rapid current. We encamped upon the river bank, after a march of 21 miles, having come up with the party from the village of Ponka whose wagon tracks we had seen a day or two since. They were on a hunting excursion, but had thus far met with poor success. The latitude of our camp is 41° 59′.

Friday, September 28.—To-day we have advanced for 22 miles down the valley of the Elkhorn, and are to-night encamped upon its banks, near the point at which it changes from its easterly course to southeast. Sixteen miles out we crossed a small tributary, being compelled before so doing to repair an old and dilapidated bridge. The valley continues wide, and the surrounding hills are gently undulating. Its soil is an alluvial deposit of exceeding richness and fertility. Timber is scarce, however, a few cottonwoods growing in the immediate vicinity of the river, some of fair size. There is far too little to even meet the wants of the section in which it is found, much less to afford any supply to the barren plains around.

Saturday, September 29.—Our course to-day has been generally east-southeast. For eight miles we continued down the valley of the Elkhorn, which remained unchanged in its character, and then passed through the hills and over a level and slightly undulating prairie to the banks of Plum creek, upon which we encamped for the night. The march has been rendered very disagreeable by a cold east wind and frequent showers. After encamping two houses were seen upon our right, distant over two miles. I visited them, and found the people to be of a better class than the ordinary frontier farmers. They seem to be doing well with the ground they cultivate, and were troubled with no scarcity of food. The great lack are educational and religious facilities. I obtained from them some potatoes, poultry, and butter, which have been decided luxuries in our supper.

Sunday, September 30.—The day has been stormy and disagreeable, and our last Sabbath in camp has been observed as usual.

Monday, October 1.—We resumed our march this morning, with a chilling east wind blowing, and, crossing Plum creek, advanced to the southeast over a prairie identical with that traversed on Saturday. We ultimately reached the wide, fertile valley of Logan's creek, and came to the banks of that stream, which is 40 feet in width, and possessed of a very rapid current. We crossed it by a substantial bridge, erected by the settlers of the vicinity, and advancing two miles further encamped upon a small tributary of the creek, after a march of 21 miles. The valley of Logan's creek is poorly timbered, containing only a few scattered trees, with here and there a small grove. Its soil is very productive, however, and we passed some beautiful corn belonging to a farmer living near the bridge. Our latitude this evening is 41° 48′.

Tuesday, October 2.—We have followed an excellent road to-day, running in a rather crooked course along the divide between Logan's and Belt creeks. The general characteristics of the surrounding country have remained unchanged. After a march of 17 miles we suddenly came into the settlements, houses bursting into sight at a dozen points, and the country assumed all the peculiar beauties due to cultivation, unknown to us for so long a time and therefore the more thoroughly appreciated and admired. We advanced two miles further to a spring in the vicinity of the village of Fontanelle, which contains about 50 houses, and here encamped. Our latitude this evening is 41° 34′.

Wednesday, October 3.—Our march to-day ended on the Platte road, where we soon found indisputable proof of our having again reached the influence of civilization in the fact that the party speedily procured liquor, which produced a general disturbance in camp. The soldiers and citizen employés became engaged in so heated and senseless a dispute that it became necessary to separate their camps, and I thought at one time that the drunken quarrel might end in fatal consequences. Prompt and vigorous measures were taken and alone quelled the disturbance, and I heartily rejoiced that throughout our long journey we had been beyond the reach of this terrible curse, which has occasioned the only difficulties which have disgraced the expedition.

Thursday, October 4.—We this morning effected an early start, and after a brisk march closed our arduous labors by entering Omaha, where I found Lieutenant Maynadier waiting, and consolidated the expedition for final disbandment. Our friends received us cordially, and those at a distance were promptly notified of our arrival by telegraph, and by mails and despatches awaiting us we were soon in possession of intelligence of our homes and families, the want of which had constituted one of the chief deprivations we had been compelled to undergo.

As soon as possible the expedition was disbanded, all its affairs settled, and its members dispersed to the various duties and avocations that succeeded their life on the plains and among the mountains of the Great West.

Report of First Lieutenant H. E. Maynadier, 10th infantry, on route between the Yellowstone and Platte rivers, 1859.

WINTER QUARTERS, DEER CREEK, N. T.,
January 27, 1860.

SIR: In accordance with your instructions, I commenced, on the 2d of September, 1859, a reconnoissance of the country between the Yellowstone and the Platte rivers, by the way of the Rosebud, Tongue, and Powder rivers. The party under my command separated from the other on Tullock's creek, and proceeded up that creek. This is a small tributary of the Big Horn river, running obliquely through the Wolf Hills, in a northwest course.

It flows in a narrow valley in a very crooked channel, so that it was difficult to find a road for wagons along it, it being necessary to cross the stream frequently, and to cut the road in many places through heavy cottonwood timber and willow thickets.

The stream was dry, except in holes at long intervals, and we had no good water during our march along it. The surface water was so stagnant, and so strongly impregnated with alkali, that it could not be used, and the supply obtained by digging in the bed of the creek was very little better. Our success in obtaining water by digging was precarious also; for while at one camp an abundance, such as it was, was had at the depth of a few feet, at the next, only 12 miles above, a pole sunk 19 feet failed to procure a drop. The bottom of this creek is of stiff blue clay, varying in thickness and resting on sand and gravel, from which water can be obtained when the clay can be removed. At one camp (September 6th) we found a pond of beautiful clear water, and were congratulating ourselves upon the discovery, when on trial the water was found to be bitter with alkali, and produced violent nausea upon all who drank it. Fortunately, the animals drank it freely, and with no bad effects.

Near its head Tullock's creek divides into three forks, and the hills change from their ridge-like, precipitous character into gently sloping declivities, clothed in luxuriant grass, and dotted here and there with groves of pine trees. On the 7th September we left this creek, and following its left branch, guided by an old lodge-trail, we crossed the divide between it and the Rosebud, whose clear, running water and beautiful valley formed a delightful contrast to what we had left behind us. Resting here a day, we proceeded up the Rosebud, the lodge-trail guiding us as before, and travelled by a very fine road along the valley of the stream. Our route lay along this stream until the 11th September, and I may say generally that a finer natural road cannot be found. The valley traverses two ranges of the Wolf mountains almost at right angles, and is sometimes in its abrupt turns to all appearances closed by some lofty peak; but only in appearance, for it has a uniform width of about half a mile, and is level and free from ravines. The stream runs in a deep, narrow bed, fringed with willow and box-elder, the only timber, and would be difficult to cross with wagons. This, however, can easily be avoided, without materially lengthening the road, and in fact it was necessary to cross it but twice in the 30 miles which we travelled on it. The Rosebud also divides near its head into numerous branches, some dry, some constant streams. Just before leaving it the road enters a valley so narrow, and shut in by such precipitous hills, that it may be called a cañon, and forming a view rarely equalled in picturesque grandeur. The tops of the hills are densely covered with pines alternating with bare castellated cliffs of red clay and sandstone, presenting in the combination of dark rich green and glowing scarlet a contrast of color highly pleasing. Indeed, among all my recollections of the trip, the valley of the Rosebud holds the highest place for beauty.

At the point where we left it on the 11th September the course of the stream changes abruptly to the west, while the road continuing southeast ascends a ridge, affording a view of the tributaries of Tongue river. To the north the surface of the country is one mass of barren peaks, filling the whole space between Rosebud and Tongue rivers, and forming the middle of the three ranges of the Wolf mountains. Any attempt to traverse it with wagons is useless, as we came very near finding to our cost; the southern chain of the Wolf mountains was in plain sight, and our route lay in a valley along the foot of it; but happening to bear too far to the north, we soon found ourselves in a pocket, with no escape except by the way we entered. Retracing our steps we gained the proper road at an expense of five or six miles, which lengthened the day's march to 22 miles, and made it near night when we reached Tongue river, having a good road in its valley, only interrupted in a few instances by ravines not very difficult to cross, and with good crossings of the stream when they became necessary.

The character of this river at this point is similar to that below. It is 30 yards wide, flowing in a bold stream over a bottom of stones and coarse pebbles. Its general course is east of north, though its bed is very crooked and winding. It is well-timbered, and an abundance of good grass is found on its banks. The hills bordering the valley are low and rounded, but immediately behind them comes the chain of barren clay peaks which had hemmed us in from the start.

You had expressed a wish that I should go directly across from Tongue to Powder river, if it was possible, and I made an examination of the country with a view to ascertain whether I could do it. My experience of the day before among the hills, and the appearance of the country, satisfied me that it would be hazardous to leave a water-course, and impossible to take the wagon and carts over the hills Accordingly our route lay up the valley of Tongue river. I should mention here that near where we struck the river there is a large and unfailing spring. It is immediately on the river bank, and issues from beneath a bluff.

On the 13th September, after travelling along the main river six miles, we came to the mouth of the East fork, a stream about the size of the Rosebud, and resembling it in its general features. Tongue river here turned to the west, the course along the fork being south of east. Finding a good road along its banks we travelled to very near its head, finding it also dividing into several branches. Near its head, water was scarce, and our last camp on it (September 16th) was quite as bad as any on Tullock's fork.

On the 17th we went from this fork to the Clear fork of Powder river, crossing a divide very different from those previously crossed. There was no well-defined ridge, but a high plateau of undulating hills, three or four miles wide, to which the ascent was steep and short, and from which it was difficult to descend. We found a tolerable road, however, along a dry ravine running into the Clear fork, travelling sometimes on its banks, sometimes on its bed, and having no greater mishap than an occasional upset.

The Clear fork of Powder river, where we struck it, has a wide valley, but for some miles is destitute of timber. Being instructed to get to as low a point on Powder river as possible, I determined to follow down the Clear fork to its mouth, and accordingly on the 18th and 19th September our route lay along that stream. About 12 miles below the point where we struck it, the valley of the stream contracts between cliffs of clay more barren and broken, if possible, than any we had yet seen, and the road becomes very difficult. The stream runs from side to side of the valley, under steep bluffs, and the only road to be found crosses and re-crosses continually, making it very laborious and tedious travel.

The most marked feature is the occurrence of an immense bed of lignite, showing on each side of the stream to a thickness of four feet above the surface of the water and extending apparently much deeper below it. Masses weighing as much as 500 or 600 pounds are seen lying in the bed of the stream and along its banks. At one spot at the foot of a bluff it was seen in a state of combustion, and in many places there were appearances of its having been entirely consumed.

On the 20th September we reached the junction of the Clear Fork and Powder rivers, and took a route along the valley of the latter. This stream flows through a densely timbered bottom, over a bed of soft mud and quicksand. The water is very turbid and the current sluggish, and it is difficult to find a place where it can be crossed without sinking animals and wagons in its slimy, treacherous bed. There was no choice, however, for a glance at the hills and the ravines forbade any attempt to keep on the higher ground, and we were forced to make our way along the crooked banks of the river the best way we could. To avoid frequent crossing the wagons and carts were sent around the bends, cutting the way through cottonwood and willow, and making, with great labor, only three or four miles a day. The river was crossed four times, and each time the wagon sank in the quicksand, and had to be unloaded and dragged out by ropes. On the 25th September we reached the mouth of Sandy fork, or Crazy Woman's fork, as it is called by the Arapahoes, and that offering some prospect of better travelling, I determined to go up it until I struck the trail of the other party. In addition to the experience of the last five days I was influenced in the determination to leave Powder river by a rise of water, which took place on the 24th, as well as because I had ascertained, to my entire satisfaction, that any further effort to go up Powder river would be entirely useless.

From September 26 to October 2, the route followed Crazy Woman's fork a distance of about 60 miles. At first it was repetition of the troubles of the main stream, heightened by raw, rainy weather, but as we ascended the creek the country opened and we came into a very fair road. On the 30th September we came to a village of Arapahoes of about 60 lodges, under the chief Little Owl. They were very well disposed, and one of the principal men (Friday) being able to speak English fluently, I obtained from him much information about the remainder of the route, and news of the other party. I made a feast at my camp for the principal men, and they seemed perfectly satisfied with their treatment. Next day, October 1, we moved camp to a branch of Crazy Woman's fork, and were followed by a number of Arapaho lodges. On the 2d of October, at 10 o'clock a. m., we arrived at the trail of the party under your command, and followed it until the 12th, when the two parties united at the Red Buttes on Platte river. It is unnecessary for me to enlarge upon that portion of the route which was upon your trail, further than to refer you to the intinerary accompanying this for each day's march. The reconnoissance, although unmarked by any occurrence of great importance, was not without incidents of minor character, and I am sure it will be pleasantly remembered by all who were engaged in it. As matter of natural history I may mention that the entire route was through a country abounding in game, and our tables were abundantly supplied with mountain luxuries, while many valuable and choice specimens were collected by the gentleman in charge of that department. For the details of the topography and meteorology, &c., I refer you to the maps, sketches, and records of the gentlemen respectively charged with those branches. It affords me great pleasure to bear witness to the industry, activity, and zeal displayed by the gentlemen associated with me in the performance of their several duties, and at the same time to report the excellent conduct of the hired men and the escort, a detachment from the 2d infantry.

Very respectfully, your obedient servant,

HENRY E. MAYNADIER,
First Lieutenant 10th Infantry.

Captain WM. F. RAYNOLDS,
Commanding Yellowstone Expedition.

CHAPTER I.

FROM SWEETWATER RIVER TO THE YELLOWSTONE.

The expedition commanded by Captain Raynolds left its winter quarters on the 10th of May, and on the 12th reached the Red Buttes, where a snow-storm prevented further movement until the 14th. At this point the command was to separate, and the party under my charge to travel up the Sweetwater and across the Big Horn mountains to the Yellowstone.

The morning of the 14th of May dawned clear and bright, though the air was cold and the mantle of snow upon the surrounding hills was more suggestive of January than of May. Captain Raynolds started first with his party, and soon after the rest were on the way. I had for assistants Mr. Snowden, topographer, Mr. Fillebrown, meteorologist, Dr. Hines, physician, Messrs. Trook, Waring, and Lee, general assistants, and Paul Deval, guide. In addition to these were 23 packers, herders, and drivers. Our baggage and stores were packed on mules and carried in carts, the latter destined to be abandoned when the the road became impracticable for wheels. Rising the hill from the Red Buttes, we took our way along the well-worn road toward the Sweetwater and soon lost sight of the Platte, and the cliffs which give name to the locality. After a tiresome march, made very disagreeable by the cold wind in our faces, and the slippery, muddy road, we reached the summit of the divide between the Platte and Sweetwater, and camped at the Willow spring. This name is given to a spring which issues from the top of the ridge, and though the willows are gone, the roots and stumps furnish a scanty supply of fuel. Next day, May 15th, the cold wind from the west continued, but it was impossible to stop where we were, and we set out for the Sweetwater.

The road descended gradually and was broad and smooth, but the gravel made the mule's feet sore, and the dust and sand blown up by the wind were very painful to the eyes. It was a relief to reach the bridge, and after crossing, to camp in the shadow of Independence Rock, on the banks of the beautiful Sweetwater.

This river has been the theme of nearly every traveller on the plains, and well deserves all the praises bestowed on it. Its valley forms a continuation of the noble valley of the Platte, and seems especially located by nature for a passage-way across the dry and barren "plains" from Independence Rock to the South pass. The road in the valley of the Sweetwater resembles an avenue in width and smoothness, and all, too, without the aid of man.

Independence Rock is a large isolated mass of granite 90 or 100 feet high, elliptical in shape, and covering about an acre. A short distance from it is the Devil's Gate, one of the most striking features of the landscape; it is a gap with vertical sides of solid granite, through which the river has forced its way, and now it thunders through, leaping and foaming from rock to rock as if in triumph at its victory over the massive stone.

The road winds round the point of the cliff, and passing a low hill, the beautiful valley breaks upon the view. Far ahead is the pass of the Pilot Butte road; to the left the South Mountain fills the landscape, with its rounded form relieved against the distant blue ridge of the Medicine Bow Hills, and to the right the Split Rock tells the traveller where his day's journey will end. The valley is bounded to the north by the Rattlesnake Hills, a ridge of bare rocks made up of spurs, running obliquely to the course of the stream, and forming hills at regular intervals along the road. In places the road passes close under the towering rocks, and again they recede, until at about 100 miles from the Platte the ridge turns to the north, and is lost among the more imposing shapes of the Big Horn mountains.

On the 20th of May we had reached a point on the Sweetwater above the turn of the hills, and had an open horizon to the north, indicating that here we were to leave the road and proceed towards the Popo-Agie. At first we travelled over a sage plain, sloping upwards to a ridge of clay hills terminating abruptly in a regular-shaped butte of clay, capped with sandstone. Reaching this, the valley of Wind river was visible, and there seemed to be a gentle, regularly sloping prairie from where we stood to the valley of the stream. The Wind River mountains bounded the view to the west, and formed a picture rarely witnessed; their summits glistened with the whitest snow, while their bases were seamed and wrinkled by dark cañons and precipices black with pine trees.

The anticipation of a level road to the Popo-Agie was not realized, for we had hardly gone three miles from the butte, before our journey was stopped by the verge of an abrupt precipice, which had been concealed by a slight swell in the surface of the prairie. After looking in vain for some place to descend, night came on and we camped on the side of a mountain which we had reached after skirting the precipice for four or five miles. This was a singular feature even in this land of anomalous scenery, and deserves a detailed description. Looked at from the plain below, it has the appearance of being a ridge or bank of baked red clay, with a cornice of sandstone worn into a thousand fantastic furrows by the storms, and buttressed in places by the cones and slopes of detritus. This line or bank extends about 13 miles in a curved course, connecting a range of low hills with the spurs of the Wind River chain, and bounds a valley containing the Big and Little Popo-Agies.

The camp we were compelled to make was on the side of a hill at the northern end of the precipice, in a grove of pines, clustered round the head of a ravine which contained a spring. Next day, May 21st, we descended the hill with great labor, breaking the axle of a cart in the effort, and reached the Little Popo-Agie. Here we remained one day to send back for the broken cart, and determine the best course to the junction of the Wind river and Big Popo-Agie. The plain was so broken up by ravines that it was difficult to travel, but by heading some, and crossing others, we reached the mouth of Popo-Agie May 23d, after a long day's march, and a very round-a-about, crooked line of travel.

At the mouth of Popo-Agie Captain Raynolds was encamped, and had been waiting for us for three days. On the morning of the 24th he left to continue up Wind river, while I was to descend the stream and try my fortunes in the mountains, which were already in plain sight before me. Lieutenant Mullins joined me with a detachment of men for an escort, and on the 25th the party set out down the Big Horn. I shall use the name Big Horn to designate the river formed by the junction of the Wind river and Big Popo-Agie. Of these two, the Wind river is the larger and longer.

On the 26th of May we reached the foot of the mountains at the opening of a cañon, which seemed to promise a practicable pass, and we accordingly entered it. For a mile and a half it was good enough, and finding a good spot we camped. Next day we reached the summit of the mountain, after travelling three miles over a road so steep that the mules could carry only half packs, and could draw only the empty carts, their loads being packed.

Here we camped on a small stream, and encountered a very severe storm of rain. When night fell, the spot where we had camped on the mountains was shrouded in a mist so thick it could almost be felt, and during the night it dissolved into a pouring rain, soaking through tents and completely saturating everything. The morning of the 27th set in clear and bright, though cold from the great elevation, and enabled us to dry ourselves and our things by noon, when we set out to descend the mountain. After proceeding a short distance we struck upon a stream of fine water descending rapidly, but flowing in a fine valley, along which the carts proceeded without difficulty. This valley, although so near the summit of the range, contained an excellent soil, and was well stocked with grass, which even at this time had attained full growth. This is to be attributed to the fact that the valley was in the angle between the main range and a spur, being protected by the latter from the north wind, and not overshadowed by the former, so that the sun even in a low declination had full action upon it. The descent of the valley was so considerable, that the wagons and carts required no pulling, and in places the wheels were locked. In about five miles we had descended to a dry ravine, heavily timbered, and running along the foot of a vertical ridge of red sandstone; here our first stream turned abruptly to the south, and after the fashion of water-courses in this region, plunged in a cañon, and was lost to sight. Passing on to the dry ravine, which was from 10 to 15 yards wide, and five feet deep, we travelled down it and camped about sunset on the Big Horn river. At this place there was a flat bottom on the river of four miles in length, and half a mile wide in its widest part, which was where the ravine we travelled down came into it. At the southern end the river emerged abruptly from a cañon, and to the north and below our camp it passed around the foot of the sandstone spur, cutting off all travel in that direction.

On the morning of the 29th of May I despatched three men to search for a route along the river, and went myself to visit the cañon, or rather the end of it. The range at this point presents a bold face of rock on the southern side, through a cleft in which the river enters. From the summit it has a slope of about 15° to the plain in which we were camped, and through this mass the river runs. The total length of the cañon is four miles; its width nowhere more than 200 yards; and its depth in the centre must be 1,500 or 1,600 feet. At the northern end there is a valley which closes rapidly in until the end of the cañon is only as wide as the stream, and has the appearance of a gate. The sides are vertical, and stratified with such regularity as to give the idea of artificial masonry. The valley, or, as it might be called, the approach to the cañon, is bounded by a cliff of sandstone, worn by wind and storm into arches resembling casemates, the tops and sides covered with the nests of swallows, and the caverns resounding with their cries when we disturbed them. Though deficient in the elements of vastness and grandeur which had been the characteristics of the scenery for the previous six days, the picture was none the less beautiful, and I almost imagined myself looking upon the ruins of an ancient fortification.

At the foot of the cliff, and near the opening of the valley, a fine spring of sulphur-water bursts out. It is strongly impregnated with sulphur, and has the greenish-white appearance and pellucid clearness of that kind of water. Its temperature is considerably above that of the river, but it cannot properly be called a hot spring. Within a few yards of it is a smaller spring of good sweet water, which unites its waters with those of its neighbor, and both flow into the Big Horn. The messengers returning informed me that no road could be found along the river, and the only way was to return along the dry creek, and keep in its valley until the summit of the spur was reached.

This we accordingly did; and after a toilsome day's march encamped on a small stream of water near the summit of the spur. Next day, May 30th, we crossed the divide and descended a very steep rocky hill to a dry ravine, containing some cottonwood timber.

The river affording the only water to be had, we continued along the ravine until we reached it about half-past 6 p. m., after a day of excessive toil. It now became evident that our further course must be made without wheeled vehicles, and also that no road even for pack-animals could be found entirely in the river valley. For three days we had been laboring in the broken region, making very little progress, and using up animals and men. Accordingly on the 31st of May I gave orders to remain in camp and prepare everything for packing, reserving only the light ambulances for instruments; all heavy and unnecessary property was abandoned, and the carts broken up to make pack-saddles and axe-helves.

We had now penetrated beyond the highest spurs of the Big Horn mountains, and were in a region of low barren hills, broken in every direction by tortuous ravines, and interposing a cliff or a chasm wherever we turned. From the summit passed yesterday the view was sublime. Immensity was the idea that filled the mind when gazing upon the scene, and no sketch can do it justice. The upper or northern range of Big Horn mountains closed in the picture in that direction, their shapes rounded by distance into an undulating outline, save where some lofty peak reared its snowy crest so high that the eye could not distinguish where the solid fabric of the mountain ended, and the vaporous substance of the cloud commenced.

Far in the blue haze of the northwest the Snow mountains appeared, and beyond them, barely discernible, the Rocky mountains, the limit of our labors. Between all was barren, dry, broken, and heaved up as if some sea had suddenly congealed into waves of earth, crested with rocky foam. Yet, as my fancy warmed with this wealth of desolation before me, I found something to admire in the calm self-denial with which this region, content with barren magnificence, gives up its water and soil to more favored countries. The immense net-work of ravines, and aggegation of peaks and cones, gave evidence of the torrents poured out by the melting snows of the mountain tops, and the great rush of waters which makes the Missouri and Mississippi what they are in the spring.

Within the curve of the main range the spurs are crowded and confused, producing this strangely broken country I have endeavored to describe, which continues westerly with a gradual ascent to the Rocky mountains. Though of no great height, the broken ridges effectually bar travelling, and it would be expensive and difficult to construct a road through them.

June 1.—Started early with only the light ambulances and one wagon belonging to the escort, besides our pack-mules. The valley of the river afforded a tempting path, and I had strong hopes of being able to travel without climbing; but, in about three miles, the inevitable bluff stopped the way, and again we turned into the hills.

The valley by which we entered soon narrowed into a ravine, and finally stopped abruptly. We scrambled on, however, and by many a turn and twist reached the summit of the spur.

The descent was as difficult as the ascent, but by dark we were camped on the river again, with the satisfaction of knowing we had passed the last spur, and would have, for a time at least, a comparatively easy journey.

June 2.—Found a good road for seven miles in the valley of the river, and stopped at a place which appeared to present a ford. For some days the river had been rising, and in many places I had tried unsuccessfully to find a fording place, but at this point I found I could ride across by taking an oblique line down stream. The greatest depth was about four feet, but the current was so strong that I thought a raft would be safer than risking the mules with packs on in the water. Accordingly, a raft was made, and all our heavy packs crossed on it in safety, but with much greater labor than I had anticipated; the lighter articles were packed on top of the saddles, and by hurrying the mules through the deepest parts, nothing was injured more than by getting slightly wet. I breathed freer when everything was safe on the other bank, and ordered a move. Leaving the timber on the river bank, we ascended a terrace and found a level plain, on which we travelled with great ease about 12 miles, and found a good camp on the river. This evening the river rose suddenly and became very turbid, but we were safe across it just in time.

June 4.—Proceeded down the Big Horn river 17 miles over a plain nearly level, and broken only by few narrow gullies not difficult to cross. We passed to-day creeks well timbered on the west side, and saw No-wood creek on the east; it is about 50 feet wide at the mouth, and well timbered, though above it has no timber on it. It rained to-day all around us in the mountains, but none fell on us.

On the 5th of June we left the Big Horn river, having got to a point as low as was suitable for the end proposed in the exploration; the entrance of the lower cañon (the northern) was plainly visible, and the northern range was so near that trees and rocks could be easily distinguished with the naked eye. We took a northwest course, and following a lodge-trail over a low hill, came to Gray Bull creek, and camped. This is a fine stream, rapid and shallow, running over a gravelly bed. It is heavily timbered and runs in many channels, forming numerous islands with fine groves of cottonwood.

During the last two days the nature of the country has changed for the better, though it is still far from being a fertile or cultivable region.

June 6.—Crossing Gray Bull creek, we proceeded nearly parallel to it in a westerly direction for four miles to turn a spur of barren hills, and then turning to the north came upon a rough, broken series of clay ridges similar to that which we had been in a few days back before crossing the Big Horn.

After a laborious journey of 26 miles we camped without wood or grass, and only a little water in a puddle, so muddy as to be almost unfit for use. The mules were turned out and herded all night to enable them to make a scanty meal from the sparse grass.

Early on the morning of the 7th we started, hoping to reach Stinking creek. After crossing three bad ravines and several bad land spurs, we came on to a plain some three miles wide and perfectly dry and barren, except a thin growth of sage. About three miles ahead appeared a line of low trees, which so much resemble those which line the dry ravines that no very great confidence was placed in them. They proved, however, to be on Stinking creek, which was sunk to a depth of 70 or 80 feet below the plain, and flowing in a narrow valley; the trees grew on the margin at the foot of the bluff, and it was their tops that we had seen. Our hunters had killed three fine buffalo cows, and here was plenty of wood and water, with better grass than we had seen for weeks. Although it was early I determined to camp, and much to the relief of all hands. The animals were soon stripped and enjoying a meal that must have awakened pleasant reminiscences of the Platte, while the human part of the command prepared for a feast to which late privation and toil gave double zest.

Fires crackled in every direction, and hump-ribs, marrow-bones, tender-loins and steaks, stewed and sputtered in the fervent heat. Extra particular epicures were deliberate and careful as to the exact quantity of salt and pepper, and the inclination of the roasting-stick, while the hungrier part were content with a roast on the coals, with a slight sprinkling of ashes for a condiment. We had afterwards many such merry feasts, but this is especially remembered on account of its being the first, and coming so directly after hard work and actual privation.

The stream was rushing and roaring along in its gravelly bed, and looked only two or three feet deep, but it was found on trial to be deep enough to swim a horse, and not fordable.

June 8.—Ascending from the bed of the stream to the plain, we travelled along the creek about 15 miles and searched several places for a ford, but found none. Camped on the bank of the stream, at the foot of a bluff, in a grove of cottonwood, and with pretty good grass.

June 9.—Finding no good ford, I determined to ascend the stream as far as practicable, hoping to be able to cross it higher up; but on attempting to leave the plain on which we were travelling we got among some bare clay hills which were utterly impassable, and were compelled to return to the stream and camp on it about one mile above our camp of the 8th. As a last resort an attempt was made to cross by a raft. This was made by a wagon body calked and wrapped in a tent, which kept out water very well. On the morning of the 10th we collected all the chains and ropes and made a line, by which I hoped to be able to cross the stream. One end being attached to the wagon body, it was pushed off into the angry current, and four oars vigorously plied, but the force of the water was such that the body could not be got across the current, and it went rapidly down stream. The chain stretched and snapped and left the crazy craft helpless in the stream. Borne furiously on by the current it struck the rocky shore, when three of the men in it leaped out, leaving myself and one man to share the fortune of our impromptu boat. Swift as the wind we went on, and by some providential chance escaped the rocks that thrust themselves here and there above the foaming waters, until at about a mile below where we had started we managed to get into an eddy and made the shore.

A second attempt was equally unsuccessful, and we narrowly escaped going over some rapids that would have swamped the boat. Leaving it in the stream where it had lodged on a reef, we prepared to get ashore, and found that the reef extended to the shore we had left, and probably entirely across the stream. I determined to try it, and getting my horse, found that I could ride without getting deeper than to the knee when on horseback. Still it was a hazardous, almost a desperate, resort, and I scarcely dared attempt to ford in such a current. My own horse was a very large one, while nearly all the others were small and would have great difficulty in keeping their footing. Yet it was the only alternative, and, on consultation with my assistants, it was determined to try the ford; accordingly we moved down to our camp of the 8th and got everything ready for a passage next morning.

June 11.—After an early breakfast we commenced to ford, and in order to render more plain what follows, I will here give an account of the stream at the point where we forded it. It was a double bend like the letter S, and we were in the upper part. The breadth straight across was about 250 yards, but the reef on which it was fordable ran obliquely up stream, making the distance to be travelled by the animals from bank to bank about 500 yards. The reef had a breadth of 10 or 15 yards, sloping gradually up stream, but going off abruptly down stream into twenty feet water. The depth of water on the reef was about four feet, except for a space of about 30 yards, near the further shore, where it was nearly to the back of a medium-sized mule, and it was in crossing this 30 yards that the main difficulty lay.

I will not attempt to describe the swiftness of the current, for what I shall say of its effects will abundantly show its power and force. The largest mules were selected and a single pack placed on the top of the pack-saddle, and each mule being led by a man mounted on another, they entered the stream. They succeeded better than I anticipated in keeping the mules up stream, and crossed the deeper part with no other damage than an occasional ducking. Finding that the animals could keep their footing, I determined to bring the chronometers and instruments across in the ambulance so as to prevent wetting them by the water which surged up against the sides of the mule and splashed over the pack. About half past three in the afternoon I had the instruments and some other light articles placed in the ambulance on the seats elevated entirely above the water. Four strong mules were attached, and two men detailed to ride along on the down-stream side of the mules to force them to keep up against the current. My horse being very strong and tall, and perfectly accustomed to the water, I took charge of the leaders and led them by a strap; the wagon-master led the wheel mules in the same way; one of the most careful men was in the ambulance to drive; and having thus taken every precaution, we started.

Through the shallow part there was no difficulty, except that it was as much as the mules could do to draw the wagon through the roaring current; but when the deep part was reached, and the wheels were more than half submerged, nothing could resist the force of the water. The hind wheels were washed down, without being lifted from the bottom, until the fore wheels were locked under the side of the body. It was necessary to turn the leaders to get the wheels loose, and in doing it they slacked the traces, the hind wheels could not hold the carriage, and in a moment it was swept into deep water. The mules, being entangled in the harness, were soon drowned, and finding them dead, I let go and my horse swam ashore. The men riding below, and the wagon master, got ashore in the same manner, excepting that one had a very narrow escape, having in some way got off his mule, and being obliged to swim he fortunately passed close enough to shore to be rescued by Duval, the guide, and Mr. Warring. The man in the ambulance jumped out when it filled and swam to a shallow part of the reef, from which he was rescued and brought on shore on horseback. As soon as I ascertained that the men were safe I crossed the stream and followed it down at a fast gallop. At about two miles I saw the wreck lodged on an island, the top of the ambulance broken off and everything out of the body. A little further down I found the top washed ashore, and got the odometer, which had been fastened to it. Returning to camp I found that only a box of stationery, which had floated, had been recovered; everything else must have sunk as soon as the ambulance turned over, and any effort to recover anything at the bottom of the river would have been madness. It was now dark, but I thought it possible to obtain the harness off the mules, and went down with three men to where the wreck was lodged; after cutting some of the straps and loosening others the whole thing moved off, and it was beyond our power to hold it. We returned to camp wet, cold, hungry, and dispirited, and I passed the most wretched night it has ever been my lot to encounter; still I felt that the accident was not to be attributed to any want of care on my part, and I must here acknowledge my indebtedness to all the party under my command. They were calm, cool, and industrious, and faced the dangers of the day quietly and bravely. It is a matter of congratulation and thanks to Heaven that no human life was lost, when each person in the party was repeatedly exposed to a danger against which no human efforts could have availed. As a matter of obvious precaution I had directed that no man should carry a gun or anything that would prevent him from swimming if he should be washed off his horse; hence there were several Maynard rifles in the ambulance, with other articles and weapons habitually carried on the person. There were also a sextant and horizon, three chronometers, and three barometers, which were all lost.

June 12.—Notwithstanding the dangers and fatigues of yesterday, the camp was astir at the usual hour, and we found that although our losses were heavy we could still get along. The remaining ambulance was on the other side of the stream and in a very weak condition; besides, there was no harness to suit, and after yesterday's experience I had no desire to attempt to get it across the stream; but, as we had the odometer, I sent three men to bring over the wheels and an axle, which they succeeded in doing with some difficulty. Harness was made of odd straps and pieces of canvas, and a very respectable and useful sort of cart rigged up. This cart shared the fortunes and dangers of all the rest of the journey and played no unimportant part in our labors, as it enabled us to keep up a continual odometer measurement. By 12 o'clock everything was ready, and we set in a northeast direction, over a dry barren plain, broken by ravines and spurs of clay and rock. Our course was nearly parallel to a range of high rocky mountains, distant 18 or 20 miles to the west, and containing a singularly-shaped mass called Heart Mountain. It is a mountain capped by an immense square rock, leaning slightly, and forms a prominent landmark.

After a weary journey of 23 miles we reached Sage creek at dark. This is a small stream 8 or 10 yards wide, and completely hidden between its banks. It has no timber except willow, and had recently overflowed its banks, leaving them so miry that we could not get to the creek, and were obliged to use the water in holes and sage for fuel; there was no grass, and our animals suffered very much. The water in the creek was very muddy, but it was doubtless owing to the recent freshet.

June 13.—Travelled along the valley of Sage creek over a fine level plain sloping gently upwards to the northwest, and from three to five miles wide. Crossed a branch of Sage creek flowing across the plain and issuing from the mountains to the north. The other branch runs along the valley for 12 miles, then crosses it and flows through a canon or gap in the mountains. We camped about a mile below the gap. An immense herd of buffalo was in sight all day, and the hunters were successful in furnishing meat. The day was warm and sultry, and a curious effect of mirage was produced, making buffalo loom up like shapeless black masses 20 feet high. Thinking the gap near camp was the one known as Pryor's gap, I examined it. It was about 100 yards wide, with sides nearly perpendicular of rock. For a little way in there was a good road, but the very broken appearance of the country further on led me to believe that no good route could be found through it.

June 15.—Crossing Sage creek and leaving it we travelled northwest, and in four miles came to the divide between Sage creek and Clark's fork of the Yellowstone. Crossing the divide, found good travelling over a rolling country, with a few scattered pines growing along rocky ravines. We had some difficulty in crossing one of these ravines, but finding a dry gully we followed it, travelling in a buffalo path, and came out on Clark's fork. This is a bold, rapid stream, 150 yards wide. Its valley is level, well timbered, and produces good grass. Looking up it from this camp we saw the Heart mountain, and, apparently, the stream runs very close to it. No one has ever visited the head of this river, which lies in a region of mountains covered with perpetual snow, and absolutely impassable to man or beast. Since leaving the Big Horn river we have seen no trace of Indian camp or lodge trails, and have many times been obliged to travel in buffalo paths and sheep trails. This part of the valley of Clark's fork shows signs of Indians, and is, no doubt, a favorite resort for them. The stream is very high and too deep to ford. It seems to have a depth in low water of four or five feet, but is now 15 or 20. The current is gentle, and the channel, though crooked, is not broken by islands or reefs, so that it would be possible to navigate the stream in batteaux or small steamboats from its mouth to the foot of the mountain, a distance of about 60 miles. I mention this because, if the valley of the Yellowstone should ever become inhabited, Clark's fork would be a means of obtaining wood from the mountains, besides the mineral treasures which I have no doubt are abundant in them.

June 16.—Travelled down Clark's fork to a point where the valley was terminated on the east side by a high bluff cutting off further progress in that direction. A short distance below a well-timbered creek came in on the west side, and I determined to cross and travel up its valley near to the foot of the mountains, so as to be able to cross the other tributaries of the Yellowstone, near their heads, where they are generally in two or three branches and can be forded.

Camped in a willow grove with an abundance of fine grass, and set about making a boat to cross the river in. The hunters were sent out, and returned late at night with the skins of three buffalo and an elk. Meantime the people at camp were busy collecting poles of cottonwood and willow, and cutting thongs of parfliche, so that on the morning of the 17th we commenced to construct a boat. A stout cottonwood pole is laid for the keel with knee-pieces lashed at each end to form the bow and stern, then other poles are bent and tied at each end to the keel and to the upper ends of the bow and stern-post, cross-pieces and ties are inserted at intervals to stiffen the frame, and as the whole is fastened with strips of wet parfliche it becomes, when they dry, as rigid as if put together with iron; then willows of about an inch in diameter are bent over the frame, passing from one gunwale to the other over the keel, and placed about three inches apart; finally, two or three buffalo skins are sewed together and stretched tight over the frame, hair-side in, and the boat is complete. The skin covering is firmly lashed to the framework, and when it dries, it is stiff and tight. Our boat was 18 feet long by 5 feet wide, and carried a good load besides the two men who rowed and a steersman. By the evening of the 18th everything had been safely transported across the stream, and we camped on its left bank.

June 19.—The boat was dismantled by taking off the skins and cords, to be carried along for future use, and we started up the valley of the branch of Clark's fork, which we called Bull-boat creek. It is a fine stream of clear water with a densely timbered bottom, and a depth of 2 or 3 feet; its width is 25 yards. After going up it 12 miles we crossed it and travelled up a branch, which we left and kept a northerly course over high, rolling hills covered with good grass, and broken by ravines generally containing water and a few cottonwood trees. Camped at the head of a ravine, with a scanty supply of water.

June 20.—Soon after leaving camp we struck a lodge trail, apparently much travelled, though with no very recent signs, and following it came to a bold and very rapid stream of clear water. The trail crossed the stream, but upon trial it was found to be too deep to ford, and too rapid to swim. I hoped to be able to head it or cross it higher up, and started up it, crossing a branch and travelling in a very fine level valley which abounded with antelope. After making 18 miles, camped on the stream, with excellent grass and plenty of wood.

This stream is known as Big Rosebud by the trappers; Bonlon de Rose, by the Canadian voyagers, and Bils-Kopay-agee, by the Crow Indians. It is ordinarily about 100 yards wide, and 2 to 3 feet deep, it is now, however, high from the melting snows, and has a depth of 5 feet. The great obstacle to crossing it is the great rapidity of the current, and the rocky character of the bottom, which is a mass of large round boulders, some entirely under water, others protruding. No horse that we have yet tried can keep a footing or swim against the force of the current. Just at this point and below us there is a fine valley perfectly level and producing fine grass, through which the stream marks its winding course by a hedge-like row of cottonwood; but not more than 10 miles ahead we can see the cañon from which the river emerges, a black gap in the high snowy mountains. Our only hope is to ascend the stream until it becomes shallower and less rapid.

June 21.—After a few miles in the valley we were forced to take to the hills, which were very rough and rocky. Before doing so an experiment was made to fell a tree across a place where the stream was narrow, in the hope that the tree would lodge against the boulders and give a starting point for the construction of a bridge. A tall cottonwood, some three feet in diameter and immediately on the bank, was selected. After a good deal of cutting with our dull axes it fell, the butt end lodging against another tree and the top falling in the water about three-fourths of the way across. It had no sooner reached the bottom than the upper branches were broken like pipe-stems, twisted off, and the huge trunk turning with the current moved off bodily down the stream. I was amazed at this result and reluctantly gave the order to try the hills. The stream impinged against a rocky precipice, and this was to be climbed by a sheep path; on top the travelling was little better, being over a series of high rocky hills covered with pine. The trouble of getting the odometer cart through the pine and over the rocks can scarcely be told, but, through the persevering efforts and unremitting labors of Mr. Snowden and his assistants, it was done without damage. At last we got back to Rosebud and camped. The mountains were now only four miles off and we had a share of their snow, which fell for some time during the afternoon; at night there was a heavy frost and ice. The water of the stream was very cold, and, notwithstanding the rapidity of the current, trout of finest flavor and great size abounded in it. Many were caught 15 and 20 inches in length and formed a valuable addition to our table. We had seen, also, in the woods herds of mountain sheep, but the hunters were not very successful in killing them.

June 22.—We were fortunate enough to find a ford about four miles above camp and crossed everything safely, but we were now in the heart of the snow mountains and the only way out was by climbing. We ascended and descended places where mules were never made to go, and after many slides and slips, and rolls and tumbles, which fortunately did no serious damage, camped in the bottom of a deep narrow ravine near some deserted Indian lodges. The ravine, though narrow and completely shut in by the high hills, furnished excellent grass, and our animals recovered well from the unusual fatigues of the day's journey.

June 23.—To get away from camp it was necessary to climb a hill almost vertical by making a winding path along its side. Several of the mules slipped and rolled from top to bottom, breaking pack-saddles and packs, and especially the poor mule whose unhappy lot it was to carry the boat skins. They had become by this time anything but agreeable in odor, and being stiff and hard it was very difficult to pack them securely. It was touching as well as ludicrous to see the poor creature's look of suffering resignation whenever his disagreeable load would fall to the ground.

After great labor and toil we succeeded in getting up the mountain and down it to a small stream in whose valley lay our only course, for the mountains were out of the question. The timber on the stream was very dense and it was no easy matter to get through it, but, by turning about and crossing and recrossing, we at last got out on a flat prairie, and saw about three miles ahead a heavily timbered stream into which the one we were on emptied. On reaching it I found it to be a wide deep river flowing to the northeast, and knew it could be no other than the Yellowstone. Thus we had at last reached one goal, and I hoped to be yet in time to meet Captain Raynolds at the Three Forks by the 4th of July. I felt satisfied that we could have no worse travelling than we had had, and, moreover, as I knew I would return by the Yellowstone, I determined to cache at this point some bales of goods for Indian presents, which had been a sad drawback. I accordingly cached the goods and remodelled the packs by distributing our provisions, now reduced to a very inconsiderable weight, equally among the serviceable animals; this gave only a light load for each mule.

CHAPTER II.

THE YELLOWSTONE RIVER.

On the 24th of June we commenced a journey up the Yellowstone in a fine level valley on the south side of the stream. After crossing two small streams we came to a large and very rapid creek, called the Rocky, and camped on it to reconnoitre and consider the best plan of crossing it.

June 25.—Finding no ford, we moved about a mile down Rocky, and camped at its mouth on the Yellowstone.

June 26.—The camp was at a place favorable for a passage, the river being only 507 feet wide and running in one channel. The bank on each side was low and the water deep from bank to bank, the current was rapid but smooth, and I entertained no doubt of our ability to make a safe passage even with the limited means at command. The boat skins, by this time hard and dry, were put to soak, and timber selected for a boat frame; during the 27th the boat was completed, and by 1 p. m. on the 28th the last man was crossed. Having no other large streams to cross I determined to leave the boat here, and had it placed on a scaffold high enough to be out of the reach of wolves. At 2 we started and followed a lodge trail running along the river bank. At first the road was level, but at one place, where a spur reached down to the river, there was a very ugly hill to descend. We camped at dark on the bank of the river.

June 29.—Leaving camp early and following the lodge trail, we left the river and struck off northwest over rolling hills gradually ascending and increasing in height. These were the foot slopes of a snowy pile about 15 miles distant which we called the Short mountain. For two or three miles the route lay on a stream filled with beaver-dams and spread out by them into quite a lake. After making 22 miles we came to a stream called Twenty-five Yard river, the same I think that Captain Clark calls Shield's river; it is a narrow, shallow stream flowing from the Belt mountains into the Yellowstone. The dividing range between the Yellowstone and Missouri was in plain sight, and only about 10 miles distant; and the lodge trail which we had been following led toward a well-defined gap.

June 30.—Travelled up the Twenty-five Yard river, crossing two forks coming in on the right, we then crossed the main stream and, leaving it, went towards the gap. Camped about five miles from the foot of the mountain on a small spring.

July 1.—Following the lodge trail we entered the pass by a well-defined road with evident marks of the recent passage of a large band of Indians, probably the Flatheads on their hunt. The pass followed the winding of a small stream, and gradually ascended by its crooked course until it was lost in a dark narrow cañon. Then turning abruptly the trail led up a very steep hill through a dense pine forest, and in about half a mile the divide was reached. Notwithstanding this was higher than the limit of snow, the surrounding peaks towered loftily above us; the white snow glistening through the pine trees, and the wind keeping up a monotonous roar, as it swayed the myriads of pine boughs to its course. A halt was called on the summit to allow all hands to breathe, and to prepare for the descent, which bade fair to be worse than the ascent. I was surprised to find the mosquitos very troublesome at this great elevation, and while I was eating a piece of snow held in one hand, the other was kept busy brushing them away. The descent was very steep and rocky, and there were many places where the mules had great difficulty in keeping on their feet. At one point, near the bottom, the gorge opened and presented a charming view of the broad plain in which the three forks of the Missouri unite, and soon after we came to a beautiful mountain stream which provided an easy road into a fine valley, where we camped on the ground of some deserted Indian lodges, which promised a plentiful supply of wood. I shall speak again of this pass in a general summary. It is known as the Blackfoot pass; but must not be confounded with one of the same name in the main range of the Rocky mountains.

July 2.—We were now on the waters of the Gallatin fork of the Missouri, and I knew we could be no great distance from the place of rendezvous, the junction or head of the Missouri, where we were expected to be by the 4th. We therefore set out to reach the Gallatin, and follow it down to its junction with the Madison and Jefferson. At first we passed over rolling hills well covered with grass, but on crossing the stream down which we were travelling we came upon a miry plain so full of sloughs that the animals could not travel. Recrossing the stream, we followed it to its mouth, and camped on the Gallatin at the foot of a range of very rough low hills.

July 3.—Proceeding down the Gallatin, the road became so rough that I determined to return to the stream and cross it. Accordingly we descended, and, while engaged in fording, a shout from the top of the hill announced Captain Raynolds. The fording was suspended, and soon after both parties camped in a bend of the river just beneath a perpendicular wall of rock.

The Fourth of July was passed in our beautiful camp in an interchange of stories of adventures, and in further plans for the future. It was a matter of great thought, and, I trust, of proper gratitude to me that we had all thus united, and that all who had set out on our trip were still in life and health.

After making arrangements for further proceedings and exchanging news, we bade farewell to Captain Raynolds on the morning of the 5th, and saw his party disappear over the northern hills.

In company with my assistants I rode down to the head of the Missouri, about 6 miles from our camp. The three forks of the Missouri unite at the entrance of a gorge through a low ridge of rocky hills, after traversing a plain of 8 or 10 miles in extent.

The Jefferson, coming from the south, emerges from a chain of snowy mountains; the Madison, running nearly north, comes likewise from a distant range; and the Gallatin, from the eastward, flows from a range dividing the valley from the Yellowstone. The Gallatin joins the others below their point of union and close to the mouth of the gorge. The plain near the junction is intersected by many creeks and sloughs, and their banks are thickly overgrown with willow, cherry, and rosebushes. The only break in the level surface of the valley is a low, bare ridge lying between Gallatin and Madison. At its head the Missouri is smaller than the Yellowstone, being from 80 to 100 yards wide, and having a regular, placid current.

July 6.—Leaving camp early we proceeded up the Gallatin and its north fork, crossing the latter and passing to the east fork toward a pass further south than that which we had come through, called Clark's fork. I noticed to-day large quantities of wild flax, growing to a height of three feet, and in full bloom; also a species of geranium, and the bitter root. Our travel was much interfered with by the marshes and sloughs which met us in every direction. Camped on the east fork of the Gallatin near the pass referred to.

July 7.—Our route lay up the east fork of the Gallatin, and along its banks to the cañon from which it emerged. It was for about 300 yards narrow, and the road ran along the side of a steep, piny hill, then crossed the stream and, ascending an easy hill, came into a valley running north and south, between two ranges of high, snowy hills. The valley was from one-half to three-fourths of a mile in width, and was meandered by a small stream which emptied into the fork of the Gallatin. By a gradual rise over a very good road, and through luxuriant grass, we reached the divide, and commenced a gentle descent, which led us into a small creek flowing into Twenty-five Yard river. The valley of this stream was densely grown with pine saplings, and from evidences of cutting, &c., was a favorite place for the Indians to come and get lodge poles. I therefore called it Lodge Pole creek, and named the pass Lodge Pole pass. After a long march we camped on the Lodge Pole creek in sight of Twenty-five Yard river.

I will discuss and describe this pass more fully in my general summary, merely remarking here that it is now practicable for wagons, and would require but little labor to make it a permanent roadway. We travelled 30 miles to-day, and camped on Lodge Pole creek, about four miles above its mouth.

July 8.—Following down Lodge Pole creek we reached Twenty-five Yard river, and followed down its valley to the Yellowstone, on which we camped, about three miles below the mouth of Twenty-five Yard river. This is the river which Captain Clark calls Shield's river; and it would be well if the name were revived, but as it now goes by the name of Twenty-five Yard river I have retained it. This camp was 12 miles below a cañon from which the Yellowstone emerged. I was informed by my guide that beyond this range there was a level valley extending about eight miles to the foot of a second range, and from there to the lake in which the Yellowstone has its source, a distance not exceeding 70 miles; it flows through a narrow gorge, and no one has ever been able to travel up it.

The appearance of the mountains fully corroborates this statement; for even now the snow on their summits was receiving almost nightly accessions, and their contour was rough and forbidding in the extreme. The river has here a breadth of 250 yards and is from 6 to 7 feet deep, being at this time swelled 2 or 3 feet above its lowest stage by the spring freshets. The current is rapid but irregular, sweeping around bends with great velocity, and then slacking into broad reaches of quiet, lake-like surface. On an average it would be about 3½ miles an hour.

July 9.—After a long march through a driving rain, we reached the camp where we had left the boat. We travelled as closely along the river as possible, climbing spurs which jutted down to the edge of the water, and crossing the flat bottoms in the bends.

July 10.—The boat was none the better for its rustication, for the sun had drawn it so that some of the seams had started, and its odor was far from balmy. Spent the day in repairing her, and christened her the "Rose of Cashmere," in hope she would "smell as sweet by any other name."

By dark the Rose was serviceable, and we turned in to prepare for an early start. The mosquitos swarmed and exacted their tribute in loss of blood and sleep mercilessly.

July 11.—Despatching the land party, I started with two men in the Rose for the double purpose of examining the river and getting the Indian goods we had cached. Passed four rapids without difficulty and reached the cache, an estimated distance of 17 miles, in three hours and a half. The goods had not been disturbed, but were slightly injured by damp, which did not astonish me, as there had been rain every day since they had been deposited. Joined the land party and camped about three miles below the cache. I was able here to form an idea of the regimen of this river, and was surprised to find such a depth of water. Thè banks also indicated that the freshets in spring were neither very great nor very sudden, and I am inclined to think that the high waters in the Yellowstone extends through a period embracing June, July, and part of August.

July 12.—The road lay to-day principally in the pine hills and was not difficult. We had most of the time a well-marked Indian trail, but my desire to keep near the river led me at times to leave the trail and get into a worse road. We camped on the river in a small bottom with good grass.

I endeavored to obtain tar from the pine trees which covered the hills about us, but met with no success. The gum which exudes from under the bark answers a very good purpose for pitch, and we used it to stop the gaping seams of the Rose. This pine is of little value save in its abundance. The trees are low and scrubby and the branches shoot from the ground up. I noticed, too, that nearly all the dead trunks were wind shaken and had spiral cracks running round them, which destroyed their usefulness for lumber. The dry pine makes excellent fuel—burns well and with great heat, and can be obtained in any quantity.

July 13.—Our road to-day was very rough, as we left the lodge trail to keep nearer to the river and had several ravines to cross. Camped on the river.

July 14.—We had a fine road to-day, being all the time in the river bottom and travelling in a straight course. The day was hot and sultry, causing a murage which prevented us from seeing the details of the country. At ten miles below the camp we left we passed the mouth of Clark's fork. Its waters being turbid, produces a slight discoloration in that of the Yellowstone.

July 15.—After a few miles in the bottom the road ascended the hills and passed over a level table-land covered with a species of prickly pear, consisting of small balls covered with thorns, which caused great distress to the poor animals. The little torments really seemed to have the power to leap from their stems and stick to some luckless mule, whose sudden transition from quiet labor to outrageous kicking and plunging was the only sign of the mischief.

July 16.—The river had increased in breadth and depth, and in leaving the mountains seemed to have changed its character, becoming more and more turbid; the islands were more numerous, and large accumulations of drift, like those on the Missouri, were frequent. I therefore came in the boat to sound the river, and was surprised to find a continuous channel with 6 feet at the shallowest, and 20 in the deepest places. Along the right bank there was a bluff 60 feet high and covered with pine. On the left there were fine valleys in each bend, and immense herds of buffalos were feeding in them and in the cottonwood groves of the islands. At 4 p. m. I found the land party camped in a pretty spot opposite Pompey's pillar, a well-known land-mark, and joined them. The Rose was now entirely used up, and it became necessary to build another boat. The hunters soon procured four fine bull skins, and the greater part of the timber was got. I gave orders to remain in camp during the 17th to finish the boat and prepare for observing the solar eclipse on the 18th.

July 17.—We remained in camp to-day and made a new bull-boat, which was called the Pompey, in honor of the locality. Very near our camp there was a fine grove of currants and gooseberries, now entirely ripe and very palatable. The fruit is smaller than the domestic, but would doubtless increase in size by cultivation, while in flavor it needs no improvement.

I determined to observe the eclipse from the top of Pompey's pillar, and made some preliminary observations to-day for the time and latitude. Pompey's pillar was thus called by Captain Clark, and is a high isolated rock of yellow sandstone, standing in a level valley on the right hand side of the river. The Indians believe that it fell from the bluff on the opposite side and rolled across the stream to its present place, but the real mode of its formation is plain to a more educated eye. It was formerly the point of a sandstone ridge, forming the bluff on the other side and running into an abrupt bend in the channel just below the point where a small stream enters the Yellowstone, and in time of freshet contributed towards wearing away the point on the lower side, while the stronger current of the Yellowstone was undermining the upper. Thus, in time, a cut was made. The Yellowstone usurped for a short distance the channel of its tributary, and left the point of the ridge to become Pompey's pillar.

July 18.—Before sunrise I crossed with a party and climbed to the top of Pompey's pillar. I was disappointed to find the eastern horizon bounded by the Big Horn mountains, and when the sun came above them the eclipse had begun. I had no instruments, and viewed the eclipse with only a screen taken off the sextant. I still obtained, however, a tolerably accurate record of the time of final contact, and immediately after observed for time by an altitude of the sun. The eclipse covered about 10 digits, leaving a bright portion of the sun at the time of the greatest eclipse equal in size to a new moon two or three days old. The obscurity was very marked, casting a greenish lurid hue, similar to that seen when looking through bottle glass. The animals about camp exhibited no signs of fear or other feeling, but fed quietly during the whole time.

At half past 10 we left camp and travelled over a very fair road down the river. We descended once into the river valley; the rest of the day's ride was over rolling, piney hills and across dry ravines. We camped on an island in the river with very fine grass, and in a grove of fine cottonwood. After camping a terrible storm occurred. The wind blew a hurricane and the rain fell in torrents, completely filling a dry creek near camp and even causing the river to rise. The boat did not join us, being detained doubtless by the rain.

July 19.—Continued down the river and passed the mouth of Big Horn. The road was principally over the hills, with many rough pine ravines. Camped about six miles below the mouth of Big Horn, opposite a beautiful reach as smooth as a lake. The boat joined us, having been detained yesterday by the storm.

July 20.—I travelled to-day in the boat for the purpose of stopping at Fort Sarpy and sounding. The stream is here 800 or 900 yards wide, and I found no bottom with a six-foot pole. In places the current was very swift, but there were no rapids and but few snags. Reached Fort Sarpy about 12 o'clock and found it abandoned. Soon after the land party came up and we camped about three miles below the fort. Our camp was opposite the plain on which we camped in August, 1859, and now, as then, was literally alive with buffalo.

July 21.—Along the river, through a large bottom, and over several spurs which were quite rough. The hunters killed five cows near our camp and I determined to remain and dry some meat, as our provisions were running low. We passed a muddy stream called Porcupine creek, and saw a peculiarly-shaped peak, which I called Castle rock.

July 22.—All hands were set to work cutting meat and spreading it on the scaffolds erected last night. When there is time, the meat is dried by being exposed to the sun for three or four days, having previously been cut in thin strips and slices. As we were able to remain only one day, I used fire in addition to the heat of the sun, and succeeded in curing in a single day quite a large quantity of meat. Our boat had begun to leak so much that I determined to try and make tar of the pine on the hills. For this purpose a quantity of pine knots were gathered and a kiln made according to the most approved style, but it was of no avail, and I was forced to the conclusion that this pine will not produce tar. We had used with good results the gum which exuded from wounds in the bark of the growing trees, and could readily melt it into pitch, but the supply was scanty and laborious to collect.

July 23.—We had to-day a very good road, lying principally in the valley of the river, and camped in a bend above the mouth of Tongue river. At this point there was a great deal of timber cut and sawed, and just above there were numerous Indian graves, some well protected, though with no signs of having been recently visited. This was the spot where Meldrum wintered some years ago, and intended to build a fort, but the small-pox broke out among the Indians and the project was abandoned.

July 24.—Passed the mouth of Tongue river and camped on an island. After receiving Tongue river, the Yellowstone becomes a little more muddy, but is not perceptibly increased in breadth or depth.

July 25.—After a very fair day's journey, we camped at a place called Gravelly point, below the Buffalo rapids. The boat came over these without difficulty.

July 26.—Immediately after leaving camp we ascended a high steep bluff by a buffalo path, and for eight or nine miles the road passed through very rough, broken country. Some of the clay hills were very regular in form, and the effect of the murage on the pinnacles made them loom up like tall turrets and castles. We camped on the Yellowstone below the mouth of Powder river.

July 27.—Our road commenced by ascending a series of high, bare clay hills, making very rough travelling and forcing us back from the river. We then came on to a more level plain, crossed two streams of good running water, and went down the dry bed of a third to the river.

July 28.—For seven or eight miles we had a fine road through a level bottom. We then entered a short range of very rough hills, called Henry's caches, and emerged from them on to a fine, level road.

July 29.—We had now passed the "bad land" ridges, and had a fine valley to travel in. The valley is about four miles wide and contains but little grass, occasioned, I think, by the destruction of the roots by the prairie dogs. On the right-hand side the river flows against a white clay bluff, so that the only travel is on the left side.

July 30.—Made a long march (27 miles) over a plain perfectly level and smooth. The day was very warm and the march very fatiguing from the monotony and lack of incident.

July 31.—This was to be our last day's travel, so all hands were up early and we moved camp sooner than usual. Our level valley continued with all its sameness, though a very violent and sudden rain storm contributed to relieve the monotony of the day. At last, after travelling 30 miles, we reached the Missouri, and travelling up three miles, we came in sight of Fort Union on the opposite bank. Several pistol shots were fired, which attracted attention, and soon the inmates of the fort were out on the bank, speculating upon the character of their unexpected visitors. Mr. Meldrum, the gentleman in charge, came across in a boat and received us very courteously. By his invitation I went to the fort to obtain provisions, while the rest returned to the point where we had reached the Missouri and encamped.

August 1.—After spending a pleasant night with the gentlemen of the American Fur Company at Fort Union, I started down the Missouri early this morning with supplies of flour, coffee, and sugar for my party, and found them in a pleasant camp on the bank of the Missouri about three quarters of a mile above the mouth of the Yellowstone. As I had been ordered to await the coming of Captain Raynolds at this point, I made a permanent camp, erected a flag-staff, built a corral for the mules, and after hoisting the national colors, named the camp in honor of the distinguished officer in charge of the Bureau of Explorations and Surveys, "Camp Humphreys."

During the 1st, 2d, and 3d of August we remained in camp, engaged in writing up our notes, mending clothes, and preparing camp for a comfortable reception of our friends who were expected down the river.

On the 4th, Major Schoonover, Indian agent, and Mr. Wray, clerk at Fort Union, paid us a visit, accompanied by the ladies of the fort. We prepared a dinner of the scanty materials in our possession, and made some trifling presents to our Indian friends, after which we went to the fort and enjoyed a ball given in our honor.

Although the ladies were the daughters of the forest, they were attired in the fashionable style of the States, with hoops and crinoline, and exhibited as much grace and amiability towards us, their guests, as could be found in the saloons of any city in the land.

I was as much pleased as surprised to find in what good order and geniality the people of the fort lived, and I must specially record my grateful sense of the uniform kindness and hospitality received both here and at the other posts of the company. Mr. Meldrum, who was in charge of the post, was unremitting in his attention to our wants, and was well assisted by his clerk, Mr. Wray. Both these gentlemen proved that, however rude may be the surroundings and associations of daily life, true warm-heartedness and civility can be found under the roughest exterior.

Being advised that signs of hostile Indians had been discovered, and feeling insecure in my position, on the 7th I determined to move the camp, and crossed the Missouri with all the animals and luggage. A new Camp Humphreys was established on the other side of the river, about half a mile below Fort Union, and on the same evening Captain Raynolds arrived, having come from Fort Benton by the river in a Macinac boat.

We had now descended the Yellowstone river, and I propose to give here a brief description of this hitherto unknown stream. Taking its rise in a lake in the impenetrable fastnesses of the Rocky mountains, the Yellowstone is at its outset a river, and at the highest point attained by my party has a breadth of 200 yards and a depth of six feet. It flows from the mountains to the mouth of Clark's fork in a narrow valley, frequently impinging against the points of the pine-clad ridges which hem it in. It cannot be called a crooked river, as all its bends are bold, sweeping curves, and its general course uniform. Many islands break up its channel into several streams, some of which are shallow; but there is a continuous channel with a depth of three feet at low water.

From Clark's fork to Big Horn may be called the second stage; in which the river is 500 to 600 yards in width, unobstructed by rapids, and flowing with a uniform current of three or four miles an hour.

Below Big Horn to Powder river the banks are low, except where the river breaks through the successive ranges of clay hills, and the Yellowstone gradually assumes the characteristics of the Missouri—numerous sand-bars, low, falling banks, densely timbered islands, and sloughs which run from the main stream and do not return except at high water, leaving at other times lakes and sloughs on the banks.

The main question in regard to this river is as to its navigability. In view of the fact that steamboats have been taken up the Missouri to Fort Benton, I have no hesitation in saying that the same thing can be done in the Yellowstone, as far as the mouth of Big Horn river, without having as many or as great obstacles to overcome as in the Missouri. The only serious impediments below the mouth of the Big Horn are the rapids below Powder river and the Buffalo shoals; but I am of the opinion that these are not worse than many in the upper Missouri, and a steamboat which, at the time of high water, might easily go up, could at a lower stage return and improve the channel.

In the essentials of depth of water, abundance of fuel, and velocity of current, the Yellowstone presents greater advantages for navigation than the Upper Missouri. Of course much would have to be done before boats could run with profit, even if there were any demand; but if the day ever comes when steamboats can ascend the Yellowstone with profit, it will be found as easy, and easier, to navigate than many of the rivers of the west and southwest.

The time during which navigation would be possible is from the middle of May to the 1st of August. The appearance of the banks of the river indicates that the annual floods are neither sudden nor excessive, and although the rapidity of the current is greatest at high water, it is not sufficiently great to prevent a steamer from ascending the river. It is, in fact, safe to assume that the Yellowstone is navigable easily to the mouth of the Big Horn, and with some artificial improvements, to the mountains, under the same conditions and difficulties as the Upper Missouri, the Upper Mississippi, the Arkansas, the Red river, the Minnesota river, and others, where the necessities of commerce have conquered or palliated the dangers of nature.

The question is one which nothing short of actual trial can fully settle, and it is not likely that that trial will ever be made as a mere experiment, but I shall ever cherish the hope that some day will see settlements on the banks and steamboats on the waters of the noble Yellowstone.

CHAPTER III.

THE MISSOURI RIVER.

By the 15th of August everything had been prepared for our trip down the river. Two Mackinac boats, the Jim Bridger and the Bob Meldrum, formed our fleet, and were well stocked with all the necessary stores and material.

At half past 1 we bade farewell to our kind friends at Fort Union, with many regrets, and shoved off. As soon as the bow of the boat swung round the flag was unfurled, which was the signal for a salute. The flag on the fort was run up and guns fired as long as we were in sight. We turned a bend which shut out the sight of the fort, and were once more in a wilderness, dependent on our own resources. At first the novelty of travelling in a boat was pleasing, but it it became afterwards painfully wearying, and any excitement was hailed with joy which broke up the tedious monotony of the day. The boats were propelled by oars, at which the men labored in turn, and with the aid of the current we could make from five to six miles per hour, and in a good day's run could pass over 60 miles. We started always at daylight with a supply of cooked food, having no fires on board, and travelled steadily on till dark, when we tied up and camped on shore.

Nearly every day we would strike on a sand-bar, and sometimes I was glad of the relief it afforded, notwithstanding the detention it caused. One day was so much like another day, that I shall not attempt to transcribe my journal, but shall merely attempt descriptions of important places and events.

On the 20th we reached Fort Berthold, a post of the Fur Company. This is situated on a high bluff close to the village of the Gros Ventres and Mandans. These two tribes have united on account of their small numbers, and occupy the village together under the chieftainship of Mali-Topa—"the four bears." He is a tall, fine looking Indian, and seems well disposed. The village contains 200 or 300 earth houses, clustered as closely as possible around an open area used for dances and religious ceremonies.

The day after I arrived Lieutenant White came in with a large party of soldiers and civilians belonging to Lieutenant Mullins's wagon-road expedition. I was very glad to see him, because a number of Sioux of the Blackfeet band had arrived at the village, and were disposed not to be very polite towards my small party. Lieutenant White kindly agreed to stop at Fort Berthold until I was ready to go, and to accompany me down the river, making our united force equal to any the Sioux could bring against us.

At the request of Little Elk, the Sioux chief, I agreed to have a council, and soon about 30 Indians were assembled in a room inside the fort.

Lieutenant White and myself, with the gentleman in charge of the fort, Mr. Riter, entered the room, and an old Indian opened the talk. His speech was of the stereotyped pattern. He said:

The Great Spirit has made this country for us, and has put buffalo and game in it for us, but the white men come and build roads, and drive off the game, and we and our children starve. I love my children as you white men love yours, and when I see them starving it makes my heart black, and I am angry. We are glad to have the traders, but we don't want you soldiers and road-makers. The country is ours, and we intend to keep it. Tell the Great Father we won't sell it, and tell him to keep his soldiers at home.

This was delivered in small parcels, frequently repeated, and interpreted to me in French, for our interpreter's English was more unintelligible than the original Sioux. I mean by this no disrespect to the worthy Mr. Garoux. This harangue was evidently tedious to the others, and they seemed glad when the orator was done.

The Little Elk rose with a handsome pipe which he presented first towards the sky and then to the four quarters of the earth. His attitude was very striking, and I never saw a handsomer figure or more determination in a countenance. Holding the pipe, he advanced towards me and placed the end of the stem to my lips; I took a whiff and, to show my knowledge of Indian breeding, puffed the smoke through my nose. We then shook hands and the Little Elk began:

Friend, I am a soldier, and I see you are one; you have come from the Crows and the great river, and you are going to tell the Great Father what you have seen. What will you tell him? Say to the Great Father that the Oncpapa and Blackfeet Sioux have been cheated by the agents; they have been driven from their lands; they have not received the goods promised them by the White Bear, (General Harney,) and they will not take them. We don't live on the river, and we don't want to see any white people or any steamboats, because the goods the steamboats bring up make us sick. You, friend Mato-Lopa, said he, (turning to the Gros Ventres chief,) you and your people have dwindled to a handful, because you live near the whites and raise corn.

This was followed by a torrent of invectives which Garoux would not interpret, but which was mainly in ridicule of the Gros Ventres and in praise of the Sioux. Resuming to me he said:

The Blackfeet and Oncpapas can whip the whites; you have not many soldiers, and we have enough to kill any party you can send against us. If you have any presents for us on your boats give them to us; we want to go to join our people. If you do not, we will stop your boats and take what we want.

This was pretty plain talk and well delivered, although it took five times as long as it does to read it. He then turned to Mr. Riter and said:

I see you have made a hole in the wall of your fort and intend to trade with us through it. Do you think we are squaws? Let us come inside to trade or we will burn up the fort.

The excited brave now sat down, streaming with perspiration, and commenced to fan himself cool.

It now became my turn to reply, and rising from my seat I said:

My friends, I hardly know how much of your talk to believe, for I was told when I came here that a short time ago you sent word to the Gros Ventres that you had killed me and all my soldiers. You now see me here, and I want to tell the Gros Ventres not to believe what you say, for you have double hearts, and tell these stories to make them believe you are very brave.

While this was being interpreted I watched the effect, but with all his impetuosity Little Elk took it kindly, and laughed at the imputation on his veracity. I continued:

I have been sent by the Great Father to travel in this country and in the Crow country, to see what it looks like and how the Indians are. I have been through the country, and am now going home by the river, in the boats you see at the foot of the hill. I have nothing to give you, and I wouldn't give you anything if I had, after your talk to-day. Wherever I have been I have heard complaints of the Oncpapas and Blackfeet Sioux. I know they are numerous; but that is no reason why they should steal from the Rees and Gros Ventres and from the whites. Traders are good to you; all the presents which General Harney promised have been given to you, and I see some of you now dressed in the Great Father's coats. I will have to tell the Great Father that you are very bad, and he may send his soldiers after you. Your agent tells you, and so do I, to keep at peace with the Gros Ventres, and Mandans, and Rees, and they will not molest you. The traders intend to deal fairly with you, and you will be rich enough to buy anything you want if you will send your young men to hunt instead of prowling around these villages and the Rees to kill women and dance over their scalps; you have a good country, and nobody wants to take it from you. Tell your people that my boats are going down the river, and if any of them want me to stop they may call to me, but if they fire I will land and fight them.

I now started to leave the room, but an old fellow detained me and made a most characteristic final speech: "My son," he said, holding my hand, "you and Little Elk are too young; your heads are hot, and your tongues work too easily. I am old and experienced, and you must listen to what I have to say. A great deal of the mischief that is imputed to us is done by other tribes; we never make war unless we are imposed on. We want to be on good terms with the Great Father, and I hope you will tell him a good story of us. We have to travel three days to join our people, and we do not wish to stop to hunt, and you must give us a little flour and bacon to eat on the way, and some sugar to take to our wives and children." The old rascal looked positively saintlike as he made this modest request, and held my hand as affectionately as if he had been my grandfather. "Friend," said I, "my flour and sugar and bacon will make you sick, and I have too much regard for you to put temptation in your way and send you home ill."

If it were possible for an Indian to look sheepish, I presume he would have done so, but his countenance did not betray any feeling or chagrin. Later in the day they were set across the river to rejoin their families, and that was the last I ever saw of them. The complaints against these two tribes, the Blackfeet and Oncpapas, are universal and well founded. They rob and murder indiscriminately, regarding only the size of a party and taking good care of their own precious scalps. They inhabit the heads of the Heart Knife and Cannon Ball rivers, and in case of danger take refuge in the "bad lands" between the Little Missouri and Powder rivers.

This section of country, I was told, is particularly well adapted for Indians. The streams have broad, well-wooded valleys, which abound in game and furnish good wintering places, while the intermediate ridges are so broken and rough that pursuit of Indians in them without guides is impracticable. They richly deserve chastisement by the government, and I have heard since my return to the States that their outrages have exceeded any previous ones.

I was able during the three days I passed at Fort Berthold to witness a peculiar ceremony of the Mandans, which I believe has never been described. By way of preliminary I must remark that I had made a present of my epaulettes to the chief Four Bears, and in this way had obtained the run of the village and access to the most sacred places.

In the centre of the village is a circular space some 150 feet in diameter, with commodious scaffolds ranged around it, which answer the double purpose of seats for spectators and places to dry corn and squashes. In the centre of the open space is a circular enclosure of slabs 10 or 12 feet high, and about 4 feet in diameter. This is called the "big canoe," and has a very decided reference to the flood, as the tradition which I will relate further on will show. On the first day of the ceremony the proceedings were commenced by five men, ranging themselves in front of the big canoe, with drums made of skins, shaped like turtles, and said to be filled with water. I believe, though, that they were stuffed with hair, with a hoop to keep them distended and make them give out when struck a sound like a drum. After these were arranged, a man, stripped to the skin and smeared with white clay, came from the Medicine lodge opposite the big canoe, and, walking behind the canoe, leaned against it and hid his face in his hands. At the same time a woman, in a short skirt, with her legs scarred and bleeding, her hair cut short, and several bleeding wounds in her forehead and breasts, leaned against the side of the canoe and began crying and howling most piteously, the drummers all the time thumping away and chanting in unison. This woman was the relative of a young man who had been killed a short time previously by the Rees. Having sung his praise and exhibited her grief by her scarifications, she went away, and some 10 or 15 objects bounded into the arena. These were men, painted in a grotesque manner, wearing buffalo heads with strips of fur down their backs and long branches of willow fastened to their arms. The drummers beat and howled, the buffalo men danced and capered in admirable precision, and waved their willow branches like wings. everybody shouted, dogs barked, and the motions of the dancers became more and more violent. Two of the buffalo men would run together and butt with their heads, and, indeed, they imitated all the motions of a herd of buffalo. Suddenly the drummers rose, snatched up their drums and ran into the Medicine lodge, followed by the individual who had been leaning against the canoe, the buffalo disappearing among the lodges. Then came an old man who dug a hole in the ground about 20 feet in front of the canoe and erected a stout post 15 feet high, having two cords fastened at the top and looped at the ends. The drummers came out of the Medicine lodge, took their places, and the young man who, in the first performance, had stood behind the canoe was led to the foot of the post by two villainous-looking old medicine men.

This young man had been three days without meat or drink, and being perfectly naked and smeared with clay he looked ghastly. Kneeling on the ground, one of the old men took up a portion of the skin of the young man's breast and passed a knife through it, making two apertures with a strip of skin between. The blood trickled down, and the victim winced perceptibly. A skewer of wood four inches long was passed through the two holes, and the loop at the end of one of the cords placed over its two ends. The second cord was fastened in like manner to the other breast, and the poor wretch lifted to his feet. The drummers thumped, and the young man threw himself violently back, bearing his whole weight on the cords, and swinging round the foot of the pole. The skin drew out several inches, and seemed to stretch further at every jerk of the poor fellow, who pulled, and tossed, and shouted in order to break away. It was sickening to behold, especially when, after four or five minutes, nature claimed her sway, and the poor wretch fainted and hung collapsed. He was not touched, and, seeming to revive, renewed his efforts to bring the torture to a close by breaking the ligaments of skin which held the skewers. After half an hour or more the skin broke, and he was carried off.

The next victim was served even more dreadfully, though he bore it remarkably well. The skewers were passed under the skin of the back, just above the shoulder blades, and he was hung up to a scaffold with his feet three feet from the ground. Then more skewers were inserted in the fleshy parts of the arms and legs, and buffalo skulls hung to them. I was amazed to see how far the skin would stretch, puffing out to a distance of 12 or 15 inches.

These disgusting scenes were repeated during two days, varied by races round the big canoe by troops of young men and boys, dragging from four to ten buffalo heads attached to skewers in their backs. Some fainted and did not recover; some were violently nauseated, and proved conclusively that their three days' fast had not been faithfully kept; others held out to the end, and leaped, kicked, and struggled until they were free from their disagreeable attachments.

All the implements, skewers, bull heads, cords, and willow branches were deposited inside the big canoe, and were considered sacred from that time out. I endeavored to ascertain what all this meant, but could only get a meagre account. The idea of the big canoe is common among several tribes, and Catlin and others infer that it is based upon some tradition of the deluge. The Mandans relate a story agreeing in many respects with our account of the flood. They say that their fathers came to this country in a large canoe, and after having been many days on the water a bird flew out to them, bearing a willow branch with fresh leaves on it. They soon after landed, and drew the canoe on land to live in. The bird remained with them, and showed them how to build earthen lodges, and where to find game and fruit. This bird is even now held sacred, and enters largely into their religious symbols. The self-torture and mutilation which accompany their mysteries cannot be explained, except by the supposition that it is a course of preparation for the hardships and dangers of war. I noticed that every male over 10 years old had the scars of the skewer holes on his breast and back.

There are a few men who refuse or fail to undergo the trial, and they are banished from all society with men. They wear women's dress, do women's work, and can only be distinguished from the women by their coarser features, and the contempt exhibited towards them. They are called by the traders "bundashes," a word of which I am unable to find the derivation. It is not Indian, and, so far as I can ascertain, is not French.

Captain Raynolds reached Fort Berthold on the 22d of August, and on the 23d we resumed our voyage down the river. On the 25th we arrived at Fort Clark, an abandoned post of the Fur Company, and the site of the Ree village. The name Ree is universally used now, and is an abbreviation of Aricara. These people are but the degraded remnant of the once powerful nation, and are at the mercy of their enemies, the Sioux. Going on shore, I summoned the chief, and told him I had some presents for him. The village was notified, and after the necessary toilets were made, the chief and his officers appeared at the boats. Bread and coffee were served to about 70 of them, and I then told them that I had some cloth and calico to give them, but as I could not stay to distribute them I would leave it with the chief. This seemed satisfactory, and I left three pieces of calico, one of cloth, and a miscellaneous assortment of beads, feathers, flints, fire-steels, awls, buttons, ribbon, and other trinkets which Indians value. It made a large bundle, and seemed to please the women and children especially. To the chief I gave a small quantity of sugar, an article of which Indians are passionately fond. The chief made a speech returning thanks for the presents, and complaining bitterly of the Sioux. He said that the young men of the Rees could not go to hunt, because the Sioux were always prowling about to kill them, and even in the cornfields at the village women had been shot and scalped. He begged that the Great Father would protect them; the Rees desired peace and tranquility, for they were but few and would not last much longer; they did not get their share of the goods the Great Father sent them, and each person's allowance was so small that it would be better to keep them away, because they were only a cause of quarrel and theft. In conclusion, he hoped I would have a pleasant trip, and soon see my friends and the Great White Chief.

The languid and despondent air of the old man, with the deep, unvarying tones of his gutteral language, contrasted strongly with the fiery manner and clear ringing vowels of the Little Elk, and gave good evidence of the difference in the condition of the two tribes. I told the chief that I would report to the Great Father what he had said of his troubles; I knew the Sioux were bad, but the agents did not intend when they advised the Rees to keep the peace that they should not defend themselves, on the contrary, he should arm his young men, let them go together and fight together, and the Sioux would soon find out that their hearts were not dead, and would cease to molest them. The Great Father had no objection to their defending themselves, and if they were not strong enough he would help them.

No reply was made to this, and as everything was in readiness we shoved off down stream.

At Fort Clark I took some articles on board to be transported to Fort Pierre, and I was glad to be able thus to reciprocate, in a small way, the politeness I had received at the hands of the Fur Company's agents at all their stations.

Our journey down the river continued as monotonous as before, and each day resembled the other in all save the progress we made. Occasionally the wind would hold us at bay, and force us to lie under a bank for hours and days. This detention was extremely annoying, and I would have preferred the greatest hardships we had ever encountered upon land to the wearying listlessness of our wind-bound boats.

The river was in places so filled with sand-bars and snags that it was difficult to find a channel, but as our experience increased we became more skilful, and at last could avoid nearly every shoal and snag.

On the 30th of August we had come sufficiently far to be out of the way of the Blackfeet Sioux, so Lieutenant White determined to push on. With our best thanks for his kindness and good wishes for his safe voyage, he left us and was soon lost to sight. We continued, baffled by winds and sand-bars, and finally succeeded in reaching Fort Pierre, by dint of hard work, on the 2d of September.

This was our starting place in June, 1859, and we were welcomed by many who had seen us set out. The story of our massacre, set afloat by the Blackfeet Sioux, was believed, and already the prairie "quid nuncs" had been telling how they knew it would be so. I must do all of them the justice, however, to say that they welcomed us as warmly as if our coming had established, instead of refuted, their prophecies.

On the 8th of September Captain Raynolds's party arrived, and preparations were made to continue the journey, which were completed, and we sailed on the 10th.

Until the 15th, our journey down the river was of the old stamp, each day dragging after the other unbroken by incident, unmarked by any special circumstance. Sometimes I got so nervous at the perpetual splash and creak of the oars that I could scarcely contain myself; and even at night my dreams were of rowing, and the dreary ripple of the water against the boat sounded always in my ears.

At last, on the 15th, we reached Fort Randall, and were gladdened by the sight of familiar faces and the hospitable attentions of the officers of the post. The sudden change from the late uncivilized mode of life and flatboat fare to the delicate refinement of the gentlemen and ladies at the fort, and the luxuries that loaded their tables, was like magic. It did not prevent me, however, from enjoying myself, and the week passed at Fort Randall was to me a constant succession of feasting and pleasure. The land party again met us here, and on the 21st we set out again with but one more meeting to anticipate, and that at the end of our labors. Our friends at the fort escorted us to the river bank, and cheered us as we fell off into the stream. The flag streamed out in the breeze, but soon we were again reduced to our flat-boat condition, when a bend shut us out from the sight of the post.

The next day we reached Niohara, the new village at the mouth of Niohara or L'eau-qui-court river. Here our survey was to end, and the time spent waiting for the arrival of the land party was occupied in finishing the plot of the river, filling up notes, and preparing generally for a wind-up.

The remainder of the trip to Omaha was more interesting than the upper river, as there were numerous settlements on the banks of the river; and we obtained vegetables and butter and eggs at very reasonable prices.

At last, on the 3d of October, we reached Omaha city at 3 o'clock in the afternoon. I hired a house from a Frenchman, near the river bank, and had everything taken from the boats and stored. This took until dark, when, after a final search to see that nothing valuable was left on board, I left our boats with a hearty wish that I might never again be called on to make such a long voyage in such craft.

CHAPTER IV.

Having now detailed the most important events in my journey, I will submit a few general remarks upon some of the inferences to be drawn from the reconnoissance.

The total distance travelled between the 10th of May and the 4th of October, by my party, was 2,500 miles, including 1,400 miles of river travel.

The line of travel is a sweep from the Platte through the unexplored region about the Big Horn mountains, and the hitherto unknown streams of that section, down the Yellowstone and Missouri rivers.

This line encloses the present territory of Dakota, and its projection serves to correct some very great errors that exist on the maps even of the latest compilation.

The country within this line is about equally divided into a mountainous and prairie section; the former composing the western, the latter the eastern half. The whole water-shed of this immense region is through the Mississippi.

Throughout the mountains, during the months of May and June, the number of water-courses is immense. The mountains rise from rolling, broken hills into peaks and ranges of unbroken granite, seamed with millions of furrows, each of which contains a tiny rill. These unite and recombine into rivulets, gradually increasing to rivers, which again are enlarged by the constant additions they receive, until the wonderful volume of the Missouri is complete.

The rock and clay of the mountains preserve every drop that falls, and deliver their floods in torrents, producing sudden rises and freshets, which cause constant changes in the courses of the streams as soon as they reach alluvial valleys.

The process in the prairie is different. The snow in winter is packed by the wind into the depressions in the surface, where it melts under the suns of May and June, and is absorbed into the alluvial surface, forming a slough which is quickly grown up with grass and weeds. By the fall the water has evaporated, the vegetation dries up, and when by any chance it is set on fire it burns like tinder. Still a good deal of the water which is deposited on the prairies must find its way to the streams, for in nearly all of them water is found in holes. All the constant prairie streams have their sources in the mountains. This condition of things will go to show, what I have no hesitation in asserting, that the greater portion of the whole country embraced within my line is unsusceptible of profitable settlement or cultivation.

The few arable valleys in the Big Horn mountains are inconsiderable in size and separated from each other by rocky ranges difficult to cross. The prairie is too destitute of timber and water to attract or sustain settlers.

The valley of the Yellowstone offers the greatest advantages of any part of the country explored. It is fertile enough to yield generously to the hand of the farmer, and the capacity of its hills for grazing is unlimited. It is the paradise of the Indian, and in every direction it is marked by the tracks of the vast herds of buffalo, antelope, and elk which are subsisted upon it. This will apply to the Yellowstone from the mouth of Big Horn river to the mountains. The tributaries in this part are clear mountain streams; while from Big Horn down they are, with few exceptions, sluggish, muddy currents, flowing through barren clay hills, known as Mauvaises Terres, or Bad Lands.

Nearly all the country inside the curve of the Big Horn mountains is also of this description. There is every reason to believe that the mineral wealth of the mountainous portion is very great. I purposely discouraged any desire among those under my command to search for gold, but, in several instances, small quantities of the sands of some of the streams were washed and found to yield gold. Moreover, the geological features of these mountains are precisely similar to those of California and the neighborhood of Pike's peak, which abound in gold. But it is hardly probable that the gold could be obtained profitably, except by large outlays of capital, and concerted operations of organized companies.

For the details, however, of the geology, meterology, and natural history of the region, I must refer to the reports of those of my assistants who were in charge of those branches.

The exploration also shows that any route, either for a railroad or wagon road, through the Big Horn mountains, or by the valley of Big Horn river, is impracticable, except at immense cost.

A road connecting the Platte and the Yellowstone is easy and practicable, but it must go round, and not through, the Big Horn mountains.

It is necessary in crossing the prairies, or "the plains," as they are termed, to travel by water-courses; hence, from the Missouri westward, three routes offer —that by the Platte, which is well known; by the Cheyenne, which I do not think practicable, and by the Yellowstone.

So far as engineering problems are concerned, nothing difficult occurs in the latter. A road with easy grades could be made from the mouth of the Yellowstone to the head of the Missouri at a cost within reasonable limits, and a full supply of fuel, pine, and cottonwood timber, and, possibly, coal could be obtained. The valley of the Yellowstone would form a good continuation of a route from St. Paul to Fort Union, into Oregon and Washington, and might be a profitable location for a telegraph if a northern line should be projected.

The sketch of the route will convey a good idea of the topographical features of the country, for I can vouch for the correctness with which the topographer has recorded the results of his labors. To my associates generally, I beg to return my best thanks, and I will conclude my report by saying, that in all dangers and all emergencies I felt that I was surrounded by men on whom I could most fully rely.

Respectfully submitted.

HENRY E. MAYNADIER,
Captain 10th Infantry.

REPORTS OF DETACHED PARTIES.

Report of J. Hudson Snowden on explorations from the Platte to the head-waters of the Shayenne, 1859.

CAMP ON DEER CREEK, *October* 18, 1859.

SIR: You will proceed with the party that has been organized for that purpose to make an examination of the country between this point and Powder river, so as to ascertain the sources of the two forks of the Shayenne. To do this the best way will probably be to start from here so as to strike near or at the western end of Pumpkin butte, thence easterly, or northeasterly, to the heads of the streams mentioned, then to return to the Platte by a route east of that followed on going out. Circumstances may, however, indicate a better route, and should this be the case you will pursue such a course as will best accomplish the end in view, and to fill up the topography of the section of country between the routes passed over by Lieutenant Warren, topographical engineer, in 1857, and ourselves the past season. As a matter of safety, you will take with you rations for twenty days; but will aim, if possible, to be absent not more than fifteen days.

Very respectfully,

W. F. RAYNOLDS,
Captain Topographical Engineers.

J. HUDSON SNOWDEN,
Topographer, &c., Yellowstone Expedition.

WINTER QUARTERS, DEER CREEK, *April*, 1860.

SIR: I have the honor to submit the following report of a reconnoissance to Pumpkin butte and the source of the two forks of the Shayenne river, made by me in October last, in pursuance of your orders, a copy of which I append.

Dr. Hayden and Messrs. Schonborn and Waring accompanied me, and the whole party consisted of eight persons. Five animals were packed with provisions and bedding. I started October 19, and travelling down the valley of Deer creek to Bissonette's trading-house, picked up Michael Boyer, who, by your authority, I had employed to accompany me as guide and interpreter. Leaving the trading-house about noon, I crossed the Platte at a good ford, the water coming a little above our horses' knees; this is a lodge trail crossing, and is about a half mile below the trading-house.

Passing over a sandy ridge I came, in 4½ miles, into a valley of a dry creek, which emptied into the Platte five miles below Bissonette's; crossing this and following parallel to it over sandy spurs, I came, in 13½ miles, to the summit of a high ridge which divides the waters of the Platte from those of the Shayenne. From this point I could see Laramie Peak, bearing by compass south, 35° east, and all the intermediate range of mountains; this ridge has an elevation of about 800 feet above the Platte, and a short distance to the west of where I passed another higher ridge of more broken character, covered to some extent with pine, joins it nearly at a right angle. Running off in a direction a little west of north, extending to near Powder river, I followed a dry creek which comes down in many branches from the angle of these ridges. After pursuing it in a northeast course some six miles, and finding no water, I was forced to camp. There was no wood on this creek, and wild sage is the only resource for fuel.

The country passed over was sandy, covered with sage, cactus, and bunch grass; the high ridges show white sandstone in places. Travelled 21½ miles from Bissonette's, from which place I commenced the reconnoissance.

As soon as it was light on the morning of the 20th, I started down the valley of this dry creek, and in 3½ miles found a place where the water rose to the surface through the sand; here I remained until afternoon. The creek is destitute of timber at this place and above, but about 1½ mile below, and plainly visible, is a clump of cottonwood trees, where Boyer says there is water, and called by the Sioux, Mini-t-him-ki, or the Last Spring.

Leaving this creek I ascended and crossed a tolerably high ridge, and in three miles came upon a small creek in two branches, water springing up amidst salt-weed and rushes. Camped on this creek; the water good; no wood. The country had recently been set on fire and all the grass on the hillsides destroyed; that in the valley, however, was good. Travelled 6¾ miles.

The morning of the 21st was cool and pleasant. Travelling up a gently sloping ridge, and attaining the summit in 2¼ miles, we stopped to enjoy the view that presented itself. Ahead, Pumpkin butte showed plainly, and the high peaks of the Big Horn mountains; to the east, a faint outline of the Black hills; Laramie Peak, in the southeast rose up prominently above everything else in that direction.

Descending from the ridge and crossing a few gullies, I passed another of about equal elevation, and came to a creek with a sandy bed some forty yards wide. A little water forced to the surface by the impervious underlying strata runs for a short distance then sinks again in the sand; a few scattered cottonwoods fringe the banks.

Crossing a low sandy spur, I came upon several deep gullies with steep clay banks of black "bad land" earth; in the beds of these gullies I found springs of water with salt-weed growing in and around them.

In 8½ miles I came to the summit of another ridge, from which I could see the timber of a creek ahead; following down the valley of a small drain with water in holes here and there, I came, in three miles, to the head of a dry creek with considerable cottonwood growing in the points; the bed of the creek, about 40 yards wide, was as dry as a powder. We found some water about a mile below, and I camped in a clump of cottonwood trees. The hills we passed are composed of sandstone, and in many places resemble the sand hills of Loup fork; sand rock occurs on the summit of the ridges or where a gully washes a hillside; grass tolerably good; sage and cactus in abundance.

About seven miles distant, and parallel to the course I travelled, to the west, runs the pine ridge in which all the creeks we crossed head. Travelled 13 miles.

The morning of the 22d was fresh and cool. Light cirri clouds covered the sky, and the sun gave little warmth. Crossing a low spur of hills I came upon the dry bed of a tributary of the stream we camped on.

In six miles we reached the summit of a high ridge and, in passing over a gentle depression in the high prairie divide, we came to the north end of the ridge where it breaks off into drainage leading to Powder river.

Descended rapidly, and crossed deep and precipitous gullies, difficult in places to cross a pack mule. Followed a broken spur of a ridge, which led to a creek closed in by high perpendicular bluffs of clay rocks. Water in holes was impregnated and rendered bitter by a decoction of leaves falling from a few large cottonwood trees that fringe the banks. The grass here was good, in small quantity. Camped here for the night, having travelled 16 miles.

Starting early on the morning of the 23d, and crossing several broken spurs and deep gullies, I camped close under Pumpkin butte, where Michael Boyer found a small quantity of good water standing in basins washed in the sand-rock. Our camp was in a deep gully enclosed by perpendicular walls of red sand-rock 40 or 50 feet high. A few cottonwood and cedar trees furnished fuel, and the hills were covered with good grass. It was early when I camped, having travelled only 5¾ miles.

Leaving two of the men in charge of the camp and animals, I ascended the second butte from the south; the ascent was not steep until near the top, which is surrounded by a grayish sand-rock, with pine and dwarf cedar growing in the crevices, presenting a sheer face of from 25 to 30 feet, and it is only in a few places, where masses have fallen, over which you can reach the summit. On top it is flat, covered with buffalo grass, with an elevation not more than 1,000 feet above our camp, and breaking off on all sides in the same manner as the side we approached. The butte is comprised by four separate shafts, all bearing the same general character, but somewhat different in size and shape, joined at the bases, and rising up from a ridge which divides the waters of the north and south Shayenne, and both of these streams form the Powder river; the drainage of the first and last of these rivers rising within a few feet on either side of the butte. On the west side, after the fall of perpendicular rock, and below this the debris, comes a smooth, gentle slope, which is traversed up to the very base of the rocks by deep and narrow gullies; these joining a short distance below form creeks running northeast into Powder river, while, on the eastern side, the fall, after leaving the butte, is much less precipitous, and the drains that you see leaving the butte in that direction, after following them a short distance with your eye, are lost in a plain only bounded by the horizon.

A most magnificent view presents itself from the top of this butte. The whole range of the Big Horn mountains, from the head of Clear fork to the head of Powder river, all the higher peaks, now covered with snow, could be distinctly recognized, and many familiar localities along the foot range. Turning to the south the Laramie mountains were also plainly visible; from Laramie Peak to the Red buttes, also, a few points, but not so distinct in the Rattlesnake range.

In the east it was more hazy. A dim, blue cloud-like ridge, I took to be the

Inyan Kara of the Black Hills, was all I could distinguish. A band of mountain sheep were seen, and Michael killed a fine black-tailed deer. Pumpkin butte is called by the Sioux Indians "Wa-ga-mu Pa-ha," or Gourd hill, as some of the mountain men say, on account of a small species of gourd that grows upon it; but this is not the case as far as I could ascertain, and I presume the name is derived from some dance or ceremony in which the rattling gourd holds a position. Mr. Schonborn took observations on the butte, as he did along the route; but the results have not as yet been computed, and I am unable to give the proper elevations of points at this time.

Leaving our camp on the morning of the 24th, and passing between the two most southern buttes, I followed parallel to the course of drain running in northeast direction, (which I found was the head of "Belle Fourché,") crossing rolling spurs of the high prairie on my right. The grass was good over these hills, and recent signs of numerous herds of buffalo and a few butchered carcasses showed that the Indians had been hunting here not long since, and now there were none to be seen. In 10½ miles we crossed a creek, destitute of timber, with a broad open valley and large holes of water. The valley was filled with antelope. This creek runs in a north and northeast direction, joining the first drain that we followed down, forming, with others, the head of the Belle Fourché, or north fork of the Shayenne. Crossing two ridges, I camped on a drain with water in holes, running into the last mentioned creek.

There was no wood here, but a little sage, and a great quantity of "bois du vache." The water was slightly impregnated with salts, but not unpalatable. Travelled 15¼ miles.

Crossed a ridge on the morning of the 25th, from the top of which I could see ahead of us a singular ridge, running at right angles to our course, some six miles distant, covered with a multitude of red cones and miniature pumpkin buttes, resembling very much in character the hills to the northeast and east of your route on the head of Tongue river, and Clear fork of Powder.

Following down a prairie drain, with a wide open valley covered with herds of antelope, now running in every direction frightened at our approach, I crossed a creek with water in holes, very salty, running in northeast direction along the base of the ridge, with open valley on the west side. No wood on this creek. I passed through the hills on the east side, composed of cone buttes and square hills, forming minor spurs to the main ridge. These hills are whitish indurated clay, capped with red lignite rock; steep near the top, but taking a gentle slope near the base; drained by steep and broken gullies into the creek we last crossed.

Emerging from these hills and turning more to the southeast, over a slightly concave basin draining in a northeast direction, I passed a ridge, from the top of which we took our last look at Pumpkin butte, which presents the same appearance from this side as it does from the west. Here, too, we could see the high peaks of the Big Horn mountains. This is the dividing ridge between the north and south fork of the Shayenne.

A spur led us rapidly down to the valley of a creek that rises in many branches in a basin of the ridge; a short distance below the juncture of these branches two spurs close in on the creek, leaving a narrow opening for its passage into the plains beyond. I camped just above the opening in the ridge, where the timber commenced, in a barren little valley covered with sage, and with poor grass. The small quantity of water in the holes was very bad, thick, muddy, and filled with animalculæ, requiring straining through a handkerchief before you could drink it, and what remained in the handkerchief would be much more interesting to a naturalist than to a thirsty traveller. The ridges around were sprinkled with pine. In many places the hills are denuded of vegetation, and the black, "bad land" soil presents a very barren appearance. I saw a small band of buffalo bulls, and a pack of large prairie wolves. Travelled 18 miles.

On the 26th I travelled down the valley of the creek. As we proceeded the timber increased in size and quantity; the valley was covered with sage, grease-wood, and cactus, crossed by narrow deep gullies that run out from the piney ridge. After passing through the narrow opening left by these ridges, the country was more rolling and the hills were covered with grass. Several drains empty into the creek, some of which are thickly timbered. I had been travelling on the south bank, but in 11½ miles crossed where the water was running, but sinks again a short distance below. I camped in a bend in a thick grove of large cottonwood trees. Water in a large hole, with which we supplied ourselves and animals.

The bed of the creek here is 20 yards wide; grass not very good. Boyer says the name of this creek is Mini Pusa, or Dry Creek, a name well adapted to all the creeks in this section of country. It is, in fact, one of the most northern branches of the south fork of the Shayenne, and is called, together with a larger branch below, the North fork, by the men living along the Platte, in contradistinction to the more southern branches of the south fork of the Shayenne. These men only know what we call the North fork as the Belle Fourché. Travelled 13 miles.

Leaving the river bottom on the 27th, I travelled along the valley on the north side, crossing deep ravines. We came in seven miles on to a large fresh lodge trail that turned off here to the north. Michael told me this was the trail of the Ogallalah going to the head of the Missouri, and he could not conceal his joy at not meeting them. I proceeded on this trail for several miles, when it turned toward the creek. Leaving it, I camped below at a good hole of water.

The country passed over was more open and rolling. . Several branches came into the creek from the south side. The creek bottom is heavily timbered with large cottonwood, and a great deal of dead timber lies scattered about. The bottom is sandy, covered with good grass all around. Where we camped, and in places, it was still quite green. The Indians have made this a camping ground. Wood was piled up, lodge poles lay scattered about, and numbers of trees felled. Travelled 13 miles.

October 28.—The morning was cold, with a raw wind from the southeast, cloudy, and looked very much like snow. The water in the holes was frozen hard. Leaving the valley, in a short distance I passed over a low point of hills coming in two and a half miles to the main south fork, the same creek that I camped on near its head on the 21st. Crossing it a short distance above its junction with the creek I had just left, where the bed is 150 yards wide, dry and sandy, the banks are fringed with willow and young cottonwood. I travelled down through a well-wooded bottom, the trees growing over sand ridges; the same character as Lewis and Clark's fortifications on Bon-Homme island, and similar to those on Platte river and along the Loup fork. The river made a sharp bend to the northeast. I camped, and we prepared to weather a storm that appeared ready to descend upon us.

We could not have found a more sheltered position. Our camp was surrounded by a dense thicket of young cottonwood, protecting us from wind, and furnishing bark for the animals. The river here has a bed about 200 yards wide; is dry in places, but rises in a ledge of rock below our camp, runs for a short distance, and again sinks beneath the sand. This must be a formidable stream during a wet season, and, when running any quantity of water, must be difficult to ford on account of quicksand. Very few places afford a better wintering ground for a large party than this.

A bottom enclosed and protected by hills, filled with large cottonwood, and young groves that would furnish sustenance to almost any number of horses; good grass covers the bottom and neighboring hills. The Indians have taken advantage of these natural facilities, and from appearances have frequently wintered here in large numbers. Much to my surprise it cleared up, and in the afternoon, when going out to a high hill south of camp, I could see the windings of the South fork for some distance. After running past our camp in a northeast course, it turns to the south, continuing in that direction for about five miles, then again turns to the east, pursuing that course as far as I could see. Travelled 4½ miles.

The morning of the 29th was cold and cloudy. Striking off in a southwest direction I followed a spur which shed off into deep gullies, the drainage on the right going into the South fork, which could only be traced in the distance and cloudy atmosphere by the depression of the valley and the high bluffs on the opposite; on the left the gullies joined, emptying at the bend six miles below our last camp.

The spur led towards a point of a prominent ridge having two cone buttes, and a series of sharp projecting rocks standing out from the ridge on the divide. The ridge is a continuation of the same we camped under the night of the 25th; it is covered to some extent with pine—is cut through by the South fork, and this point of rocks extend out on the divide between that stream. Descending from the divide over a sandy slope, thence across a sage plain, I camped on the tributary. This creek is fringed with large cottonwood, and has good water in holes, with a deep narrow bed; greasewood and sage covers the bottom ; grass good and abundant. It runs east towards the South fork, taking its rise far back in the Lignite hills. Travelled 22 miles.

October 30.—Travelled in a southeast direction toward another point of the Lignite ridge, projecting out on a divide similar to the place I had passed. I crossed a dry bed of a small creek which rises in the ridge on the left, thence over a low sandy spur, where a few pines grew, and many stumps and dead trees showed that a good deal of the timber had been destroyed either by the fires or atmospheric agencies. In about five miles I attained the divide close under the projecting spur of the piney ridge. From this place I could see a very broken country ahead, relieved in the distance by a high ridge which divides the South fork from the Platte, and beyond this the Laramie mountains stood up in bold relief.

The Lignite pine ridge takes a sharp turn here to the west. Between me and the Platte divide I could see several branches of creeks, separated by spurs of hills heading in a mass of sand-hills far to the west, running east and northeast to the South fork. Leaving the ridge, over some very rough and bad lands, we crossed two well-wooded branches near their junction with each other; both were dry, with high steep banks; the valleys barren and filled with greasewood, and enclosed by broken "bad land" spurs. Crossing a ridge I camped on another of these branches ; here we found good water in the shallow ; timber sufficient for camping purposes, and grass good, but not abundant. Travelled 14½ miles.

October 31.—I travelled up the creek for a mile, then leaving it and taking to the hills on the left, I reached the crest of a spur of the Platte divide. This spur is high, intricate, and so narrow in places as barely to admit one animal to pass; breaking off on both sides into gullies leading to the creek on which we last camped, on the right, while the drains on the left run into another branch of about equal size which heads in the divide we were approaching. Pine and cedar grow in the heads of these gullies ; here I saw several black-tailed deer. As we proceeded the ridge flattened out, and off to our right the country was rolling and covered with grass.

We crossed paths made by antelope that were very fresh, and from the well-worn trail and multitude of tracks they must have passed recently in great numbers. Michael Boyer told me that they migrate every fall to the sand-hills on the heads on the branches of the South fork of the Shayenne. I camped on a creek near its head, close under the Platte divide, where we found water in a hole covered with ice two inches thick. Cottonwood grows along the banks, while the ravines and spurs from the divide are covered with pine. Sage covers the valleys; grass not very good. Travelled 16½ miles.

The morning of November 1st, was cold and cloudy, with a raw southeast wind blowing.

We ascended the divide by a spur, following deer paths that wound among the pines and cedars. I saw ten black-tailed deer, and the signs show that many inhabit this ridge. In three miles we attained the summit. A short distance to our right, on the top of the divide is a long white ridge, resembling very much a new rock-railroad embankment, which Dr. Hayden found to belong to the "White river tertiary formation." The Sioux call this ridge "Tak-che-cua-paha," or Antelope Park hill, from a pen built of pine logs near the base, in the form of a circle, ending in a narrow lane which leads to a pit about eight feet deep surrounded by pickets. Many antelope paths pass through this pen, which is now destroyed, only a few logs marking the outline of the fence; the pit, however, is in a good state of preservation. Michael told me that eight years ago the Indians used this pen to trap antelope, and that it was built by the Arapahoes. Descending from the divide by a pine spur, I camped on a creek which runs into the Platte. Good water springs up in the creek bed, and our camp was surrounded by a fine clump of young cottonwoods; grass was good, but not much of it. Travelled 8¾ miles.

Travelling in a southwest direction on the 2d, in a mile and a half we crossed a branch of the same creek with water in holes. Coming upon a spur of the main divide, I could see the Platte about 10 miles distant.

Passing over "bad land" gullies, running from the divide, separated by hills of the same white or rather flesh-colored marl and coarse sandstone, some washed and denuded, others covered with bunch grass and some buffalo grass, I reached the Platte road about noon, crossed the Platte and camped at the mouth of "La Bente" creek in a beautiful little valley surrounded by high steep hills. Travelled 14¾ miles.

Striking the Platte road on the morning of the 3d, at the crossing of Wagon Hound creek, I followed it all the way to Deer creek, camping the night of the 3d on a small creek between La Prele and Box Elder. One of the pack mules giving out on the road, and being unable to get it along, even after having relieved it of its pack, I was forced to leave it at La Prele in charge of a trader, where it subsequently died. I reached Deer creek on the 4th, having been absent 17 days, and during that time travelled a distance of 247 miles. The animals were weak when I started, from the long tramp of last summer, and the miserable pack-saddles, although lightly packed, soon used up the backs of two of them; these saddles have no pads and are too narrow in front; the two evils combined render a bad back unavoidable in a very short time.

The season I travelled through this region was a very dry one, no rain had fallen for a long time, and when I mention finding water, might be relied on as permanent.

Sir St. George Gore, in the summer of 1855, took a large train of ox and mule wagons from the Platte near the mouth of Box Elder to Powder river, passing near the west side of Pumpkin butte, demonstrating that wagons can be taken through; but I would not recommend the route, both on account of scarcity of water in a dry season, and the rough nature of the country between Pumpkin butte and the Powder river.

Should a road ever be needed from this vicinity on the Platte to the head of the Little Missouri river, I think the best route would be over, or a little east of, my trail to Pumpkin butte, striking the head of the Belle Fouché about 12 miles east of the Pumpkin butte, thence along the Belle Fouché. At least, as far as I could see, there was no serious obstacle that would reader it impracticable.

The want of timber on the head of the Belle Fouché and the high elevation might render travel through that portion dangerous in winter season. The eastern portion of my route was through a very broken region, unfit for wagon travel. The whole of this region is barren and desolate, totally unfit for the uses of a civilized being—interesting to a geologist, and a splendid Indian country.

Very respectfully, your obedient servant,

J. HUDSON SNOWDEN, *Topographer.*

Captain W. F. RAYNOLDS,
Topographical Engineer, Commander of Expedition.

Report of First Lieutenant John Mullins, 2d dragoons, on route from Fort Benton to Fort Union, between the Missouri and Yellowstone rivers, 1860.

HEADQUARTERS MISSOURI AND YELLOWSTONE EXPEDITION,
In camp opposite Fort Benton, N. T., July 18, 1860.

SIR: As it will be necessary for your command to march from this point to the mouth of the Yellowstone, while I propose to descend the Missouri in a boat, you will proceed by way of the south side of the Missouri, and are charged with the duty of making a topographical examination of the country through which you will pass.

The whole country between the Missouri and Yellowstone rivers is unknown. The objects to be attained are to ascertain approximately the dividing ridge between the two rivers, the sources of the streams flowing into each, the character of the country, its agricultural and mineralogical resources, and the practicability of running wagon and rail roads over it. Careful topographical notes should be taken and such barometrical observations made as will enable you to give a profile of your whole route. A field map should be kept up so as to provide in a measure against the loss that would result from the destruction of notes. Such observations of latitude and magnetic variation should be made as is possible with the instruments I am able to furnish you.

A portion of the Indian goods belonging to the expedition will be given you for the purpose of securing the good-will or services of any Indians you may meet. The following persons are assigned to your command to aid you in the discharge of duties in the capacities named:

James Bridger, guide; Dr. F. V. Hayden, naturalist; A. Schonborn, artist and meteorologist; W. D. Stuart, topographer.

A sufficient number of packers will also be sent to take care of the animals belonging to the expedition. In addition to this, you will take with you the whole detachment of the escort that accompanied me to this place.

You will use your utmost endeavors to reach the mouth of the Yellowstone in season to leave there by the 20th of August for Fort Randall. A report will be required of you, and you will therefore keep your notes in such a manner as to be able to make it.

Very respectfully, your obedient servant,

WM. F. RAYNOLDS,
Captain Topographical Engineers, Commanding.

First Lieut. JOHN MULLINS, *2d Dragoons,*
Commanding Escort to Yellowstone Exploring Expedition,
Camp at Fort Benton.

CAMP AT FORT BENTON, *July* 20, 1860.

SIR: In obedience to the above order I left Fort Benton to-day, having with me the whole party detailed by yourself. After ascending the bluff skirting the valley of the Missouri river on the south, I pursued the easterly course, and after marching one and a half mile arrived at a clear running stream, its valley bordered with a fine growth of young and thrifty cottonwood. The stream is called the , and heads in what is called the Highwood spur of the Belt mountains. The course of the stream is about north-northwest, and it empties into the Missouri river a short distance below Fort Benton.

Leaving the stream, I struck upon and followed for 13½ miles an Indian lodge trail which led to a fine spring, where I encamped, having made a day march of 15 miles. The weather during the day was quite pleasant, although it clouded up, and we had a slight sprinkling of rain about noon. The country was favorable in character, being a high, rolling prairie; the soil rich, and grass excellent. The spring, near which we encamped, gushed out from beneath a high precipitous ledge of rocks, towering up for some 300 feet. The water was excellent and abundantly sufficient in quantity for men and animals. The grass was excellent in quality and abundant. A remarkable feature about this spring was the fact that its waters sank at a distance of some 200 yards from its source, and probably, by a subterranean passage, joined its waters to those of a small lake about 500 yards from camp. The borders of this lake were thickly covered with a deposit of alkali from the evaporation of its waters, although the water of the spring was entirely devoid of any saline or alkaline taste.

From our camp we had a most delightful view of the Belt mountains to our right, terminating in two high, round buttes; and far away to our left rose the peaked tops of Bear's Paw and the Judith mountains in the east and northeast, sloping down to broad, table buttes.

Between these points all the intermediate country appeared rough and broken. The weather was cloudy at night, and I got no observations for latitude.

July 21.—Weather clear and pleasant; left camp at 7.10 a. m. and travelled east by south. Travelled about three miles and was then forced to abandon the cart, as the country was too rough, and I had no suitable harness. As this step rendered the odometer useless, I was forced to determine my distance by time and rate of travel. The barometer was also accidentally broken, but Mr. Schonborn was enabled to ascertain the relative elevation and depression by means of the boiling point of water. The character of the country to-day changed gradually, as we increased our distance from last night's camp, from a high, rolling prairie to a rough broken character; soil poor and of a whitish color. About three and a half miles from camp passed two high, round buttes to the south, and distant about five miles. At five miles from camp crossed a dry creek, heavily timbered with cottonwood; course east. Followed down this creek on an Indian trail, made by the Flatheads, who had preceeded us some weeks on their annual hunt to lay in their winter supply of buffalo meat.

After following down the valley of this creek four and a half miles we crossed a small, clear, running stream putting into it. A mile and a half further brought us to the mouth of the stream, it emptying into a deep, bold stream called Arrow river. This stream runs along the base of a long range of precipitous bluffs, which reach an elevation of 250 feet above the valley of the river.

Finding an abundance of fuel at this point I camped, having made a day's march of 11 miles. Grass was scarce, but I did not see any chance of bettering our condition. The soil here contains much lime and gravel.

July 22—Leaving camp this morning we followed the Indian trail, which led in an east southeast direction to the top of the bluff. I then changed my course to due east, and travelled in that direction for 13 miles over a series of high, level table-lands covered with excellent grass. The soil was dark in color, and contained a good deal of sand intermixed with a little gravel, After travelling

13 miles over the country described above, we crossed a clear running stream, with fine wide valley and good grass, but not a stick of timber either in the valley or in sight.

After making the crossing, we travelled over a rolling prairie for two miles further, and then crossed another creek which had no timber in its valley, and the waters of which were saline. At this point I changed my course and travelled east by north over a broken country much cut up by ravines. A march of five miles up this course brought me to a deep dry creek bed with precipitous banks; following down the bed of this creek for one and a half miles we came suddenly upon a bold swift stream, which the guide informed me was called Judith river. The stream is about 30 yards wide, and the valley varies from one half to three quarters of a mile in width, heavily timbered, principally cottonwood, with a thick undergrowth of cherry and serviceberry. Here we found traces of large Indian camps, showing the place to be the favorite winter resort of the Blackfeet. The location is excellently adapted to this purpose, as it is so completely sheltered. In fact, you are not aware of the existence of the stream until you are within a few yards of it; for so very precipitous are the bluffs that skirt the valley that you cannot even see the tops of the trees in the valley until you are within a few yards of the edge of the precipice. Latitude, by meridian observation of the sun, 47° 17′ 56″.

Ascending to the top of the bluff near camp I was enabled to get a fine view of the country. Bearing east-southeast from my position I noted a high range of the Judith mountains circling in irregular outline to the north northeast, terminating near us in high, detached buttes, covered with pine and cedar, while far to the south-southeast rose dimly the broken outline of the Belt mountains, stretching away to the south and terminating abruptly upon the valley of the Missouri. By the aid of my field-glass I could see distinctly what is called "Devil's Gate," on the Missouri river, as well as an indistinct view of the valley near the position of the Great Falls. The whole presented a very picturesque appearance, and there seems to be quite a valley between the Judith and Belt mountains, showing the existence of a stream, which is probably a tributary of the Yellowstone.

July 23—Made a short march to-day, travelling southeast. After making three and a half miles I encamped on one of the principal branches of the Judith, about half-a-mile above its junction with the main river. The fork upon which we encamped has a north-northwest course and appears to head in the Belt mountains. The other branch which is nearly the same size, has a westerly course, and heads in the principal range of the Judith mountains. Both these branches have the same character as the main river—narrow valley, well wooded, and being clear, bold running streams. The soil of the valley is rich and the grass is excellent. This locality is well adapted for stock-raising and agricultural purposes. Latitude 47° 14′ 13″.2.

July 24.—Weather clear and warm. Left camp this morning at 6 a. m., and travelled, east by south, up the left hand fork of the Judith, crossing it several times in order to avail ourselves of the best country for travelling. The country was more broken than during yesterday's route, and the route consequently rougher. I was gradually ascending a depression in the Judith mountains, where I expected to find a pass. At five miles from camp we crossed a stream putting in from the south. At half-past 9 a. m. I observed a large band of Indians approaching us down the valley of the stream we were ascending; I sent an advance party with my guide to ascertain who they were. They proved to be the "Little Robes," a band of the Blackfeet Indians. They were delighted to meet me, and I accompanied them to their village, half a mile distant, where, to my surprise, I saw waving from the top of the chief's tent the "Star-Spangled banner." I counted 54 lodges, and estimated the number of Indians to be about 150 or 200. They insisted upon my stopping with them, saying that they wished to eat, smoke, and talk with their white brethren. I concluded it was best to stop, and after selecting a good position for defence in case of treachery, I ordered out a stronger guard than usual, and had the animals hoppled within gun-shot of camp, and the packs, parfliches, saddles, &c., piled up in such a manner as to form a defensive work, to be used if necessary. The chief invited me to his tent and set out something to eat, of which I partook, although it was not very palatable in its nature, still I did not want to offend the feelings of our red brothers. I was enabled to talk with them through my guide and interpreter, James Bridger, who spoke the Flathead language and was readily understood, as there were several members of the band who were Flatheads and could interpret to the rest. I distributed a portion of the Indian goods that had been placed in my hands, with which they were highly delighted. The chief, a cross-eyed Indian, said that "his heart was full of joy," and that he loved his white brethren. He then harangued the people, and they gathered together a large quantity of buffalo meat and carried it down to my camp; we found it, just then, to be a very valuable and acceptable addition to our stock of provisions.

The country now becomes more broken and we are increasing our elevation rapidly. The Judith mountains are now in front and to the south of us, while several high buttes are in sight to the north. Got a meridian observation of the sun to-day for latitude, 47° 06′ 39″.2.

July 25.—Weather clear and pleasant; left camp at 6 a. m. and continued our course up the creek,.which had now dwindled down to a small branch with but little timber upon it. Followed this creek but a short distance, and then leaving it to my left I marched over a h gh rolling prairie, ascending gradually. At a distance of 14 miles from camp we arrived at the summit of the "Judith Pass," or the divide between Muscleshell and Judith rivers. We found this pass to be much lower than we had anticipated and the route was far better than we had anticipated, as we met with but few obstructions to impede our progress. Crossing the divide we proceeded 11½ miles further and encamped on the waters of the Muscleshell river, after a day's march of 25½ miles. The Muscleshell at this point is a beautiful, bold, running stream, and heads in the highest range of the Judith mountains. The country over which we passed to-day, after leaving the divide, was beautifully diversified in its nature. All the higher hills were covered with dense groves of yellow pine, extending in some instances down the slopes to the rolling country beyond, with now and then, at intervals of two or three miles distance, clear streams of running water. The soil throughout this region is rich, and there is an excellent growth of grass. I think this neighborhood is admirably adapted for agricultural pursuits.

Game is now becoming more plenty, and to-day we saw signs of buffalo. From a position near our camp this afternoon I could see the mountains of Twenty-five Yard river far away to the south, as well as the dim outline of the Yellowstone valley and the mountains beyond.

July 26.—Weather mild but cloudy. Left camp this morning at 6.30; our route for the first 14 miles was through a descending country, similar in every respect to that passed over after crossing the Judith Pass. All the high points were covered with beautiful groves of pine and we were constantly crossing valleys covered with fine grass, through which ran clear streams of excellent water. The soil was rich, sand with occasional outcroppings of sandstone, which is well adapted for building purposes. During the last six miles of our march the country changed gradually from the nature described above to that of the "Mauvaise Terres;" the soil containing a large constituent of lime. Very little vegetation except a few cedar and pine reefs. The whole country during the last six miles of our route presented a strong contrast to the rich and arable country that we had just emerged from. During the latter part of our march we struck upon an Indian lodge trail, which led us to a small stream running northeast, upon which I camped, although there was but a scanty supply of water. There was a little cottonwood, sufficient for fuel, but little grass. I considered myself very fortunate in striking this trail, for the chances were that otherwise we would have been obliged to camp without water. Our hunter was fortunate, too, and succeeded in getting a good supply of fresh meat, so that, notwithstanding the barren appearance of our position, we were enabled to pass the night very comfortably. Marched 20 miles to-day, and camped at 2 p. m. While en route I halted and obtained a meridian altitude of the sun, which made our latitude 46° 55′ 55″ 92.

July 27.—I changed my course a little this morning, bearing more to the northward and making an east-northeast course. I marched in this direction for nine and one-half miles over a barren country, occasionally broken up by precipitous bluffs and ravines, with no vegetation but sage bushes. After accomplishing this distance I arrived at Yellowwater creek and determined to camp there, as my guide informed me that it was 25 or 30 miles to the Muscleshell river, with no water intermediate. This creek furnished us with an ample supply of good water, very yellow in color, hence the name of the creek. We had barely enough timber for camping purposes and but little grass. The valley of this stream is wide, with however but little vegetation, except sage and greasewood; the soil is clayish and very sticky. The whole country in this neighborhood appears barren, with the exception of a few pine groves on the higher bluffs. Got no observation for latitude to-day.

July 28.—Left camp at 6 a. m., shaping my course east-southeast over a barren and cheerless country, which was much cut up by hills and ravines; no wood nor water, soil sandy, and containing a large proportion of lime. Our march to-day was one of the most fatiguing that we have ever encountered, as we made 28½ miles, the day being warm and sultry, the country dry and dusty. Fortunately, at 2 p. m., we discovered the valley of the Muscleshell river, and a weary march of eight miles, with animals nearly broken down, brought us to the river—a bold, beautiful stream, about 25 or 30 yards wide, with a fine valley, which was diversified by the appearance of groves of cottonwood. The Muscleshell runs north from this point to the Missouri, and its head seems to be in the mountains of Twenty-five Yard or Shield's river. The country east and south of us seems very much broken, with constant appearance of pine and cedar reefs. From this point, as far as the eye could reach, the country seemed covered with immense herds of buffalo, all moving toward the valley of the Yellowstone. I selected a good camp for the night, and then sent out my hunters, who killed several fat cows. We then had a general feast on humpribs, marrowbones, tenderloin, &c., and all the party, beneath the genial influence of the feast, seemed to recover their pristine spirits. The grass being tolerably good, I determined to lie here to-morrow for the purpose of recruiting animals, and preparing for another march through the "bad lands" by which we are completely environed, and which present anything but a welcome appearance.

July 29.—Remained in camp all day; at noon got a meridian altitude of the sun, which made our latitude 46° 48′ 34″.27.

July 30.—Continued our march this morning, keeping a general easterly direction of a barren, rough country. Passed a number of herds of buffalo, who seemed to have eaten off every sprig of grass; we met with no water after leaving camp, until after a march of 23 miles we camped near the bed of a small creek containing water in holes; no grass, and but little wood. To our left we could see high reefs of cedar and pine timber, while to our right we could see the timber in the valley of the Porcupine, distant about 12 miles. During the night we were much annoyed by the buffaloes running through camp.

July 31.—Left camp this morning on a northeast course, which we continued for five and one-half miles, and then changed our course to due north, travelling in that direction four miles further. Our first march of five miles was over a gradually ascending country toward the cedar reefs to the northeast; arriving at these we found that they skirted the bluffs adjacent to the valley of the Porcupine river and its three principal tributaries. From this point I had a magnificent view of the valley and country beyond, as far as the eye could reach in every direction. Large herds of buffalo were visible in the different valleys. The three forks of the Porcupine were seen almost to their source, winding through white hills and cedar reefs, all coming in together near the same point and forming the main Porcupine. Their green timbered valley contrasted with the white rocky bluffs and broken highlands; all the valley, being filled with buffalo, presented a striking variety in natural scenery. After considerable trouble in getting down the steep rocky bluffs, we at length reached the main river; but, to my great surprise, I found it nearly dry, there being but a few holes of water in its bed, and the water in them rendered undrinkable by the constant wallowing of the buffaloes. I therefore marched up the valley of the Porcupine four miles and encamped upon one of its tributaries, where I found better grass and purer water, although I estimated that one-third of the fluid that we dignified by the name of water was buffalo urine. Travelled nine and one-half miles. At noon I halted and got a meridian observation of the sun, which made our latitude 47° 01′ 42″.

August 1.—We continued our march to-day up the right-hand fork of the Porcupine, the general direction being northeast, gradually ascending to the divide between the Yellowstone and Missouri rivers. I reached the divide after a tedious march of 18 miles, crossed it, and proceeded for six miles further down a tributary of what is called the Big Dry Sandy river. The whole country traversed to-day was dry and barren; no wood, water, nor grass; the latter having been entirely eaten off by the buffaloes. I now began to feel quite uneasy about my animals and feared seriously that they would not be able to make the trip; near the divide two animals broke down and I was compelled to leave them behind. Fortunately I found a camping place near some large holes of brackish water, but we had very little wood or grass. I shot a fine young cow near camp, and had barely gotten in when we were visited by a sudden and very severe hailstorm. The waters of the little creek upon which we were encamped raised suddenly so high as to overflow its valley, and force us to remove some portions of the camp to higher ground. Some of the animals were very much injured by the pelting of the large hailstones.

August 2.—Left camp this morning at 6 a. m.; our general course was along the Missouri slope of the divide over a country that is entirely and emphatically worthless, being principally made up of "white bad land" hills and precipitous ravines, with occasional outcroppings of the lignite or semi-coal beds. No wood nor grass, but abundance of water, the result of the recent hail and rain storm. After travelling 13½ miles I encamped on Dry Sandy, without wood and with very little grass.

August 3.—One of my men being sick I was unable to proceed far, so I camped after a march of three and one-half miles, on a small tributary of the Sandy coming in from the northwest, which was well timbered and seemed a favorable location in which to lie over. Just before reaching the timber I discovered, by aid of my glass, a large body of Indians approaching us rapidly; I selected a camp in the timber under cover of the cottonwood trees and dead timber. Very soon about 12 Indians galloped up to the crest of the hill above my camp, and halted, as if to reconnoitre my position. I sent out the guide (James Bridger) to ascertain what they wanted, and in the meantime had all my animals hobbled and tied up close to camp. Bridger soon returned bringing the Indians into camp, saying that they were Crows and friendly. I observed that they were all dressed in war-costume; their bows strung, and arrows and rifles in their hands, and seemed to have an unfriendly scowl upon their faces. Having with me only

14 available men, I stationed half of them as a guard over the animals under under charge of a sergeant, and the other half placed over the property in camp. In a few minutes three of the Indians fired their rifles in the air, and on my asking what it meant, they informed me that "their hearts were bad," and they had come to avenge themselves upon the white men. The answer was hardly given before my camp was charged upon by about 250 Crow warriors, yelling at the tops of their voices and firing about 30 shots into my camp, but, fortunately, doing no damage except shooting a few holes through one tent, and riding over another. I cautioned my men not to fire on the Indians unless some one of my party was hit. The object of the Indians in charging in this manner was to stampede my animals, and by that means get possession of them, but as I had taken the precaution to have the animals hobbled and tied up, the Indians failed to accomplish their object.

It was with the greatest difficulty I succeeded in getting the Indians sufficiently quiet to hear what I had to say to them. By the aid of Bridger, who understood their language, I was enabled to talk to their chief, "Great Bear," or "Mato-Luta" I will submit, verbatim, as translated, his conversation on this occasion. He said: "Our hearts are bad. The white man is no longer a friend to the Crow Indian. The Great Father has deceived us. We have not received our annuities. My people are sick and dying from eating bread given to us when the Great Father sent three steamers up the Missouri river. We made a treaty with the Great Father many moons ago, in which the Great Father at Washington told us that we must not leave our own country, and that our annuities would be delivered to us every year in our own country. They have not been sent to us this year, but the Great Father has sent them to our enemies' country, [such is the fact; their goods were sent to Major Twiss, in Ogallalla, Sioux country, by some misrepresentation on the part of persons interested against the American Fur Company,] where we cannot get them; for our enemies are stronger than we. The white man has set our enemies upon us; some of our warriors have been killed, and we have lost many horses. They have taken our trading post [Fort Sarpy, on the Yellowstone river] away from us. We could go there and trade with the whites without being killed by our enemies, the Sioux; but now we have no presents; we cannot trade our robes for blankets anywhere. The Sioux will not let us trade at Fort Union; and now, our hearts being black, we have come out to fight *you*."

I informed the chief that it was not the fault of the Great Father that their goods had been sent to the Sioux country, but the fault of their agent. He replied that they had not seen the agent, but that Major Schoonover, at Fort Union, had talked well to them.

I am of the opinion that this matter should be looked into by the department. Some one ought to be responsible for these open violations of treaties with the Indians on our western frontiers. Treaties and promises have been neglected and violated so often with these tribes that treachery on their part may be expected at any time.

Having succeeded in pacifying the Indians sufficiently to prevent a fight, the chief desired me not to go near their camp, as the hearts of his young men were still black, and he knew that he could not control them. Seeing the justice of his advice, I followed it.

I got observations for latitude to-night, circum-meridian altitudes of ———, which made my latitude 47° 05′ 18″.72.

August 4.—When we left camp this morning we were followed by about 300 Indians—men, women, and children; all anxious to see the soldiers of their Great Father. Their village being about five miles below us, on the Big Dry Sandy, I bore off to the east-northeast, in order to avoid them, and at the same time endeavoring to travel by the route possessing the best natural advantages to enable me to repel an attack, if a second one were made. The country passed over was much cut up by dry creek beds and ravines.

A distance of six miles brought us to the Big Dry Sandy, below the bend in which the Crows were encamped; crossed the river and pursued the same course, which two miles further on brought us to the well-timbered valley of a creek, in which, however, we found no water. This creek headed in the divide a short distance to the south. After making a day's march of 15½ miles, we encamped near some ponds or small lakes in the prairie, near a small, dry creek. Water poor; grass scarce.

August 5.—At 6 a. m. we set out from camp, pursuing a due east course over a broken country near the divide, between the Yellowstone and Missouri rivers. I was gratified to observe the great change that took place in the country as we travelled eastward. The soil became better, grass more plenty and of better quality, and wood and water in the ravines. At a distance of four miles from camp we recrossed the dividing ridge, and then travelled along near its crest for five miles further, and encamped at a clear, cold spring, the waters of which sank again ere they reached a distance of two hundred yards from camp. Plenty of cottonwood and black-ash timber, and excellent grazing for the animals. From a high point on the divide I was enabled to get a fine view of the country. The valley of the Yellowstone was distinctly visible, a long blue line of cottonwood timber marking its rounding course from the Big Horn mountains, while the country toward the Missouri broke off from the divide by precipitous bluffs; the drainage marked by deep ravines, all having more or less timber in them.

To the eastward the White Hills seemed to rise even higher than the elevation of my location, breaking off gently towards the valley of the Yellowstone in white bluffs and low round buttes. In the southwest, where the country was less broken, I noticed a large number of Indians chasing buffalo, of which many herds were in sight.

August 6.—Marched only four miles to-day. Followed the divide for three miles, when finding that it wended off to northward I left it, still pursuing my easterly course for a mile further. I encamped on a bold, running stream, containing cold, clear water; valley well timbered with black ash and cottonwood; soil along the valley excellent; grass good in quality and plenty. As the animals were considerably worn out, I determined to remain here to-day for the purpose of giving them a chance to recuperate. Shot a fine buffalo cow, which gave us ample material for a feast, to which we did justice. Weather cloudy, with high wind. I was however enabled to get a set of observations up the Polari to-night, which made our latitude 47° 03′ 14″.62.

August 7.—Having arranged everything yesterday for an early start, by arranging strap packsaddles, &c., I was enabled to start this morning at 6 a. m.; course east-northeast, near the divide, and leading over a high rolling prairie; crossed several dry creek beds, and saw a great deal of fresh Indian sign, such as fresh horsetracks, dead buffalo, &c. After travelling 25 miles, I found a camp at some water-holes, where we found but little grass and no wood. The "bois de vache" served us for fuel. Just after we camped we discovered a body of Indians (about 15 or 20) approaching us. They proved to be one of the lower bands of Crow Indians, and were very friendly in their manner. I gave them the remainder of the Indian goods in my possession, with which they were well pleased, and they sent me in return some very fine dried tongues.

August 8.—Weather warm and cloudy. Set out at 6½ a. m., course northeast over a high rolling prairie country. Crossed many dry creek beds and ravines, and after a day's march of 14 miles, encamped on a stream of running water. As the water was very muddy I supposed it was the effect of the recent rain. Grass and wood good, but not abundant. The country in the direction of the Yellowstone appeared less elevated and very rough, while toward the northward it gradually rose to the divide, which I judged to be about six miles from our position.

August 9.—Upon leaving camp this morning I changed my course to east by north, bearing more toward Yellowstone river. The country over which we passed had a gradual descent, but was much cut up by deep ravines and high red hills, with large lignite deposits near their tops. In crossing these "bad lands" we met with several streams with running water, but they had little or no timber in their valleys. They appeared to head but a short distance to our left in the divide, and ran in a northeast course towards the Yellowstone. After gaining the top of the bluff breaking off into the valley of the last creek we crossed, we found ourselves upon a broad flat prairie, sloping off gradually towards the Yellowstone valley, which was in plain sight. A march of 8 miles across this prairie brought us to the Yellowstone, where I found a good location and camped. The bands of buffalo are now less frequently met with, and I determined to lay in a supply of meat to last me to Fort Union. I succeeded without much difficulty in procuring the desired amount.

The Yellowstone valley presented an agreeable change in appearance when compared with the rough and barren country we had just traversed. The valley of the Yellowstone, wide, rich, and well timbered, and the river being navigable far above this point by steamboats of light draught. Obtained observations of Polari, which made our latitude 47° 25′ 07″.39.

August 10.—Pursued our march down the valley of the Yellowstone, meeting with no obstacle to impede our progress. The slope of the country is very gradual on this side of the river, and presents a strong contrast to the opposite side, which is rough and broken in the extreme. During to-day's march we crossed the beds of several dry streams, which at certain seasons must pour in a tremendous volume of water to the Yellowstone, as is plainly indicated by the appearance of driftwood, &c. After marching 25 miles we encamped a second time upon the Yellowstone, having an ample supply of grass and wood.

August 11 —Left camp this morning at an early hour, as usual pursuing a north-northeast course. A march of 12 miles in this direction brought me to the bank of the Missouri river opposite Fort Union. Finding that I could not cross the river at this point, and receiving your message, I marched down the river about two miles, where I found the boat which you had ordered to be placed at my service. I ferried over my command and all of my government property; I then had my animals all driven into the river and they swam across safely, and at 3 o'clock p. m. I was able to exchange congratulations with my friends from whom I had parted at Fort Benton.

The whole distance passed over in travelling the route prescribed by yourself from Fort Benton to Fort Union was, according to the estimation, 363½ miles, but I am inclined to believe that the distance is a little underestimated. The country passed over on my route, with the exception of that portion in and near the Judith mountains, and lying contiguous to the streams forming the drainage of the same, is worthless. Although it is a much nearer route from Fort Union to Fort Benton than on the other side of the river, still I think the latter route would be far preferable for military purposes. A railroad could be constructed along my route at a comparatively slight cost, as there are no very great elevations to overcome throughout the route. A reference to the barometric notes of Mr. Schonborn will enable you to get a profile of the whole country passed over.

I cannot conclude, sir, without expressing my appreciation of the services of the gentlemen assigned to my command as civil assistants; of Bridger, the guide, it is unnecessary to say anything, as his reputation is not confined to our own country. The geological report of Dr. Hayden will be the best commentary upon the value of his services and the manner in which his duties were performed, although the duty was with him a "labor of love."

Mr. Schonborn was indefatigable in his endeavors to procure a correct barometrical profile of the country; and, after the barometer was broken, he did all in his power to compensate for the defect in our instrument outfit. His life-like views of the country speak for themselves.

To Mr. Stuart my thanks are also due for the manner in which he discharged the onerous duties of topographer. I consider it my duty, and it is a pleasant task, to pay this token of respect to the gentlemen composing my staff.

Very respectfully, your obedient servant,

JOHN MULLINS,
First Lieutenant 2d Dragoons.

Captain WM. F. RAYNOLDS, *Topographical Engineer,*
Commanding Missouri and Yellowstone Expedition.

Reconnoissance for a wagon road from the Platte to Powder river, by J. D. Hutton, 1860.

March 29.—Left winter quarters on Deer creek at 8 a. m. Bissonette's, near the mouth of Deer creek, at 9.15 a. m. Crossed the Platte at a point north 12°, 900 yards from Bissonette's. The river at this point is about 80 yards wide, and two feet eight inches deep in the channel; rocky bottom. Leaving the river, the road ascends a high hill to the left of the ford, passing around its summit and descending again to the Platte one-half mile below the lower ford. Thence along an old road up the river 2 600 yards, where the Powder-river trail leaves the emigrant road. At this point the camping ground is good for wood and water; grass is poor at this season. Thence the trail follows a course north 62° west, to the top of the first range of hills; then turning north 57° west, over rolling, sandy, sage-covered hills, to the valley of a dry arroyo, (Willow Springs creek.) Thence north 37° west, keeping close to the hills on the right and towards three remarkably shaped peaks or buttes, to Willow Springs, a distance of 15 miles from the Platte, and 19.05 miles from Bissonette's. At 5 o'clock p. m. camped at Willow Springs. Wood (willow) and water good, grass scarce. A good wagon road the whole of this day's march, with the exception of two ravines near the spring, which may be made good with very little labor.

OBSERVATIONS FOR TIME AND LATITUDE AT THIS CAMP.

[J. D. Hutton, observer; G. H. Wallace, time keeper; chronometer, Bannard, 1905; sextant, Troughton & Simms, 2812.]

* PROCYON.

Chron. time.			Obs. D. Alt.		
h.	m.	s.	°	′	″
7	50	59.6	105	02	50
	56	04.4	104	52	40
	58	40	104	45	35

* ε URSÆ MAJORIS.

h.	m.	s.	°	′	″
8	43	32.4	103	41	50
	15	24	104	47	15
	21	07.6	106	28	10
	23	50	107	11	40
	32	28.4	107	59	00
	34	56	108	34	10

* ALDIBARAN.

Chron. time.			Obs. D. Alt.		
h.	m.	s.	°	′	″
8	43	32.4	64	33	50
	46	26	62	31	10
	50	55.6	60	54	10
	52	23.2	60	20	20
	53	32.8	59	56	10
	55	30.4	59	11	50

* POLARIS.

h.	m.	s.	°	′	″
9	08	08	84	44	10
	11	47.6	84	41	50
	15	53.6	84	39	30
	17	59.2	84	39	00

March 30.—Left camp at 7.30 a. m., following up the most eastern drain running to Willow Springs about half a mile, crossing it and ascending the spur between the two forks, course north 14° east, distance $2\frac{1}{4}$ miles. Thence north $1\frac{1}{2}$ miles, over low rolling spurs of barren land, to a range of sand hills running from the divide between the Platte and Shayenne rivers, toward the Platte, in a southwesterly direction. The land-marks, on entering the sand hills at this point, are of some importance as guides through them. They are, on the left, a high, round hill of yellow sand, entirely destitute of vegetation, and beyond it, half a mile distant, and to the right of the trail, a rocky bluff point facing west.

The best road found through the sand hills was on a general course of north 28° west from the before mentioned rocky bluff; winding about among the hills to take advantage of the ground without deviating much from the given course. The distance through them by the road followed was three and a quarter miles.

These hills appear to be a spur between two drains running to the Platte, the summit having no perceptible surface drainage; the basins between the hills having no outlets to the valleys on either side. The whole ridge is composed of a light shifting sand, covered in places with a scanty growth of sage and greasewood.

The trail, after leaving these hills, passes over a gently rolling prairie across the heads of a drain running to the Platte to the dividing ridge between the waters of Powder river and Platte, two and three quarter miles on a course north 28° west. Thence along the divide north 75° west three fourths of a mile. Then turning down a spur between two drains running to Salt creek to their junction, north 16° west, 6 miles from the last turning point on the dividing ridge. Camped at this point at 3.15 p. m. Wood (cottonwood,) water, and grass good and abundant. A good wagon road the whole of this day's march, excepting through the sand hills, where it is bad, without any capability of being made better. The wheels sinking deep in the sand and there being many unavoidable sharp pulls.

OBSERVATIONS FOR TIME AND LATITUDE AT THIS CAMP.

[J. D. Hutton, observer; George H. Wallace, time keeper; chronometer, Bannard, 1905; sextant, 2812.]

* PROCYON.

Chron. time. h.	m.	s.	Obs. D. Alt. °	′	″
7	38	57.2	104	43	20 cl'dy.

* POLARIS.

h.	m.	s.	°	′	″
8	06	12.4	85	47	20
	09	45.2	85	44	30
	12	04.8	85	43	50
	15	08.8	85	41	00
	17	08.8	85	39	30 cl'dy.

* β AMIGÆ.

h.	m.	s.	°	′	″
8	25	18	86	02	50

* ALDIBARAN.

h.	m.	s.	°	′	″
8	29	09.2	67	00	00
	31	04.4	66	38	40
	33	02.8	65	55	20
	34	04.8	65	35	50

* ε URSÆ MAJORIS.

Chron. time. h.	m.	s.	Obs. D. Alt. °	′	″
8	45	32	79	41	30
	50	51.6	81	77	10
	52	06.8	81	39	20

* α HYDRÆ, (south.)

h.	m.	s.	°	′	″
9	14	49.2	79	19	10
	16	43.2	77	20	40
	19	16.4	77	24	30
	21	20.4	77	24	40
	26	21.6	77	27	00
	30	23.6	77	26	40
	32	21.2	77	25	00
	34	06.4	77	24	30
	36	06.4	77	22	10
	38	11.2	77	21	00
	39	57.2	77	17	10
	42	15.6	77	12	20

March 21.—Left camp at 8.30 a. m., following the trail down the bed of the stream, which it leaves for the high land on the banks at a point about 11 miles from the morning camp; passing around the head of the deep ravine, and returning again to the creek within a mile and a half. This part of to-day's march was not practicable for heavily loaded wagons on account of the steepness of the ravines, but very little work will make it good.

Apparently the traders and Indians have several other trails at this place which may be better than the one travelled. One down the bed of the creek is probably the best when the creek is dry, as at present. Water may be found in holes all along the creek on this day's march; no timber, grass good. The country on both sides of Salt creek is a mass of broken "bad land" ridges, runningto the northward, only one tributary ravine of considerable size running to this stream.

Vegetation, sage, greasewood, and bunch-grass; a few rushes in the creek bottom.

Exposed strata of lignite and sandstone, (21) dipping 70° southeast.

Camped on Salt creek at 3 p. m.; no wood, but drift; water, alkaline; grass good and abundant.

April 1.—Left camp at 8.30 a. m. and followed the creek bed; about three miles from camp passed a remarkable bluff on the west, which is visible from the dividing ridge at the head of Salt creek. Its summit-line is straight and level, with two abrupt and squarely formed notches; bears from the divide north 40° west.

At 10 miles from last night's camp the creek turns and flows due west for a distance of one and a half mile, where it receives a tributary drain from the southwest. The traders have a trail turning to the right, leaving the creek bed where it commences to trend west, and passing over the hills descends again to the creek five miles below, saving in distance about two miles. It is said to be practicable for wagons. Camped at 3 p. m., with good wood and grass. Water plenty; but as everywhere else on this creek is slightly alkaline. The latter part of the day's march passed several small groves of stunted cottonwood. Water in holes at intervals of one or two miles. The road passed over to-day, like that of yesterday, constantly crosses and recrosses the creek, passable for loaded wagons in dry weather, but after heavy rains the creek crossings are probably miry.

Big Horn mountains are distinctly visible from the hills on either side of the road.

High peaks (cloud and snow peaks) bear north 50° west; end of spur at Willow creek, north 72½° west.

April 2.—Left camp at 7 a. m. and followed the old trail down the creek, which flows northwesterly for about four miles, where it bends off to the eastward. At this point the trail ascends the hills to the left, crossing a spur and descending again to the creek about two miles below, cutting off a large bend. From this point the creek trends to the northeast to its junction with Powder river, a distance of 19¼ miles from last night's camp.

At 18 miles, where Salt creek enters the bottom of Powder river, left the trail, (which strikes Powder river four miles below,) crossed Salt creek and camped on the right bank of Powder river, 300 yards above the mouth of the creek; 100 yards below the camp there is a good ford on the river, 40 yards wide, one foot deep, with gravelly bottom; good banks on both sides. The road to-day has been more direct than the two previous days, the bends in Salt creek being larger and more open, affording many opportunities of cutting across points, thereby saving distance.

At seven miles from last camp Salt creek receives a large tributary from the southwest, which heads in Mildrum's Pine hill; called it Pine Hill creek.

Exposed strata of lignite, &c., dipping about 10° northeast along the first part of to-day's march, and gradually increasing to 40° at five miles from the mouth of the creek. The only perfectly black lignite seen was three thin stratas, about 30 feet apart at the point of greatest dip.

The valley of Powder river, at the mouth of Salt creek, is well timbered with cottonwood and willow.

April 3.—Left camp at 7 a. m. and went down Powder river to examine the crossing of the old trail; found the crossing at the extreme southern bend of the river, at which place are several deserted houses. The crossing is miry, and scarcely passable on horseback at this time; the traders having crossed on the ice in December. All trails between the upper and lower fords lead to a low gap in the hills about three miles north of the upper and two miles northwest of the lower ford, all apparently running to Crazy Woman's fork of Powder river, a distance of about 35 miles; said to be without water.

From the upper ford to the Portuguese houses the distance is about three miles, course due west.

NOTE.—To strike the upper, and by far the best, ford: on emerging from the broken bluffs bounding the valley of Salt creek to the more open valley of Powder valley, the road ascends a low hill, from which Pumpkin butte is distinctly visible. From the summit of this hill keep north 20° west, cross to the left bank of Salt creek, and follow it down to a lone cottonwood standing directly on the creek bank; here the lodge trail to the ford, 250 yards distant, is distinctly visible, being apparently much travelled by Indians. The river is not fordable at other points than those mentioned, even at low water, on account of the miry banks on each side of the channel, of a different character from any seen on the same river below.

Returned to camp at 10.30 a. m., and moved camp up Salt creek 13.5 miles; camped, with wood, water, and grass.

OBSERVATIONS FOR TIME AND LATITUDE AT CAMP ON POWDER RIVER, APRIL 3, 1860.

[J. D. Hutton, observer; George H. Wallace, time keeper; chronomter, Bannard, 1905; sextant, 2812.]

* *β* AMIGÆ.

Chron. time. h.	m.	s.	Obs. D. Alt. °	′	″
8	31	00	95	52	10
	33	09.6	95	03	30
	36	08.4	94	00	30
	37	48.4	93	23	40
	39	00	92	58	00
	40	38.4	92	23	40
	42	24	91	43	50
	45	03.2	90	45	00
	46	16	90	20	10

* ARCTURUS.

h.	m.	s.	°	′	″	
10	09	33.2	72	02	50	(2)
	13	46.4	73	33	20	
	15	32	74	12	00	
	17	38	74	55	30	
	19	20	75	33	20	
	22	39.6	76	35	00	
	24	07.2	77	16	30	

* *a* HYDRÆ.

h.	m.	s.	°	′	″
8	51	28.4	75	55	00
	53	17.6	76	01	00
	54	48	76	03	30

* *a* HYDRÆ—Continued.

Chron. time. h.	m.	s.	Obs. D. Alt. °	′	″
8	56	32.8	76	09	00
	57	42.4	76	11	20
	59	05.2	76	14	40
9	00	27.6	76	16	20
	04	15.6	76	23	20
	07	09.6	76	26	30
	11	03.2	76	30	00
	12	38.4	76	31	00
	15	56.4	76	31	30
	19	59.6	76	30	30
	21	57.2	76	29	20
	24	16	76	28	30
	25	45.6	76	25	50
	23	40.8	76	22	00
	29	56	76	20	00

* POLARIS.

h.	m.	s.	°	′	″
9	48	56	85	29	00
	51	42	85	27	20
	54	06	85	26	00
	55	24	85	25	20
	57	49.6	85	24	40
	59	08	85	23	10
10	01	04.8	85	23	00
	03	16.4	85	21	10

April 4.—Left camp at 8 a. m., following the old trail of Salt creek 19.5 miles, and camped, with water and grass; no wood but drift.

April 5.—Left camp at 7.30 a. m., following the old trail up creek 20.7 miles, and camped at the nearest water to the head of Salt creek. Cottonwood and grass abundant.

April 6.—Left camp at 8 a. m. on the old trail over the dividing ridge between Platte and Powder rivers. Five miles from camp, where the spur leading to the water on the head of Salt creek leaves the main spur, marked the spot with a pile of stone, the trail being scattered and indistinct at this point. Examined the divide for a trail leading towards Platte bridge. Found an old lodge trail which appears to keep the ridge in a westerly course to get around the sand hills, which extend to the Platte, striking that river a short distance below the bridge.

Crossed the sand hills by the same road followed before, and camped at Willow Springs.

April 7.—Left camp at Willow Springs at 7 a. m., following the dry bed of the stream. At one and a half mile crossed a small spur from the sand hills, impassable for loaded wagons. At eight miles struck the trail followed in going out.

Crossed the Platte two and a half miles above the place where it was crossed going out. The river here is about 150 yards wide, two feet six inches deep, with gravelly bottom, only fordable at low water.

Arrived at winter quarters, Deer creek, at 3 p. m. Distance to Powder river by the road travelled ninety-six (96) miles.

www.ingramcontent.com/pod-product-compliance
Lightning Source LLC
LaVergne TN
LVHW011235110826
845150LV00006B/1641

* 9 7 8 1 4 2 5 5 1 4 7 8 5 *